Siren's Song

SIREN'S SONG

THE ALLURE OF WAR

ANTONIO M. SALINAS

Deeds Publishing • Atlanta

The views expressed in this book are those of the author and do not reflect the official policy or position of the Department of the Navy, Department of the Army, Department of Defense, or the U.S. Government.

Some of the names in this book have been changed.

Printed in the United States of America
Published by Deeds Publishing, Marietta, GA
www.deedspublishing.com

Cover and design by Matt King
Cover Photo Courtesy of Eros Hoagland
Photographs from the author's personal collection or used with permission by those noted on the acknowledgements page.

Library of Congress Cataloging-in-Publications Data is available upon request.

ISBN 978-1-937565-17-6

Books are available in quantity for promotional or premium use. For information, write Deeds Publishing, PO Box 682212, Marietta, GA 30068 or info@deedspublishing.com

First Edition, 2012

10 9 8 7 6 5 4 3 2 1

To the men of 4th Platoon, Dagger Company, 2nd Battalion, 12th Infantry Regiment, 4th Brigade Combat team, 4th Infantry Division:

I will never forget you.

TABLE OF CONTENTS

THE ALLURE OF WAR:	15
A LONG PATH TO WAR:	19
ANTE BELLUM:	21
USMC:	23
US ARMY:	31
WAR TRAINING:	37
JANUARY 2009, JRTC:	43
TO WAR:	53
CONTACT!	65
JULY 2009:	103
AUGUST 2009:	143
SEPTEMBER 2009:	167
OCTOBER 2009:	203
NOVEMBER 2009:	233
DECEMBER 2009:	259
JANUARY 2010:	283
FEBRURAY 2010:	323
MARCH 2010:	337
APRIL 2010:	365
MAY 2010:	381
USEFUL PASHTUN:	405
ACKNOWLEDGEMENTS	409

USEFUL ABREVIATIONS AND TERMS:

120 MM: Big mortars.
155: Massive artillery.
240 B: A machine gun. Awesome.
81 MM: Mortars.
ABAD: Asadabad. The base in the capital of Kunar province.
ANA: Afghanistan National Army.
ANP: Afghanistan National Police.
ANSF: Afghanistan National Security Forces (Army and Police).
APACHE: Large attack helicopter.
ASV: Armored vehicle: Armored support vehicle. An armored truck.
BN: Battalion. Typically 700- 1,000 soldiers.
BLACK HAWK: Medium size helicopter. Transport and MEDEVAC.
BLUE FORCE TRACKER: Advanced American system that shows location of friendly forces.
CO.: Company. Approximately 100 soldiers.
CO: Commanding officer of a company.
CHINOOK: Big helicopter. Transport, has guns.
COP: Combat outpost. Fort. Base.
CROW: Commonly Remotely Operated Weapon. A remote control Machine gun.
ETT: Embedded Training team. Soldiers and Marines that train the ANA.
FOB: Forward operating base. Big Outpost.
HESCO: Essentially a large steel basket filled with dirt. Used as a fortification.
HLZ: Helicopter Landing Zone
IBOLC: Infantry Basic officer Leaders Course.
IDF: Indirect fire. Mortar or artillery.
IED: Improvised explosive device.

KLE: Key leader engagement. A talk or meeting with locals.
KIOWA: Small helicopter. Reconnaissance and attack.
M2/.50 CAL: A big Machine gun.
MEDEVAC: Medical evacuation.
MK 19: A fully automatic Grenade launcher.
MOS: Military Occupational Specialty. Your job in the military.
MRAP: An armored vehicle. Hummer on steroids. Mine Resistant Ambush Protected.
NODS/NVG: Night optical device/ Night vision goggles
OP: out post. A small checkpoint. With 5-20 troops.
PLT: Platoon. Approximately 20-30 soldiers.
PKM: A Soviet model Machine gun.
QRF: Quick reaction force.
SHURA: An Afghan Meeting of elders or important leaders.
TCP: Traffic control point. A traffic checkpoint used to deny enemy freedom of maneuver and to demonstrate presence on the road.
TOC: Tactical Operations Center. A headquarters
TOW: Tube launched, optical wire guided missile.
TRP: Target reference point. A known target for artillery.
UAV: Unmanned Aerial Vehicle or drone.
XO: Executive officer. Assistant to the company commander, second in command.

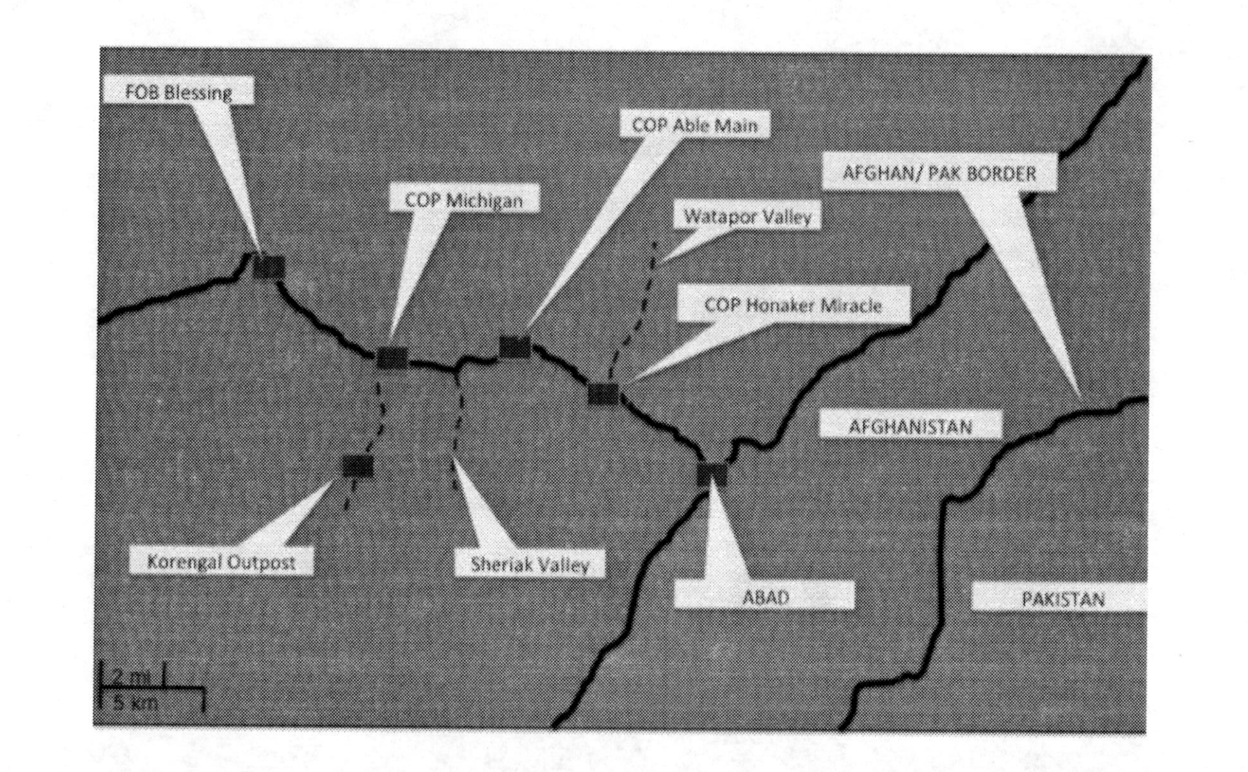
FOB Blessing
COP Michigan
COP Able Main
Watapor Valley
AFGHAN/ PAK BORDER
COP Honaker Miracle
AFGHANISTAN
Korengal Outpost
Sheriak Valley
ABAD
PAKISTAN
2 mi
5 km

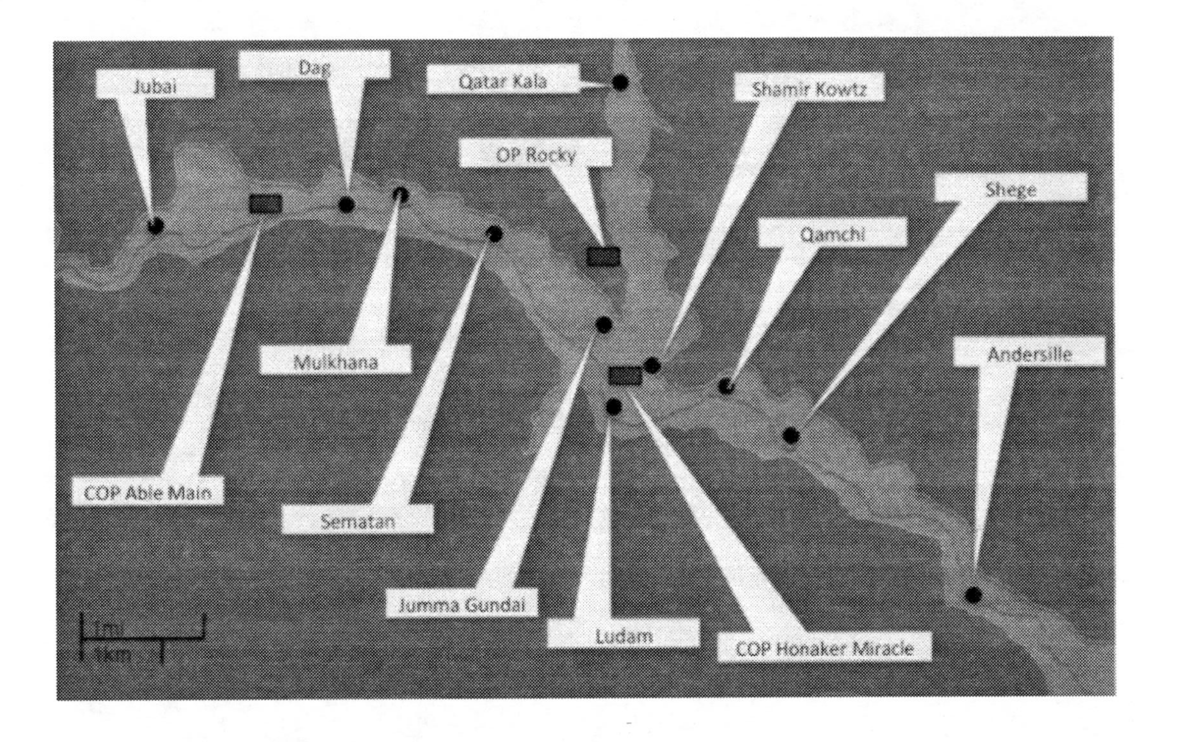
Jubai
Dag
Qatar Kala
Shamir Kowtz
OP Rocky
Shege
Qamchi
Andersille
Mulkhana
COP Able Main
Sematan
Jumma Gundai
Ludam
COP Honaker Miracle
1mi
1km

THE ALLURE OF WAR:
A SIREN'S SONG

"First you will come to the Sirens who enchant all who come near them. If anyone unwarily draws in too close and hears the singing of the Sirens, his wife and children will never welcome him home again, for they sit in a green field and warble him to death with the sweetness of their song.

There is a great heap of dead men's bones lying all around, with the flesh still rotting off them. Therefore pass these Sirens by, and stop your men's ears with wax that none of them may hear"

(Odyssey. Book 12, 188-191).

It seems that one truth, if any exists, is that mankind has a deep fascination with war. To some men, the allure of going to war can be addictive. War itself can be addictive. War seems to have a Siren's song's hold upon much of mankind, in that some of us are drawn to it like nothing else in life. The Sirens were mythological women-monsters who were rumored to live on an island in the Mediterranean Sea. In the *Odyssey*, ancient Greeks tell us the Sirens sang a song which enticed men to the brink of total desire. It called to them in a way more potent than the strongest lust, and lured men to their deaths. Men were warned to stay away from the Sirens, lest they be shattered upon the rocks surrounding the isle and meet a terrible end.

Yet, some men would brave the temptation. They would tempt the Fates to see how close they could get to the Sirens without dying. Odysseus, the wise war hero from the Trojan War, wanted to get as close as he could to them. Through his famed Greek ingenuity, he found a way to come close to the Sirens, though they teased his ears to near the brink of insanity.

War in the 21st century seems to have the same ancient allure that attracted men from all ages of history to the Siren's rocks, so to speak. As we grow older, we are warned through a variety of forums, including literature, movies, and media, that war is a very dangerous thing. We know that to go to war might mean death, loss of a limb, or less desirable ends, like burning to death. The common knowledge of war and its outcomes is especially prevalent in this age of Internet sites such as "youtube.com", where users watch real battles unfold via video footage. One would think, given the possibilities inherent in battle, it would seem logical to avoid this perpetual human drama known as war.

Yet, many men* still crave this experience. Men flock, by the thousands, each year to serve in armies. Others, having tasted the strong wine called war, continue to serve as modern day mercenaries in the booming market of private security companies. For those of us who have slept with the Sirens and lived to tell the tale unscathed – we still fantasize about them. They tempt me still.

So perhaps we are not so different from those Greeks who volunteered centuries ago to sail to Troy. As later generations in the antiquities read the *Iliad* and the *Odyssey*, young men fantasized about going to and fighting in war. They looked inside themselves and wondered if they had the mettle to stand in a line and face the horrors of hell with their mates. They wondered what it would be like to stare death in its face. They wondered what it would feel like in the first moment when they laid eyes upon their enemy and to have adrenaline pump through their veins as they collided with him. They imagined the shouts and screams of men in battle. They wondered if they had what it took to lead others into the fray of combat.

This scene is not so different in the 21st century, as young men today watch the stories of war unfold in movies such as *"Black Hawk Down"*, *"Braveheart"*, *"Saving Private Ryan"*, and *"We Were Soldiers."* The next time you look upon a young man, or even a man fully grown watching a war movie, look into his eyes. You will see it on his face. He is wondering what it would be like to be in battle. Do you ever wonder what it's like?

(Today, thousands of women also crave this experience and seek combat. They serve with honor on the modern battlefield. However, this book is only a narrative from my eyes – a man that searched for war all his life.)*

A LONG PATH TO WAR

The song of the Sirens has played in my ears all of my life. As a child, I imagined battle. For years on end I wondered what it would be like. Perhaps many of us do. For me, I found myself imagining what it would be like to stand in a formation amongst soldiers, preparing for battle. In particular, I imagined the sounds of battle. Growing up, my father taught me to hunt, and I still remember listening to our footsteps as we quietly walked in the woods or through open fields in search of our prey. I listened to the sound of our boots as we stealthily stalked upon the ground and heard the jingle of extra ammunition in our pockets. These are the memories which I held of those early morning patrols in the wilderness of Michigan. All of this I loved.

Unbeknownst to me, parts of my life foreshadowed what I would later experience in battle. Hunting provided some of the emotions I later experienced in combat. The adrenaline that your heart pumps at the sight of prey, the deafening roar of a shotgun blast followed by smoke slowly rising from the end of the barrel. Your ears ring and all other elements of sound seem to cease. You fire off a few more rounds, locking you into the moment, attempting to kill the beast that is your prey.

I searched for glimpses of this song of war before I was a man that could see battle. I found some satisfaction in combative sports such as wrestling, football, and karate. When I wore football equipment, I imagined myself as an ancient warrior. I reveled in the deafening noise of muscle and bone crunching when hitting an opponent. There was something about the noise in my ears the first time I got my bell rung after a hit on the field. I loved the exhilaration of taking an opponent down, and destroying his will to fight. Yet, this was not battle.

Following high school, my road led me to the United States Marine Corps (USMC). In the Marines, I learned to shoot, walk, run, talk, and drink like a warrior. I was fit, brave and tough. But no battle came during my years of service. I fought other Marines in combative contests. I shot at numerous marksmanship ranges. Yet, there was no battle.

In college, I attempted to leave behind this quest of war to earn a degree and eventually teach high school history. However, I had never heard the sound of enemy fire about my ears. I had never known battle. I had never known contact with the enemy. In graduate school, I enrolled in Army ROTC. I began preparing myself for the taste of battle I so badly yearned for.

After a decade of searching, I finally saw the waves crashing upon the rocks as I neared the Sirens. I finally was close enough to hear their song of war. Yet, the Sirens were not in the Mediterranean, as I was led to believe. Rather, they waited for me in the Pesh River Valley of Kunar Province, Afghanistan. There in Kunar, I finally learned the truth about war. There, I found out what it was like.

ANTE BELLUM
1998-2007

UNITED STATES MARINE CORPS

My search to experience what war was like led me to the Marines. I was a recruiter's dream. I was fit, smart, and motivated. Only a week after walking into the recruiting office, I swore into the delayed entry program, set to ship off to boot camp upon graduating high school. In the summer of 1998, I reported to Parris Island, SC. After a plane ride to Charleston, SC, I found myself on a bus, surrounded by other young men ranging in age from 18 into their mid 20's. Each of us had volunteered for the Marines. We thought we knew what we were in for.

It was the middle of July and the South Carolina air was dark, humid and hot. The bus ride from the airport to Parris Island took about an hour. I rested and drifted off to sleep. Those moments of peaceful slumber would be my final moments of civilian life before entering a life in the ranks of warriors. From that moment on the bus, it would be eleven years before I heard the sound of an enemy bullet tear the sky about my ears.

The bus crossed a dark span of highway that brought us to Parris Island. As we crossed the marshlands that separated the island from the mainland, I knew my life would be changed forever. The bus halted in front of a dimly lit building with the inscription: "Through these portals (Marine speak for doorways) pass prospects for America's finest fighting force."

The Drill Instructor approached and boarded the bus. He ordered us to dismount and move out to a set of yellow footprints painted on the ground. The drill instructor shouted: "READY! MOVE!"

Welcome to the island.

A cacophony of violent yelling began as we charged off the bus. In that moment, I felt an intense mixture of energy, aggression, excitement and fear as I moved towards the notorious yellow footprints at the recruit depot. We realized we had no idea what to expect.

Whatever it was, we were sure of one thing: it would crash upon us like a wave of human violence.

All throughout my journey at boot camp, the feeling of intensity I experienced upon dismounting the bus still coursed through my veins every time we started one of our training exercises. In my mind, the moment of the bus arriving at Parris Island created the foundation of the Marine mentality; the mindset of a Marine is one embodied as a primordial shock of brutal, visceral violence. The ingrained teachings of the Marine Corps took away my fear, and instead replaced it with a fearlessness to act in the face of danger without the slightest hesitation.

In those three months of initial training, I abandoned my civilian self and began my transformation into a Marine. I learned what it was to be a warrior. I learned how to hike, march, to pack a rucksack, shoot, and to charge a position. Aggression, speed, and intensity were the lessons I learned throughout boot camp. In that summer of 1998, through pain and sweat and fire, my steel was forged. I took easily to the Marine model of following orders and execution, building upon years of practicing martial arts.

While in boot camp, the idea of going to war was but a dream. The first taste of the decade ahead came to us in the form of the attacks on the U.S. embassies in Africa that August of 1998. Although we would not go to war then, our drill Instructors told us that if the call came, we would be sent to the rifle range and have our training cut short. I remember asking a recruit who came from Puerto Rico, *"Esta Listo para Guerra?* (Are you ready for war?)" Yet, the threat appeared to vanish, at least for a few years.

War did not come then. I wondered what it must be like to be in combat. They trained and stressed us to prepare for the rigors of battle. I imagined it as we conducted the bayonet assault course. I imagined destroying the enemy as I stabbed silhouettes in their bunkers.

War would remain obscure to me. It was this mythical creature, this Siren whose terrible beauty was shrouded in a deep mist. In training you were offered glimpses of how these mythological creatures made you feel in battle.

At times in the chaos of training, I wondered why I was there. I awoke one night in the barracks of Platoon 1084, C. Co, 1st Recruit Training Battalion. I was only 18. I was sad and missed home. I was unsure whether or not I had made the correct decision in life. I paced around in the darkness, thinking and thinking as only soldiers do when we are alone.

I looked outside.

Across the parade field I gazed and caught sight of the Iwo Jima Memorial. Illuminated in the street light were the Stars and Stripes of the U.S. Flag silently waving in the night. Although it was over 400 meters away from my barracks, I thought I heard the unmistakable sound of a flag flapping in the night's breeze. I could hear its fabric silently dancing in the wind. I stared upon my colors with both admiration and pride. I said to the flag, "I do this for you."

One of the most vivid training exercises that will forever reverberate through my head is the field fire exercise during the Crucible. The Crucible was our defining moment during boot camp. We were about half way through this final 55-hour test. We were in the wood line. They gave us live rounds. We slapped them into our rifles and made ready.

Having live rounds in our rifles changed everything. The rifle was no longer an object of burden. Instantly, it had the power to take life. I would forever remember this feeling. It would come to me again, during my first patrols in Afghanistan. You walked like a lion on a hunt. Racking a live round into your chamber changes the world for you. You seem to cross a line. You become death. You become that Grim Reaper, who you have only heard about in stories or in your nightmares. You have the power to rip muscles open and pour your enemy's blood on the earth. You are more than human. You are like a god, in a sense. You have the power to take life at hundreds of yards. In an instant you have the ability to expel breath from lungs and a soul from a body.

Although it was September, it was still brutally hot. Sweat trickled across my body from my face to my hands. We walked in single file toward our release point. Our rifles were staggered facing opposite directions as we walked – a technique derived from the echoes of Vietnam. We waited for the green smoke before charging to our positions.

The smoke emitted from a grenade and it provided concealment as well as served as our signal. We charged through the smoke that instantly blanketed the terrain before us. It was an intense moment in time, as it was the first time in my life that I ran with live ammunition. As we approached our firing positions, my fellow recruits around me screamed with primordial yells that were forged in us during our time on the island. I jumped down into a bunker. After clearing sweat from my brow, I took aim at the silhouettes and sent steel down range. I wondered if battle would be like this, sending steel under a haze of confusion and heat. I would wait many years before I would find out.

In the Marines, I learned to walk with a heavy rucksack and to carry my rifle with pride. I learned to move as infantry under exhaustion and heat. We conducted forced marches for miles on end, or what we call in the military "humping." We moved beyond exhaustion and beyond pain. After marching for what seemed like hours, we would drop our rucksacks, and practice assaulting objectives. Every assault was complimented by our primordial yells. We embodied violence. We became violence.

Soon the months of training culminated and I became a Marine. It was a title that I felt was truly earned, not given. My combat skills were further enhanced at Marine Combat Training (MCT) in North Carolina. I spent about a month conducting basic rifleman training. Here we refined our basic infantry skills of attacking and attacking. It was a fine addition to my education in warfare. I was trained as a topographic analyst. There would be no war for me. Instead, I spent time surveying airfields in Okinawa, Japan. However, regardless of your MOS (job) in the Marines, the cornerstones of discipline, violence, and aggression were perpetually fostered.

Eventually my enlistment would take me to beautiful southern California. I spent about one and a half years at Camp Pendleton, CA. Upon arrival at the unit, I was moved to HQ Co., in 1st Intelligence Battalion, 1st MEF (Marine Expeditionary Force). I would earn my corporal stripes and eventually the rank of sergeant. Here, I left the intelligence realm and fortuitously was chosen to become a martial arts instructor, and later a martial arts instructor trainer. My job was to teach Marines to become martial arts instructors. It was a dream job come true. The training that I endured for this position was the hardest martial arts training that I have ever conducted in my life. The training events forced you to combat exhaustion to the point that you were panting so much that you could barely stand. It was then that we participated in unarmed and armed combat events. I cherished every moment of this chapter in my military career. I gave Marines the ability to take life with their bare hands.

In 2001, 9/11 shook the very foundations of our country and of the martial culture of the military. My unit did not get the call to go. I continued teaching martial arts, and thought that I had fulfilled my search of understanding warfare.

Soon my first enlistment was over. In July of 2002, I decided to leave the active duty Marines and enter the Marine Reserves while pursuing my other great passion in life: history. I planned to teach high school history. I thought that my initial experiences of soldiering would be enough to draw upon to communicate the miseries of men at arms throughout time.

I began studying at Eastern Michigan University. I had already earned my associates degree attending night school on active duty. I started substitute teaching and began my course of study in secondary education. In the winter of 2003 my reserve unit was mobilized for Operation Iraqi Freedom. The idea of going to war seemed to finally come my way. Yet, my turn would not come. My unit was moved to San Diego, CA, where I would remain until June. I spent the summer of 2003 in Virginia Beach, VA – attending an intelligence school.

My first two Black Belts and me in the hills of Camp Pendleton, CA.

U.S. ARMY

I returned to university life in the fall of 2003 and was determined to pursue a career in academia, instead of the military. I dreamt of attaining my PhD and of teaching and writing about war. There was only one problem with my goal. I had trained for war and studied it for years. Yet, I had not been to war. The Siren's song continued to play in my head and I toyed with either going to O.C.S. (Officer Candidates School) in the Marines or joining ROTC (Reserve Officers Training Corps) – so that I could go to graduate school. After a great deal of thought, I joined ROTC in 2005, with the intent of earning my place in the infantry as an officer.

I attained my Masters in History during my time enrolled in ROTC. I spent hours upon hours reading about warfare through eyes of men such as Caesar, Alexander, Xenophon, and Frederick. I read about the epic battles that the ancients participated in. I imagined what it would be like to be in battle. I wondered if I would ever have my turn to face the enemy. I wondered what it was like to command men in battle and march into the uncertain shroud that is the "fog of war."

Life as a ROTC cadet was a wonderful time, spent educating me further in the military arts. I enjoyed learning the principles of leadership and tactics. We spent months learning the methods to both efficiently and effectively manage violence. We toiled over the essential skills of movement, attacks, and calling for fire. Our mentors, officers and seasoned non-commissioned officers such as MAJ Jesse Cox, provided me with the skills that I would need to save the lives of my men in battle. At the same time, they taught me to utilize soldiers to end the lives of our enemies. They taught me to lead and to keep a cool head under pressure. We practiced our battle drills in the woodlands near my university. They prepared us for war. At the end of ROTC, I had earned a place in the infantry ranks. I was commissioned in April of 2007.

Shortly following my commission and Graduate school I was sent to Ft. Benning, GA. I attended BOLC II (Basic Officer Leadership Course), IOBC (Infantry Officer Basic Course) and IMLC (Infantry Mortar Leaders Course). I had broken my leg in Airborne school before commissioning. After rigorous rehab, I was able to regain my strength and make it through the basic infantry courses successfully.

My training as an officer sharpened the blunt aggression skill set that I had honed as an enlisted Marine. I refined my ability to employ squads and a platoon into battle. It was a simply wonderful time in my life. We constantly practiced being in charge of soldiers and we took objectives. I knew that I was fulfilling my boyhood dreams.

My year at Ft. Benning, GA was a lovely time spent learning the ancient art form of the infantry. The prevalence of the infantry throughout the history of conventional war always amazed me. Although we had night vision goggles and automatic weapons, we shared many of the same miseries with our ancient ancestors, the Greek hoplites and the Romans. We learned the limits of sinew and muscle during forced marches and uphill assaults. We knew the miseries entailed on a forced march, when all you can do is bite your lip and tell yourself to keep going. We learned what it was like to see our feet minced into a mess of hot spots and pus-filled blisters after a hike. We knew the misery of the infantry.

Yet, all this we traded for victory and the assault. We know that artillery or aircraft can produce a good deal of terror. Yet, the shock of ground troops still seems to be the perpetual force behind military affairs. To place your men on the objective – in that lays glory and victory.

I completed my officer training in July of 2008. I was taught the skills necessary to employ and manage violence. I would never forget those lessons. Soon, it was time for me to move west. I was assigned to 2nd Battalion, 12th Infantry Regiment (2-12 IN), 4th Brigade Combat Team (4BCT), 4th Infantry Division (4ID), Fort Carson, Colorado.

THE BATTALION: 2-12 IN, 4BCT, 4ID

I began my drive to Fort Carson in August of 2008, knowing that I was going to war in Afghanistan in the coming spring. My drive west was a journey that was accompanied with nerves, anticipation and questions. I thought to myself, "What would war be like? How would I act in battle? Would I make the right decisions in a firefight? Would I live through my time at war?"

I stopped in the middle of nowhere, in Missouri, for a night during my drive to Colorado. That night I dreamed of battle, and the outcome in my dream did not end well. I woke up in a cold sweat and stared at my alarm clock. The clock read 2:12 AM, the exact numbers of my battalion 2-12 IN. Needless to say, I was trying not to be overly superstitious.

I arrived in Colorado and checked into my battalion. I was put on the waiting list to get a platoon. In the infantry world, you go into waiting, which meant staff-work. I worked in the battalion's S-3 section for a couple of months, assisting with various training events such as ranges and forced marches. It was a good way to learn the ropes of what it took to train a battalion for war.

One Thursday afternoon, I was told to go see my battalion commander. At the time I did not know why. I thought perhaps that I had been placed as a lead on a new project. I marched in, and he told me to be seated. He said, "Tony, I am giving you a platoon in Destroyer Company (later to be called Dagger). You will be assigned to 4th Platoon."

I was so happy that I had to hold back tears which were dwelling up in my eyes. My heart burned with such happiness and excitement. Even now as I write about it, I can recall the feeling. It was one of the happiest moments of my life. I checked into my new company and met the men that I would face the perils of death with.

I was now a platoon leader in one of the most menacing fighting forces to ever march on the face of the Earth. We were the most modern and well-equipped army the world has ever known. My turn to go to war was approaching. Soon, combat would no longer be this obscure figment of my imagination. Rather, it would become my entire world.

WAR TRAINING
OCTOBER-NOVEMBER
2008

LEARNING THE ROPES

As a second lieutenant, I began learning the ropes of the infantry. Taking command of my platoon, I knew that in about seven months time I would take 4th platoon into combat. I did my best to learn as much as I could in the short time we had before flying to war. In only a few weeks I learned a great deal about infantry tactics. I was quickly inserted into the massive training cycle that our battalion used to prepare us for combat. I led my platoon in a field exercise only days after arriving at my company. My platoon and I went through several battle drills, including ambushes, MEDEVACs, and quick reaction forces. A few missions I did well on. On others, it was a loss. I lost a few battles in these mock engagements. Our training was not easy. At times, we made training hard so that you lost. It forced you to attempt to work through a chaotic environment. It forced you to grow and seek to dominate. It seemed, in training, you learned more from losing than you did from victory. We spent weeks reacting to ambushes and creating HLZs (helicopter landing zones). My battalion prepared us to meet the dangerous scenarios we would later encounter in battle.

We also helped to train other battalions in our brigade. My platoon spent time acting as OPFOR (the opposing force, a practice force to engage American forces in mock battle) for 1st Battalion, 12th Infantry Regiment. I broke my platoon into teams and we practiced attacking infantry platoons. We prepared them for the battles they would soon fight in Afghanistan. We simulated IED attacks, meetings with tribal elders, and ambushes. We trained hard and fought tenaciously against our opponents.

On one occasion, I had a few of my men, including SPC Kruger, PVT Brenton, PVT Cortez, and SPC Warner, with me on an ambush. We sat on high ground and waited for a convoy. I remember waiting there that night for the American platoon to come within range. We were wearing the traditional Islamic garb. We waited. I remembered thinking, how ironic this was as our opponents in Afghanistan would soon do the same thing to us. The American Blue Force platoon was soon in range. We initiated the ambush with our M2 .50 cal and created chaos.

SOLDIERS AND AFGHANS

During our breaks from training, we had cultural awareness classes from Afghans who volunteered their services to train the American military. Many of them were translators at the front lines for a few years. These Afghans provided us a window into these harsh lands. They painted pictures of intricate, complex and multi-faceted battlefields.

One Afghan compared the Taliban to ants, which have their nest in Pakistan. It seemed that the permeable Afghan/Pakistan border would present the same problems to us as it did to our Soviet opponents years ago. I found it ironic – these same supply routes that we used to defeat our Cold War opponents plagued us as well.

The interpreters continued to tell us how the enemy would observe us in battle. Due to the mountainous terrain, the enemy has almost 24-hour surveillance on our movements. They explained the enemy's ability to observe us from their mountainous observation posts. Our small outposts would be seated at the foot of their mountain citadels.

We invited these Afghans within our walls. My first class on Afghan culture was an amazing sight to behold. On one side many of our soldiers were seated, listening, many of which were hardened by horrible battles in Iraq. I remembered looking at the men's faces. Some of the men were obviously daydreaming of various things far from this outdoor lecture. In some of them I saw something much different. They were undoubtedly thinking of battles fought long ago. I saw many of them preparing for the battles that were soon to come.

Across from them were seated the five Afghans that attempted to shed light into a mysterious world filled with darkness and deceit. The Afghans told us that one problem is the "fast" rate of incoming units. By this they mean the one-year rotation that we spend at war. They saw time quite differently than us. They told us an Afghan proverb to discuss this matter. "A new thief ends up in the barn."

One Afghan told us not to trust anyone – including the ANA (Afghan National Army). I did not like the idea that my men and I would be working with Afghan troops who we apparently could not trust. However, I reminded myself to stay positive and see what the future would bring.

One night during our time in the field the men made a campfire and huddled around it. They spent their time bullshitting with one another. I watched them as I was returning from our TOC (tactical operations center). They were laughing, joking and telling stories. Some of the stories were about firefights long ago in Mesopotamia. Others recounted their nightly excursions to the local bars. It was a beautiful sight to see these soldiers simply be young men and to speak comfortably to their comrades. Their faces appeared beautiful, as the shadows of the campfire danced upon them.

Our Afghan trainers watched from a little distance away, speaking in their eastern tongues. I wondered what they were speaking about. Their cryptic tongues danced in the darkness. The soldiers continued bullshitting. The Afghans listened.

JANUARY
2009

JRTC FT. POLK, LOUISIANA

FORT POLK

A few days following the New Year, 4th Brigade Combat Team, 4th Infantry Division deployed to JRTC (Joint Readiness training Center), Fort Polk, Louisiana. Our platoon came together there. I became intimately familiar not only with the men's faces and their abilities, but also their lives, hopes and fears. I was blessed with a strong crop of men.

I was blessed by my NCOs (non commissioned officers) and men in my platoon – in particular my Platoon Sergeant, SFC Staley. He blended the elements of a natural leader and tactician with a calm and patient personality. Just by speaking to him, I knew that he could bring calm and experience into any situation. He had some of the best *Coup d'oeil* (the ability to see the tactical aspects of a situation in an instant) that I have ever seen. SFC Staley's tactical abilities devised courses of actions that at times were superior to the entire number of officers combined in my company. My squad leaders, Sergeants Moffet, Wade, and Richardson, were all veterans of Iraq. My veteran specialists, Krueger, Dement, and Warner, brought the precise gunner abilities that made me feel confident. My men such as Diamante, Mendiola, Cortez, Stacey, Cofflin, Phelps, Troxell, and Brenton were strong lads and full of life.

Each day my men and I became closer. One day during training, I bought my platoon pizza. This rare field luxury was afforded to us because one of the men in the company held his reenlistment ceremony at the base Pizza Hut, so that our company could have a treat. I found it almost comical to watch them eat pizza. It was strange seeing these warriors who were capable of so much destruction show their softer side. They possessed the abilities to end life, to melt a house, and to turn a body into minced meat and muscle, yet they became like kids again.

Throughout training, I thought of my first meeting with these mysterious Sirens of war that embodied contact with the enemy. There was no doubt about it then; I was going to have my meeting with them and I wondered who they were and what they looked like. Contact has been in men's minds in every generation since the founding of armies. Men have written poems about these Sirens and libraries of books have been written describing their deadly curls and curves. When I was away from my men, I prayed that I would meet the enemy with valor, bravery, and violence. I prayed that meeting her would not cost the lives of any of my men. At times I looked at the constellation Orion. That constellation had a very special meaning to me. I first became familiar with this constellation at boot camp on Parris Island, SC, back in that unforgiving summer of 1998. It gave me hope and filled my heart with peace. It gives me hope to this day.

We spent our days going through various training scenarios. We conducted missions, interacted with Afghans, and had mock battles with the OPFOR.

Following each mission, we huddled up and held a pseudo review session regarding the action. We discussed both our successes and our failures. At times, these lessons were brutal. Yet they stayed with you and their lessons saved you.

My Platoon Sergeant continued to mentor me, fulfilling his role as the most experienced warrior in the platoon. Talking with SFC Staley about war, he said that a leader needed to be calm during combat. He said that I would have to be the one to stay calm when the chaos enveloped everything else. His words were truly wise. I tried to be that eye of the storm that he described. It was an easy concept to learn, but staying calm was a difficult concept to put into action once bullets and RPGs tore the air around you – as I would later find out.

Eye of the storm:

The beach and the waters are calm. The sky is blue and untouched. The clouds are like fields of cotton in the sky. The animals graze without care or worry. The gentle breeze kisses the earth.

Then to the east, clouds begin to gather. The wind picks up. The tidal water begins to darken. The animals sense what is to come. The trees, those silent steadfast sentries of the wilderness, can sense the coming onslaught. They have stood watch over the earth throughout the millennia. They begin to move slowly, side to side.

They know.

The rain and wind start only as a trickle – just like the initial bursts of machine gun fire in battle. It seems that within seconds the cacophony of the storm takes over. Her strong winds are the whizzing of the NATO munitions. The cracks of thunder are the impacts, where lighting emits.

The storm is our destruction.

SIREN'S SONG

I must be the eye of the storm. I must carry the storm to destroy those whom wish havoc on us.

Be the eye.

Be the calm surrounded by terror.

Training continued at JRTC, teaching my men and myself the advanced techniques of implementing American firepower on the field of battle. My platoon was detached on our own to conduct mounted training and utilize helicopters in battle. We were separated from our battalion, as well as our company. We were quartered in a small mock village for two days. I was trained to employ helicopters, OH-58s Kiowa Warriors against the enemy. My friend, LT Gabriel Dearman, and I practiced calling the helicopters in to eliminate targets. I was truly in awe of American firepower and I was glad to advance my skill set in battle.

The weather was simply perfect as we spent our down time relaxing. I felt as if I was the head of a detached unit guarding the frontier in a land long ago. It was what I always imagined. We practiced and rehearsed battle drills and just simply enjoyed the calming effects of camp life. It was such a beautiful scene, to see my men eating their MREs (meals ready to eat) near the campfire at sunset. Each man was content and only a low murmur of conversation emitted from this normally rowdy bunch. The fire was calming and peaceful. I wondered how many times through the course of military history this drama replayed itself. Men dirty from campaign and tired from practicing battle and wearing armor – enjoying their dinner around a campfire. It was my idea of peace. It was a peace that I would think about during my year in the chaos.

One night I had a dream prior to a mission. I saw an animal, which I thought was a deer on the road. I radioed it up through the convoy. As my vehicle came closer, it revealed itself to be a ram. I could distinctly see his horns and his fur. I radioed it up to CPT Louis Gianoulakis, my company commander. He told me that the ram would lead us to the objective. In ancient times, one could not have hoped for a more favorable sign, a ram. It was as if Aires himself came to smile upon my training and my war.

Soon the training segment of JRTC came to an end. My platoon's ability to perform battle had improved dramatically. We spent a couple of days completing our intense slew of AARs (After Action Reports, an overview of our past performance). I was impressed by the science, time, effort, and money the Army had invested into preparing men for war.

We soon were on our way back to Fort Carson, where we spent our final weeks of peace. It was in those weeks that I wondered if we were really that different from those ancient men at arms in ancient Greece. I wondered what it was like for them. Their preparation, at least on the psychological side, more than likely consisted of nothing more than campfire tales from older hoplites. They would talk of men in purple tunics and tiaras. The enemy spoke in babble or a barbar. They were barbarians. It was this horde they were preparing to face.

It was certainly amazing to think that the cradle of democracy was well within the sights and the grasp of the barbarians. That must have sent terror to the spines of many. Although they were outnumbered on several occasions, the Greeks still formed up and charged with honor.

The horde we faced sent scouts to our homeland. They burned down a portion of one of our greatest cities to the ground. They came into the very walls of our castle and raped us. They committed murder, with the world and our children watching. They burned civilians alive. They crushed children. They committed a great atrocity in one of our greatest cities.

Most of 4th Platoon: SPC Warner, SPC Troxell, SPC Stacey, DOC Rojas, SPC Cofflin, SPC Mendiola, SPC Cortez, SGT Dement, SPC Brenton, SPC Phelps, SGT Krueger, SGT Wade, SGT Richardson. Front: 2LT Salinas, SFC Staley. (Not in this picture: SGT Moffet, SPC Jones, SPC Diamante, SPC James, SGT Mauldin, SPC Martinez, PFC Johnson)

Now we hunted, we chased and we would kill. We prepared for our *Anabasis*, our march into the high country. I prayed for a decisive victory. We prepared for the journey to the ends of the earth to fight an enemy that will never make an army and never face us in decisive battles.

TO WAR...
MAY 2009

TO WAR

I left for war in the advance party for my battalion, acting as the temporary company XO (executive officer) for a couple of weeks, before my men would arrive in country. On a May afternoon at our Battalion Headquarters on Ft. Carson, men said their goodbyes to wives, sweethearts and children. We left the battalion that was at times a dreaded place of training and early morning runs. We stowed our gear and our armor in our baggage and soon boarded buses, carrying only back packs and our rifles. We said goodbye to our lives of peace and set off for the beast that awaited us in the Pesh River Valley, Kunar Province, Afghanistan.

We boarded aircraft in Colorado Springs, Colorado. Our first stop would bring us to Bangor, Maine where we briefly deplaned and were greeted by a happy group of civilians and veterans. They offered us smiles and words of thanks. However, in the faces of the veterans I also saw something else; they seemed to know what perils awaited us in those untamed valleys. Yet, they continued to smile, as not to worry us. We continued east, stopping in Leipzig, Germany. Again we rested and ate. We soon continued our journey and landed in Manas, Kyrgyzstan.

SIREN'S SONG

Manas was the last stopping point before we landed in a hostile country. This place was a strange hodgepodge of NATO forces. It was an interesting feeling to know that perhaps I was the first of my blood to be in this part of the world. However, perhaps, I thought, a distant relative marched within the ranks of Alexander.

Like the majority of troops waiting in Manas, I spent my time in rest on my bunk. There, far from the front in that former Soviet republic, we lounged and waited. It was carefree there. It was like a summer camp without activities. There was a gym, PX, and a large mess hall. Men and women from NATO's allies could be seen all about, lounging. We all knew that this was the last time we could walk in relative safety without the threat of attack. We were at peace there.

As I lounged about, I would write to these Sirens of war. I would write to them as if I was a young man nervous for his first date with a mature woman.

"Now you draw ever closer. I am trying to prepare myself for that first date. What will you look like? What will you sound like? What time of day, or night for that matter, will our first date be? I wonder how I should act when we first meet. Should I meet you with complete rage and aggression? Or rather, should caution and calmness greet you?

Perhaps elements of both would be more appropriate. I will strive to be brave when you introduce yourself. I am ready for you. My men are ready for you."

I thought about all the preparations that we made for war. Not only in training, but logistically. We packed for war, months before deploying. A chaos-strewn motor pool on Fort Carson became organized and shut tight.

The weapons and equipment waited in our containers. The weapons listened to the soldiers, inspecting them and re-inspecting them. They played witness to huge machinery moving them.

The sea is yet another perpetual highway for war, her waves have played witness to armies going to war for millennia. Armies since the time of Troy, Britannia, and into our modern age have sailed upon the sea. Our carefully packed equipment went to sea in a vast armada. Her waters lighten the weight for war. She eases our burden so that we may defend our homeland.

Soon our time to head to the front approached. We prepared our armor. We spent a few minutes taking our armor out of our baggage and dressed for war. We inserted our ballistic plates into our body armor and adjusted our vests to fit properly around our bodies. It was time. We were bused to our aircraft and flew into Afghanistan.

BAGRAM – JALALABAD

I landed at Bagram Airbase, Afghanistan. We arrived at night and were quickly shuffled into some tents. As morning came, the first thing I noticed were the majestic peaks that surrounded me for as far as the eye could see. They were the Hindu Kush Mountains and were gigantic, snow capped and jagged. They seemed to warn outsiders of the dangers that lay within her valleys and I wondered what exactly waited for me there.

The remnants of what was once a village lay beside the base perimeter. There were crops of some sort growing. I saw some shepherd boys tending their flock just outside the fence line. It was stunning to see shepherds amidst the tip of the spear of NATO's forces. The stunning simplicity and innocence only yards from the most modern military on the face of the earth brought a smile to my face. In one instance, the 9th and 21st century breathed upon one another. It was such a calming moment that helped to ease my nerves that come with being new to a combat zone. I saw one small boy, no older than the age of nine, tending to his flock of sheep. The boy ran into the sheep headfirst and pushed them on.

The Hindu Kush. The peaks provide warning to what lies within their valleys.

Bagram looked like a massive staging point for a great war. I thought that perhaps this was how Messina, Italy may have appeared centuries ago during the crusades. Troops from various nations and civilian contractors were walking to and from motor pools swelled with supplies. The air was charged with energy. I spent a few days conducting in-processing and training briefs. I was very anxious to get to our valley.

Once our initial training in Afghanistan was complete, we again boarded aircraft and flew to Jalalabad. We landed at Jalalabad Airfield, or what we called JAF. The further east we traveled, the more rustic were the scenes and living conditions. Jalalabad is located in the Kunar river valley, south of the Pesh Valley. JAF was attacked from time to time, but not to the extent of the valley Combat Outposts (COPs). There were still luxuries such as a PX, and a Green Bean (coffee shop), on the base. I spent a couple days at JAF, and received training on funds handling and other tasks.

ENTER THE VALLEY

My time at JAF was complete. Once again, we readied our armor and prepared for our journey. Soon we would be moving into the Pesh River Valley. I was with my company supply sergeant, SPC Wafford, and the rest of the company XOs in the battalion. We staged on the HLZ, in the hot Afghan night. We sat and waited for our Chinook helicopter to spin up its engines. I looked to the sky and prepared myself to enter the Pesh River Valley and the darkness of war. Soon the aircraft spun its mighty rotors and pushed a warm backwash of air and dust into our faces. Afghanistan entered my nostrils and mouth. I tasted the battlefield. I coughed it up and wiped the sand from my mouth. It was time. We quickly loaded onto the aircraft and flew into the dark night.

I peered into the eerie darkness, utilizing my night vision goggles (NVGs). I watched JAF as we flew away from it. JAF had lights on. The Pesh River Valley outposts did not have lights on at night, as mountains surrounded them. One could feel a tension in the aircraft as we took off. The men's faces showed concern. Each man was attempting to prevent fear from overtaking him. There was no doubt any more that we were going into harm's way. We were flying into one of the most dangerous places on earth. The heat of the spring air intermixed with my growing anticipation of moving to the Pesh River Valley. My anticipation of seeing my first war and of meeting contact continued to grow. The reality of the danger was set in as the Chinook conducted a test fire of its machine guns. The serenade of the 240Bs (machine guns), made the war real to me. With those live rounds, the reality of war set in.

We landed on the HLZ at FOB Blessing. We all piled out and spilled into the darkness. I did not know what to expect as I peered through my NVGs. FOB Blessing, like most forward locations, was a blackout FOB, meaning there were no lights at night. It was amazing to see this bastion of American firepower shrouded in darkness. We lumbered up a large hill leading from the HLZ to our quarters. The sky was clear and the air was very hot. I could not see the surrounding terrain. I soon found a bed for the night.

MORNING: A SAVAGE BEAUTY

I awoke and began my first morning in a true combat zone. I wiped dust from my eyes and walked outside. The bright sunlight beamed down upon me. I looked at the ground and waited for my eyes to adjust. I looked up and my jaw dropped as I gazed at the surrounding terrain. I thought to myself, "If this land is as dangerous as it is beautiful, we are in for one hell of a fight." Mountains on every side surrounded us. The sight was tremendously inspiring and beautiful, almost beyond description. Jagged mountains and ridgelines surrounded us from every angle. The landscape appeared daunting and brutal. It was no wonder that this place defeated the Russians; it was the most rugged terrain I have ever set my eyes upon.

Savage beauty: the Pesh River Valley

I was given a day at FOB Blessing to rest before I journeyed to COP Michigan to begin my XO duties. I lounged and rested around my quarters on the very rustic FOB. I found some time alone in solace, writing. Soldiers from 1-26 IN, 1st Infantry Division soon joined me. They bullshitted amongst themselves and I took the opportunity to ask about the fighting in these dark valleys. These soldiers were my introduction to the real fighting in the Pesh River Valley. They spoke of some very hard battles ahead. The men told me, "It's like fighting ghosts. You rarely see the enemy."

BOOM!

As I was writing and attempting to enjoy my last few moments of peace, I heard one of the loudest noises in my life. The concussion from the blast shook the shelter I was under and rattled my body. I stood up, with the intent to run and get my armor on. The men who sat next to me did nothing. That's how I learned the difference between outgoing and incoming artillery fire.

The large explosion was one of the 155's (an artillery piece) firing from the FOB. The cannons were undoubtedly supporting a firefight a few miles away. It was my first time hearing this dragon roar so close. The shock and the noise were terribly loud. It shook the building and the ground under our feet. The men near me simply continued about their business. They treated the outgoing fire with about as much regard as a man gives to the chirping of birds. Violence and destruction were normal there. I was entering the storm of the valley. I knew it would not be long until my first meeting with battle. As each day passed I grew more and more anxious.

COP MICHIGAN

The next dawn, it was time for me to move to Combat Outpost Michigan. A platoon from D/1-26 IN picked me up. I donned my armor and we drove east. Admittedly, I was anxious and excited during the convoy. I peered out through the windows of armored beasts. We first passed through the city of Nangalam, the largest village in the Pesh River Valley. It had a very busy and bustling market. Within a few minutes we were through Nangalam.

We continued east. I felt the men around me tense up when we came to an area called Tantil. The gunner of my vehicle quickly shifted his sector of fire and prepared himself. I would find out for myself one day why the tension increased there. I was in awe of the savage simple beauty of the valley floor. Beautiful terraced fields flanked these horribly rugged mountains. The Pesh River flowed through the center of the valley and the sun sparkled brilliantly upon it. The villages were a composition of concrete and mud brick walls. It looked like a scene from the Bible. I could not believe my eyes.

We soon arrived at COP Michigan without incident. COP Michigan was the gate to the Korengal valley. The mountains came very close to the COP. I assumed that the enemy came very close as well. COP Michigan was much smaller than FOB Blessing. It felt like an old outpost somewhere on the American frontier in the midst of Indian Country.

I began my XO duties on COP Michigan and began taking account for the various weapons and property that my commander would sign for. During my first evening on COP Michigan, I heard the report of an IED strike over the radio. A platoon was attacked near Blessing. Some of the soldiers were injured. It was met by acceptance in the company TOC. The idea of an IED blast was indeed somewhat frightening to me. I looked at the officers near me as I was working on some figures. Planning continued, almost without a ripple. The men around me were calloused to such things.

SIREN'S SONG

My duties continued for a few days on COP Michigan, preparing our equipment for war. I conducted my work amidst a sea of contact. The sounds of combat, only a few kilometers away, echoed down the valley. These violent echoes told me of the promise of combat that soon awaited me. The 120 mm mortars on our COP fired several fire missions daily. They helped support fire fights elsewhere in the Pesh River Valley. I grew anxious for my first date with contact. The time was approaching. I waited.

In the evenings I talked with the 1-26 IN platoon leaders and XO. They told me stories from their battles that would soon be mine. We passed the time by making jokes with one another. We smiled and laughed in the middle of this ocean of combat.

My head swelled with the plethora of new experiences that I had already encountered in Afghanistan. I was getting closer to this thing called combat. I was slowly being introduced to both the sights and the sounds of war. The mystery of warfare was slowly revealing itself to me. Although I had not seen the Sirens of war just yet, I heard their song. I was in the mists and the fog of the Siren's. I closed my eyes and I could hear their waves of war slam upon the rocks.

CONTACT!
JUNE 2009

Combat was finally becoming a reality. It was no longer this object of obscurity or myth. War became real and began to teach me its many truths. The lessons of war come quickly. The Sirens lectured to me and their lessons are never forgotten. The Siren's welcomed me to their valley and the source of chaos. These lectures are forever inscribed on the tablet of your heart and soul. It was an education that I had envisioned for years on end.

CONTACT

I was fast asleep, exhausted from the previous day spent inventorying weapons and property under the hot sun. I was sleeping soundly in the officer's barracks. Suddenly I was awakened by machine gun fire.

At once a concert of battle thundered across the valley. The ANA and our forces answered with our heavy weapons. It was my first time hearing a firefight of sorts. I have heard gunfire before at ranges or during hunting. Yet, when I heard it here, it was like hearing it for the first time. I sensed the sheer intensity of the moment. The danger and excitement swelled from deep inside me. Every fiber within me became awakened. I was alert and alive. There is no better alarm clock – as my adrenaline pumped into my veins without hesitation.

I jumped off my bunk and quickly donned my armor, grabbed my rifle, and sprinted to the TOC. The officers there began calling for fire on the hostile forces. Our 120mm mortars and the machine guns from the towers sounded in a beautiful symphony of violence. Hearing the thuds from our mortars as they impacted was very reassuring. The action was over quickly.

Our fort was attacked a few more times on that day. I found it more and more exhilarating with each action. My heart continued to inject that ancient serum of adrenaline into my body. In each of the engagements we pounded the highlands with a hail of machine gun, MK 19 (40mm grenades), and mortars.

These attacks provided me with crucial insight into combat officership. I paid particular attention to how the officers called for fire and led the counterattack. I knew that such responsibilities would soon rest on my shoulders. I learned of combat by defending COP Michigan, which routinely seemed to receive small arms fire. These initial actions confirmed that this would be a tour full of combat.

FIRST WHIZ OF A BULLET

Another day of battle greeted our walls on COP Michigan. The same concert of fire joined the atmosphere. As always, it took more than just bullets to end firefights here. It took mortars.

I followed the 1-26 IN officers outside the TOC and joined one of the platoon leaders as he adjusted mortar fire onto the enemy. We moved from place to place in our small Hesco fortress (essentially a 10' x 3' x 3' steel basket lined with felt and filled with earth). We were bounding, when we were greeted by a godforsaken noise. For the first time in my life I heard the sickening whiz of an enemy's bullet. Dirt fell from the bullet's impact on the Hesco just above my head. I asked an officer next to me, "Is that what I think it was?" I already knew the answer. He answered, "Yep."

That whiz turned volumes of blood lust and caffeine into the sheer reality that battle keeps for warriors. I felt the round break the air close to me. The dirt that fell upon me only drove the point deeper. The sound was unmistakable and unforgettable. That moment, for me, was one of the most unforgettable lessons into the reality of war.

That horrible whiz told me many things. It told me the truth of battle and the truth of war itself. It told me that I was in Afghanistan. The sound made me realize that I had finally found what I had been searching for all my life. I was at war. This was that sick Siren's song that I have searched for. The Siren's whispered to me at that moment. They seemed to tease me and made me question just how brave I was. I was sailing closer and closer to the jagged rocks of the Sirens. I knew that it would not be long before I led my own men into the darkness.

COP Michigan continued to take contact routinely throughout my stay. I was nearly finished with my XO duties and I was looking forward to the arrival of my company and my platoon. As contact continued to pay visits, my time came to join in the fight. I quickly put on my armor and ran to the mortar pits. I had attended Infantry mortar leaders' course as a 2nd Lieutenant. I knew how to gun and hang mortars. I found the mortar sergeant during the action. I asked if I could help. He said yes. I think the soldiers hanging rounds welcomed the break. I hung a total of six rounds. I loved dropping the 35-pound rounds into the mortar tube. The 120mm shock goes through your body like few things else. I was taught to open my mouth when hanging mortars, as it was supposed to reduce your internal pressure and make the shock less brutal on your body. It was truly a powerful weapon. I finally returned steel in combat, for the first time in my military career. They were my opening rounds in reply to 9/11. Those mortar rounds were my first interjection into direct combat. I wonder if they found their mark as I heard their thuds a few kilometers down the road.

I am here at the ends of land
where earth meets sky
rock meets river
men age fast

I am here where life is intense
bullets tear the sky
and the land bellows smoke

I would again hear those mind sickening whizzes of bullets tearing the sky about my ears during my final days on Michigan. Although the potential for danger was always there, I was glad that I was able to experience this prior to my platoon arriving in theatre. I will never forget these whizzes that whispered of the enemy's death.

Men from my company, including CPT Gianoulakis, LT Tom Halverson, LT John Cumbie, and LT Mark Zambarada finally arrived on COP Michigan. They landed via Chinook. I ran up to them to help with their equipment. Mark Zambarda saw me in my physical training uniform (PTs) and said, "Well it must not be that bad here; if you are wearing PTs." It was a somewhat ironic statement by Mark, who would later be awarded the Silver Star. It was quite an interesting thing to see new soldiers or officers enter a combat zone. You can see it in their faces, they try to look confident and brave – we all did. Yet it was apparent that they knew what they were getting in to.

I soon began to hand the XO duties to LT Tom Halverson. I spent my final day on COP Michigan preparing for the storm that awaited me just to the east. I was honestly a bit sad leaving COP Michigan. I had become very familiar with the faces of the Afghan workers and the surrounding terrain during my two-week stay. COP Michigan was where my first date with these Sirens occurred. The Sirens came to me and we kissed like a young man and his girlfriend in the back seat of a car. That patch of ground and outpost at the gate of the Korengal will always be special to me.

My final sunset at Michigan was spent in reflection and writing. The Muslims prayed five times a day. You could hear it clearly. Amazingly, I found it relaxing. They prayed to God, as I did. Their voices bounced off the valley floor and the mountains as the sun was setting. In the same instant, I could hear an American fighter jet tear through the sky high above me. It was a fitting moment to end my tenure at COP Michigan.

COP HONAKER MIRACLE

My platoon and I were to be attached with Chosen Company, commanded by CPT Shaun Conlin at

Combat Outpost Honaker Miracle. My time had come to finally move to my new home on the line. I again suited up in my armor and bid my goodbyes to mates from Dagger Company. CPT Gianoulakis, my company commander, wished me good luck and told me to take care of my men. LT Zambarda and his platoon escorted me east. We stopped near the village of Matin and the Sheriak valley, a place known for its constant firefights. We halted, scanned the highlands, and offered battle. Yet, no enemy bared himself to our guns.

We dismounted onto the road, and conducted observer training with 120mm mortars onto the highlands. This provided a chance to practice calling in mortars. I was given the radio and I called up the coordinates. It was my first time calling for fire in Afghanistan. It was a skill that I would use over and over again. A group of fifteen children or so gathered around us as we lobbed steel into the mountains.

It was heartbreaking to see school children walking amidst all this chaos. They walked on the road near our vehicle. They were beautiful and innocent. To me, they were the epitome of innocence wrapped in chaos. We gave them notebooks and pencils. They simply watched and smiled as we called for fire onto the mountains. War was normal to them, as it perhaps is to all Afghans.

I made the rest of the journey to Honaker Miracle and was received by the outgoing XO. After a brief tour of the COP and the surrounding terrain, I met the outgoing platoon leader, LT Ed Fox. LT Fox was a large mountain of a man who began showing me the ropes of life in the Pesh valley and the Watapor valley. My platoon had still not arrived. Instead, I had a fire team consisting of SGT Moffet, PVTs Cortez, Mendiola, and Cofflin. I was glad to see them all with me in this land of fire.

COP Honaker Miracle was located at the junction of the Watapor and Pesh River Valley. Surrounding the outpost was a savage ancient beauty, with its terraced farmlands and majestic sights. It looked like a place where western tourists would flock to for hiking excursions. It was difficult to believe that this was one of the most dangerous places on earth. However, enemy contact reinforced the danger there.

The junction of the Watapor and Pesh Valleys.

MORTARS

Following my first patrol outside Honaker Miracle, our COP was attacked with mortars. Small arms attacks seemed like only a nuisance as compared to indirect fire attacks. I have heard mortars before, while in training. It is a deep crushing sound like a "whump." Yet, in combat, it was as if I heard it for the first time in my life. Mortars shake the very ground you stand upon. There was no question that these things could tear you into shreds.

We immediately sprang into action. I joined LT Fox on an elevated TOW (missile) fighting position. The TOW was equipped with an ITAS (Improved Target Acquisition System) that had advanced optics. We scanned for our enemies as mortars continued to fall on and around our outpost. I saw one mortar round land about 150 meters from our position. Smoke and dust rose from the ground. It sounded like a small mountain crashing into the earth. It was as if the earth groaned with war.

INITIAL PATROLS

I began conducting patrols with the platoons from 1-26 Infantry, as well as the Afghan National Army, in order to learn the terrain in my area of operation. Patrolling with the Afghans who were carrying Soviet style weaponry was certainly interesting. I thought it was odd to see RPGs, AKs, and PKMs so close. They were the same type of weapons that had been used to try to kill my friends and me.

Ironically, we call this transition process of incoming and outgoing units a RIP (relief in place). During the RIP I paid special attention to the terrain, thinking where I would maneuver if we received contact. I joined these hodgepodge patrols of American and Afghan infantry moving away from our outpost and further into the different dark folds of this valley. We walked on small footpaths across farmlands that seemed unchanged since biblical times. It was a rustic scene with young men and children plowing fields with what I deemed to be some sort of oxen. I loved the sight of us moving in our heavy armor with automatic weapons. It felt as if I stepped back in the river of time.

Joint patrols with the ANA.

We soon came upon a village called Shenigam, located just to the east of our COP along the Pesh River. I felt like I was walking through an ancient village with its several mud brick alleyways. I smiled as I walked through these ancient footpaths. It was exactly what I had imagined Afghanistan would be like.

In the village of Shenigam, we soon crossed the Pesh River on a ridiculously rugged bridge. We affectionately knew this bridge as the "Indiana Jones Bridge." It was essentially a bridge made of lumber and railroad ties. I had no idea how this thing was created, let alone actually worked. The bridge shook violently over the swift moving Pesh River as we moved over in our heavy armor.

Outskirts of Shenigam village.

Patrols continued around our COP and I continued to work with the ANA. On each patrol the landscape enthralled me. I wondered if it would always have this affect on me. I ate meals with the ANA commander in an attempt to establish rapport. It was one of many cultural lessons that I received in the Pesh Valley. This was their country and I hoped that we could help to deliver them from this war torn age.

I continued to wait for my platoon and proceeded with the RIP process with the men that I had on hand. We conducted a patrol to Asadabad, which held the large base Camp Wright, what we called ABAD. My good friend LT Mike Luth and 3rd Platoon was stationed there. Mike was given the very difficult job of Route Clearance Package (RCP), a process in which they would hunt IEDs (improvised explosive devices) in order to clear the roads for our forces. We clasped arms and wished one another good luck in what we both knew would be a very difficult tour.

So this is where my war was born
Land of river, mountain and sky
Sweat, steel, and fire
Passion, fate, and destiny
This is where my war was born

SHURA – TEA AND PATIENCE

I soon had the opportunity to attend my first Afghan shura (Afghan meeting), held at the District center adjacent to our COP. It was a sight, seemingly from centuries long ago. It consisted of a circle of elders seated on a huge carpet in a plain room. Each man appeared to be the age of at least fifty years old. Some had beards as silver as the full moon, others as dark as the night's sky on a moonless night. We sat with them in this millennia old meeting ritual.

Before joining this circle, you walk up to each man; shake hands, and say, *"Salam Malekium."* I sat and listened to the outgoing company commander introduce CPT Conlin to the elders. The ringing of cell phones interrupted this sacred shura. It was somewhat humorous to see the effects of the 21st century entering this ring of ancient culture. At one point in the shura, an ANP (Afghan National Police) came up to the governor and whispered directly into his ear. It was such an ancient thing to see. It was like a scene of an ancient advisor from long ago whispering into the ear of his king.

It was difficult for me as an energetic lieutenant to understand these meetings at first. Initially, such meetings did not seem very productive. I noticed that the conversations of the eastern tribesmen did not appear to have any decisive results, and they all appeared quite lazy. The participants lounged in this circle and lay on their cushions. I honestly could not believe that this was considered a meeting. The Afghans served us tea following more of what I thought was useless circular conversation. Upon my first sip of tea I burned my mouth. I looked around and noticed that none of the Afghans in the room attempted to drink their tea. Instead, they were patiently waiting for it to cool down. They quietly smirked at me, realizing that I was another impatient Westerner.

I did not realize that I had initially judged and observed the shura with the wrong set of eyes. Months later into my tour, I learned not to judge the shura with the eyes of a Western officer. Instead, I would have to view these meetings through the eyes of an Eastern warrior, where patience is necessary. I learned that patience was one of the Afghans' greatest tools for both war and conversation. I wish I had experienced this epiphany months earlier. Yet some things in counter-insurgency cannot be learned through a manual. Rather, they must be learned upon the ground. After months of attending shuras, I learned to wait for my tea to cool.

QATAR KALA — CONTACT!

The breeze is dying down
The clouds begin to stand still
One can sense the storms
The scent of rain in the air

The heat is not heat
The cold is not cold
The elements are ready
We are ready.

I experienced my first contact with the enemy outside the protective walls of a combat outpost near a village called Qatar Kala. This village was located deep within the Watapor valley, to the north of the COP. Its control was disputed between the coalition forces and the enemy. My platoon had still not arrived. I integrated most of my men that I did have on hand into the convoy. PVT Cofflin was a driver and PVT Mendiola was a gunner of an MK19. SGT Moffet and I were in the back of the MRAP, while LT Fox served as the TC (Truck Commander). RCP under Mike Luth linked up with us at Honaker Miracle. As always, it was good to clasp arms with the familiar faces from Dagger Company, in the predawn darkness before pushing north into chaos and the unknown.

We moved east and passed the district center, the westernmost footprint of our attempt to civilize this land of tribes and to bring light to this place of darkness. We passed through the small village of Shamir Kowtz. After crossing a small bridge, we turned north onto the Watapor road, which became a rocky stream only meters from the pavement. The very rough nature of the road seemed to warn us of the hornet's nest that we approached.

Our MRAPS lumbered like giant beasts upon this barbarous road. The vehicles constantly came close to flipping on their side. Once a vehicle touches this stream you cross into danger. The Watapor valley was one of those dark places on earth that you thought you could conquer through superior technology alone. Perhaps many officers from modern armies had the same thoughts when they first enter such alien lands. The reality of these lands soon taught us that you would need more than just superior technology to claim victory.

Our element moved north on this rocky and unstable road. We soon halted near the site of where a medical clinic once stood. The key leaders from the element, including SGT Moffet and me, dismounted and moved toward the remains of the clinic. For the first time in my life I sensed the contact that would come later that day. Our meeting was long overdue. A physiological change was in my body. I felt it deep in my guts. I felt like a wolf on his first hunt.

I racked a round into my chamber. You do this on every patrol. You pull the charging handle back, and when it slams home, your rifle has the power to take life. I felt charged and alive. It was truly thrilling and I prepared myself for what would come that day.

We moved to the clinic, or what used to be a clinic. It still had 12-foot high white walls standing. However, the inner portion of the structure was completely demolished. Afghans, utilizing coalition support, built the clinic. We walked in and witnessed the full influence of the Taliban. They had rigged it with explosives a few months previously. The inside was mangled concrete and steel. The site was unforgettable. The mangled rebar and concrete looked like a slaughtered lamb with its ribs exposed to the heavens. This was a clinic that could have supported fifty patients a day. Instead, it lay there in decay.

It was a remnant of coalition support raped by evil. Simplicity and innocence embedded in darkness, evil, chaos, and carnage. The coalition built this structure, not to improve our defenses, but rather to bring life and cure sickness. Yet the enemy answered this gift of life with death. There was no mistaking the manner in which the enemy hated us and what we brought into their world. It was an introduction to our enemy that I would never forget.

I moved with the dismounted element south toward Qatar Kala. The vehicles made their way south of the village where we planned on linking up with them later in the day. Overhead, the Kiowa Warriors (helicopters) flew.

Soon it began. I heard the unmistakable crackle of gunfire. It starts slowly every time. Then after a few seconds it erupts. It was ineffective fire. We bounded toward the village and took cover behind a small wall in the northern portion of the village. From this point we began employing the helicopters as well the 120mm/81mm mortars. We began calling in a hellacious amount of firepower.

SGT Moffet and I acted as riflemen and held the right of the line. I listened to the 1-26 IN officers call in fire and helicopters upon our enemy. We watched the Kiowas and the artillery unleash their murderous arsenal on the ridgeline to the northeast. I smiled as the helicopters employed a small inferno of hell upon the enemy. The enemy kept up their fire. I kept scanning and watching our flank. I knew I would have the burden of command once my battalion took over the area. I continued scanning. The enemy fire soon died down and we continued moving south through the village.

Our dismounted element consisted of the officers and squad leaders from the incoming and outgoing units. It was a good array of the company's leadership. Soon, contact visited yet again as we began taking small arms fire. This time we could hear the impacts of the rounds near us. I heard those sickening whizzes. Our element sought cover and continued utilizing our Kiowas and mortars against the enemy.

CONVOY STALLED

While we were taking fire for the second time, the convoy was stalled. A vehicle had broken an axle and an MRAP could not pull it out. It would take a wrecker from a different outpost. This recovery operation would take several hours and many bullets, rockets, and mortars.

During the fighting, sensations were intermingled with intense pulses of adrenaline, anger, and fear. We were locked in battle with these unseen fighters who came in search of martyrdom and death. I honestly was amazed at the tenacity the enemy displayed during fighting as we hammered their positions with mortars and rocket/gun runs from our helicopters. They fought with passion and bravery, as we did. The Taliban have fought outgunned before, as they did against the Soviets.

I remembered that we were fighting for our homeland. I would do my part to defend my country and ensure that it would not be raped like it was on September 11th. Eventually, the enemy fire ceased, at least for a few moments, and we continued south.

We will roar like 1,000 lions

We will shake the valley like our city shook

They will know fear

The Watapor Valley.

MOSQUE: COMBAT AT THE FEET OF ALLAH...

Moving south, our dismounted element and the stalled convoy began taking small arms fire again. We continued to reply with our complement of air and mortar assets. We quickly established a defensive position in the center of town, near the mosque, and continuously called for fire. We remained in this position for a good portion of the day. We established our headquarters and knew that we had to stay and fight it out. We had to provide cover for the stalled convoy until recovery assets arrived.

As mid-afternoon approached, we remained in place and the contact seemed to be dying down. We thought that perhaps the battle was over for the day.

A small stream ran through the center of the village and through our defensive position. It looked almost too peaceful to be here in this battle. For a few moments I thought about how nice it would be to lie there reading a book. My small daydream was interrupted by the call to prayer and a Kiowa conducting a gun run at the opposite side of the valley.

WOMEN AND CHILDREN LEAVING...

We received reports that large groups of women and children were making their way out of the village. I had not seen any up to then so I went to the perimeter to pass the word to the men. As I was telling SGT Moffett, I saw several groups of women and children moving past us at a hurried pace. They looked like groups of frightened ducklings following their mother ducks. It was like something straight from a training scenario. I never thought that a sign of an attack would be that blatant. We prepared for contact. We manned the walls, set security and watched the rooftops and the high ground.

A hail of gunfire exploded. An RPG landed just below the wall on our perimeter. I felt the shock of the impact travel straight through my body. The shock wave knocked over a sergeant; yet he was unharmed. He immediately returned fire onto the highlands.

I did the same. It would be my first time returning rifle fire in combat. I remember seeing the smoke rise slowly from my barrel. We were in contact and it was thrilling. I smiled as I pulled the trigger. It was terribly difficult to control my breathing, as I took aim and fired. I felt a new type of combat engendered euphoria. It was what I always had wanted. I emptied a couple of magazines assisting in the suppression. The moment did not seem real. At the time I still could not believe we were in battle. My heart rate raced and my breath quickened. It was a horribly beautiful loud scene. Even in training, you don't realize how loud combat is going to be. In training you always use hearing protection. In combat, you typically don't. Your ears start ringing and you can at times barely hear the commands and shouts from others.

We poured lead into the highlands. We returned the very death that was sent toward us. The enemy kept up their fire and the air continued to whistle with bullets. In between rounds I looked over the line and saw soldiers engaging and scanning for targets. It was truly a beautiful sight, one that I had searched for my entire life. Kiowas continued to make gun runs and we sent mortar rounds into the mountains.

The 1-26 Infantry commander told me to take my squad leader and hold the right part of the line. SGT Moffet and I moved with a purpose. We sprinted from house to house, stopping before the alleyways that exposed ourselves to the high ground. We were closely followed by enemy machine gun fire and I saw impacts in the alleyways as we sprinted to cover. We eventually stopped and held our position near a barn. We scanned the mountains and watched the flank of our position.

We began taking effective fire. I could not identify where those bastards were. Our entire line was engaged. I decided to collapse our security a bit closer to our HQ. As we where bounding back, we where nearly hit by machine gun fire. I am not sure why, but I asked SGT Moffett, "That fire was for us, huh?"

He answered, "Yes."

We hunkered down and held while the angels of death lit the mountain on fire. After a few hours, the wrecker from FOB Blessing arrived and made the link-up with the disabled vehicle. The enemy fire had significantly died down. Undoubtedly some of our lead had found its mark. It was time for us to return back to our COP.

BOUNDING...

We bounded back in fire teams (bounding is a military movement in which we run in small teams over short distances, while another team provides overwatch, aiming their weapons toward the high ground). Throughout my entire life I did not think that my first time in a large firefight would be complimented by bounding in files across open terrain on a valley floor through a three to four foot trench system. It was certainly a thrilling moment as I ran in full armor through a small stream. At each stop we kept low and scanned the mountains for any threats. I tried to control my breathing and preserve my strength. The warrior's around me showed fatigue as we moved. You could see their lungs rise and lower under the armor. After thirty minutes or so of successive bounds, we were out of enemy range.

We neared Honaker Miracle at about sunset. The convoy had recovered the MRAP. I was drenched in sweat and completely exhausted. As we cleared our weapons entering the COP, I thanked God for sparing my men and me. I had survived my first of many actions outside the wire. I walked into my barracks and one of the outgoing 1-26 Infantry soldiers who did not go on the mission saw me. He asked, "So how was it?"

I said, "It was fucking amazing."

A photo of me upon returning from Qatar Kala. Once touched by battle, you are forever different.

4TH PLATOON ARRIVES

I finally received word that my platoon was set to arrive. I was overjoyed that they would finally join me. They arrived via Chinook helicopter in the early afternoon on the day following the action in Qatar Kala. I waited on the HLZ for them with a great deal of anticipation. I walked to the bird to help my men with their baggage.

SFC Staley walked off the bird and said, "I'm glad to see that you're still in one piece." This hardened combat veteran looked at the surrounding terrain and looked as if he immediately sensed the dangers there. Our war as a platoon was beginning.

That evening I briefed my squad leaders and SFC Staley on our area of operation and some of the threat areas and then dismissed them. I spent a good portion of that night in prayer and asked God for his help to give me the strength, bravery, and wisdom to lead these men with honor. I asked God to help me bring these men home alive.

SNIPER ROUNDS...

As the relief in place was ongoing, I was greeted by a new sensation – sniper rounds. I had just shaved in the early morning and was walking back to my barracks to prepare for the day's patrol. I was greeted by that mind sickening whiz. I saw the dust kick up from the bullet round's impact only a few feet from me. I instantly sprinted to my barracks and prepared my men for action. It was not the ideal way to start a morning. It was my first time touching contact while wearing shower shoes.

We moved west and we bounded there. I never thought that I would perform these old maneuvers through open fields. Truly this ancient land required the most ancient of maneuvers. We moved in our heavy armor like Greeks did in the millennia before us. We were attempting to tame this savage land called Afghanistan. We moved with my good friend LT Tom Goodman's platoon. Together, we patrolled to the Pesh River attempting to force the enemy to reveal himself.

However, these ghosts faded back into the mountains and no battle would come that day.

ANP (AFGHAN NATIONAL POLICE). SPARKS IN THE NIGHT...

I inherited several ANPs and ANP outposts in my area of operation. I diligently attempted to train and form these men into an effective unit. They were little more than tribesmen that were given uniforms and weapons. Training and teaching them became one of my primary objectives as the year continued.

One night we visited the ANP at Shege West. My platoon halted and I met these men for the first time. I walked toward their rustic outpost. It was pitch black outside and was somewhat nerve racking walking toward their outpost. These forces were known to be very trigger-happy. My interpreter shouted and greeted the ANP with a loud, *"Salam Malekium!"* As I walked into the structure, I saw various Soviet-made weapon systems. They were the same weapons initially developed by the Russians and later copied by other nations.

The ANP were very happy to see us. They greeted me in the traditional Pashtun manner, by first placing their hand on my heart, saying *Salam Malekium*, and then shook my hand. The ANP stated that they expected an attack. I assured them that we would keep overwatch for a good portion of the night.

There was something about linking up with these Afghans in the darkness that made a smile come to my face. I loved dismounting from my vehicle and walking up to their dark outpost in the dead of the night. I smiled as I walked and truly felt as if I was a character in a tale of war from long ago.

My platoon mounted up and we provided overwatch for our ANP allies. The ANP fired a burst of PKM into the darkness. The impacting rounds made sparks against the ancient boulders. It was my first time seeing sparks from gunfire. There was just something about it. I felt my adrenaline pump into my veins as I thought that a battle was imminent.

We could not see any hostile forces. We called for IR (infrared illumination) mortar rounds to illuminate the night for us, yet we saw no threats. I then called for regular illumination. The mortar rounds turned darkness into light. The illumination round burned and cast light upon the landscape as it descended down into the darkness. There was no enemy in sight. The ANP were merely jumpy in anticipation of an attack.

RELIEF IN PLACE COMPLETE

I soon bid my goodbyes to LT Fox and the rest of the officers from 1-26 IN, 1st Infantry Division. We took over the responsibility of these lands and set in for what was undoubtedly going to be a challenging year. We continued our patrols, increasing our familiarity with the surrounding villages and key personalities. The district became ours. It was up to us to free the road from the enemy and to permit our forces to travel unhindered.

The Afghan adults seemed quite leery at times toward us on patrol. Perhaps they feared the enemy who visited them when we were not present. In contrast, Children loved joining us on patrols. They would run up to us and yell, "Biscuit! Biscuit!" As an American, I honestly thought that they wanted bread of some sort. In time I learned that they were utilizing the British term for candy or a sweet. I honestly wondered, and still do, if they carried this term from the British influence in the 19th century.

Such innocence in this rugged land was nice to see. The children were like rainbows shining within a storm. They represented hope for this land and their beautiful multi-colored eyes told the story of this ancient segment of the old Silk Road. Their eyes were shades of hazel, green, and even at times blue. This beautiful collage told the tales of the great many crossroads that made up this Afghanistan.

Sparks in the night

Lead flying against stone

Gunpowder and smoke

Nerves clinch, ears open

We peer into the darkness to see the unseen

We peer into the night.

HONOR VICTIS

I soon experienced my first lesson in the dark side of combat. A man from 3rd Platoon, Dagger Company fell in battle. Steven Drees was a young man no more than 20 years old. I found the news of this unfortunate event while on mission at ABAD. My platoon was there conducting maintenance on our vehicles. SFC Staley and I paid LT Mike Luth and 3rd platoon a visit.

It was there I learned what sadness in the eyes of warriors looked like. Although no one cried, it was the most sadness that I have ever seen in the eyes of men.

Their eyes seemed to stand like dams of stone, holding back a river of tears. I felt deep sadness in the depths of my heart. I will never forget the look in their eyes. We meat-eating wolves became puppies for just a moment. Steven Drees fell for his nation and for freedom. He was the first fallen from our company that these mountains and god forsaken valleys claimed.

REFLECTION...

So much of military history must be encased in the moments prior to battle. These moments leading to battle are composed of seemingly endless minutes where one's emotions change from excitement to rage, nervousness, and then boredom. One's mindset can change in a tenth of a second. I had yet to make contact while with my platoon. It seemed that these Sirens were waiting to greet us. They continued to tempt me and I heard their voices from time to time in the distant thuds of mortars to the west. I smelled their perfume in our sweat, in the scent of CLP (lubricant) on our machine guns, and in the fumes from our vehicles.

We stood there with our heavy armor in this land scarred by untold conflict. While on patrol, one could almost sense the footprints in the land, left behind from would-be conquerors in days gone by. Those dark valleys had the ability to swallow armies. I prayed that our efforts would not merely be covered by the winds of time. I was hopeful that we could shine some light into this dark place.

QAMCHI

The village of Qamchi lay just to our east. It was a fair- sized village that was bisected by the Pesh River and joined by a footbridge. My first visits there included assessing the school's needs and meeting the elders. We moved to the Qamchi high school, which lay at the base of a mountain draw. It was a yellow building with an encased courtyard. It reminded me of a small schoolhouse near my father's house in General Trevino, NL, Mexico. A small part of me almost felt as if I had walked in these villages before.

Qamchi from a distance.

I made my first of many visits to the Qamchi girl's school. The building was very nice, especially by Afghan standards. I sat in a classroom with the teachers and headmaster. Since almost becoming a teacher myself, I have a very special affection with places of learning. I was offered a glass of cold water, which I enjoyed. Peering into it, I noticed that it was either well or river water. It seemed almost too fitting to drink a glass of water from the Afghans while seated in my full armor with my rifle in hand. I also had the opportunity to visit the Qamchi ANP checkpoint and spoke with Muhammed, the commander. He was a very charismatic and competent seeming ANP.

Qamchi High School

OP ROCKY

OP (Observation Post) Rocky was just to the northwest of our COP. It rested on a commanding height and would become very special to me. I led my platoon up this mountain citadel for the first time on a brutally hot day. We marched out of our COP and passed the village called Jumma Gundai. We passed through the market whose mud brick pavilions created a scene that looked like it came from a time long forgotten. Afghanistan has numerous sites such as this. In many respects in was like walking in a biblical time adorned with cell phones, a few cars, and machine guns.

We marched past a butcher's shop which had goat carcasses hanging for sale in the open air. Fresh blood was dripping upon the ground from the freshly slaughtered livestock. It smelled of a farm. There was sort of a biblical peace and simplicity that could fool one in these valleys. It looked unchanged from ancient times and it felt marvelous to walk past such sites.

We soon began our march up to this mountain citadel. The trail was hard going in our eighty pounds (more for some of us) of armor, ammo, equipment, and weapons. The march, combined with the heat, seemed to take the starch out of us. The mountains themselves seemed to radiate heat. Each step up the mountain required effort. These goat trails were a far cry from the mountain trails of Colorado Springs. However, we kept the pace at a smart speed. We made it to the top and were greeted by the ANPs who commanded the heights. The view was breath taking. There was that savage beauty for as far as I could see. There was just something about the ground there on OP Rocky. I knew it would always be special to me.

After setting in security, I began my key leader engagement with the ANP commander, named Khan. Khan was a fighter during the Soviet times and had scars and wrinkles upon his face that told of a life of hardship and perpetual warfare. I shared chai (tea) with these Afghan warriors. It was an enjoyable time to be in my armor with my helmet off drinking tea at sunset with them. It felt as if I was destined to be in that valley. Teatime with the Afghans is a very sacred time.

It was another encounter with the Pashtun-Wali code that ruled many of the customs practiced by the people of the Pesh valley. It was a code bound by honor and graciousness. You simply enjoyed the tea. In this land amidst war, chaos, and death, you learned to appreciate the temporary breaks without bloodshed. You simply drank your tea and enjoyed life while no bullets whistled near your ears.

Sunsets at war were especially beautiful. It was a lovely scene as the rays of sunshine slowly pulled off the ancient landscape and the heat of the day slowly dissipated into the shadows. The call to prayer echoed throughout the valley as I drank my chai. Their praises to God echoed off the majestic peaks. Sunsets became my favorite time of day at war. I think that this time of day has always seen the least amount of battle throughout human history. Sunsets seem to cool the tempers of warriors and permit them time to give thanks for yet another day of life. Dawn in both modern and ancient times was and still is the preferred time for attack. Not only does dawn provide cool temperatures and light to move into position, it also serves as a method to coordinate attacks across miles of terrain. Even in modern combat, battles rarely start at sunset.

Following my visit to OP Rocky, my platoon conducted its first night movement climbing down a mountain. It was a striking and simple time within the chaos, as we bid good-bye to our ANP allies. I loved looking upon my men in full kit set with weapons at the ready, surrounded by the Afghans in their linen clothes. We made our way down the rugged mountain. The going was rather tough as we wore our heavy armor and equipment.

We finished our climb, marching in our armor like silent dealers of death. We moved down the Watapor valley with our shadows slowly moving along an ancient streambed as dogs barked far off in the shadows of night. The night was cool and quiet. Moving silently under the stars, with only the sound of our creaking equipment, was delightful to my ears and eyes. It was all that I had ever wanted in life.

SPC Warner, PFC Martinez, SPC Jones, and me on OP Rocky.

CONTACT WITH 4TH PLT

Our date with combat had finally arrived. I was awakened early in the morning and was told to see my company commander. I quickly shaved, dressed and walked to the TOC (tactical operations center). CPT Conlin told me that the Combat Logistics Patrol from our battalion would soon be coming through our area. I was ordered to conduct a patrol to secure the route. I left the TOC with my marching orders in hand. I had been issued this order before, and that day ended without a shot. However, there was something different that day and I felt something brew deep inside of me. I moved back to our barracks and knocked at SFC Staley's door. I gave him the WARNO (warning order, a quick summary of what was going on). SFC Staley, relaxed as always, smiled and listened. He looked at me with the calm that I could always count on.

I felt what my ancient Greeks called the *enthusiasmos*. In my room, as I prepared myself, I felt as if I was possessed by God and his angels of war. I was enraged; I pounded my bed with a deep ancient anger that welled from my inner depths. I knew that we would meet contact this day. I felt it. I was certain of the battle that was to come. I have no idea how, but I was certain. I could almost smell the battle that was to come. I was ready. I felt the battle swell within me. I knew that gunfire would greet us before the sun set that day.

I left my quarters and moved to brief my men. I felt like a Spartan officer going to his phalanx prior to his first battle, knowing that he would lock shields with the enemy that day. I became ready for the contact, which I have sought for my entire adult life. I prepared myself for this date with fate and destiny.

As I walked into the briefing room I began the OPORD (operations order/ mission brief) with a question. I said, "Who is ready to kill the enemy today?"

The men raised their hands. I asked again. I told my men that we would be in battle soon. Some of them looked at me with disbelief. My combat veterans, Sergeants Rich, Moffet, Wade, Kruger, Dement, hardened by battles in Mesopotamia, stirred only a bit. Perhaps they knew it, too.

I saw these Sirens. I felt them. I do not fear you. I will control you.

I walked through the TOC on my way to my vehicle and briefly spoke with CPL Stephen Wilson to ensure our mortars were dialed in on my perceived threat areas. We mounted up and I listened closely to the strong engines of the MRAPs rumble. I checked my Blue Force Tracker (a computer system that uses GPS to track friendly movements). My throat felt dry and I waited for my platoon to give me RED CON ONE status (meaning that they were ready to move). We moved west, slowly, scanning the high ground. We passed the village of Sematan. We continued on, nothing yet. We soon approached the village of Mulkhana.

We approached a large span of open ground and peered into the large mountain draw that dominated the North. The enemy favored these draws as their places of combat. These folds within the mountains became our battlefields. As we entered this area, time seemed to slow down for me. I sensed her close.

It was quiet. It always is before a battle. It is the sort of quiet that only precludes action. Anyone that has been in a firefight can tell you about it. They will tell you that it feels like the absence of time itself. We rolled slowly and quietly under the hot Afghan sun. We scanned the highlands. My stomach clenched as I prepared for the inevitable. Then it started – another lesson into my education of warfare began.

The battle began with an explosion. An RPG exploded near our patrol. The noise was very loud and the primordial self instantly ignited. An exploding RPG is ungodly loud. It sends shockwaves through you, even through armor. The sound of an exploding RPG confirms the terror that surrounds you. My blood was pumping rapidly and my breath quickened.

My platoon opened up on them. We poured lead onto the high ground. We returned the death that was directed toward us. Bursts of PKM and AK 47 were fired upon us. I could see a few impacts on the road and the fields near our position. We returned fire in the face of the enemy and a ferocious firefight ensued. It was the first fire I heard from my men outside the training ground. PVT Cortez was my gunner. I could hear him breathe hard as he fired into the mountain with his MK19. I called to him on the intercom and calmed him down. I told him that he would be okay and that he was doing an excellent job. He continued to fire. I called up the contact report to our company, and the firefight ensued.

We were in the midst of violence. I was attempting to develop the firefight as best as I could. However, several of our gun systems malfunctioned. We pushed through the kill zone to correct the malfunctions and reload. In minutes we turned around and reinitiated contact. Kiowa helicopters soon came on the scene. We directed the helicopters to make their kill. They poured their murderous fire into the side of the mountains. We delivered several more volleys at the fighting positions. We poured waves of metal onto the highlands to destroy the bodies of our enemies. It was amazing to command my platoon. It was so utterly epic to have the earth erupt under the call of my voice. I loved it. It felt like I was meant to do this. The enemy fire soon ceased.

The CLP (combat logistics patrol) safely traveled through the kill zone. We paved them a clear way through superior firepower. 1st Platoon Chosen Co., out of Combat Outpost Able Main and led by LT Mark Harris, arrived to clear the high ground and we provided overwatch. Yet, there was no finding these ghosts. Their bodies disappeared as quickly as they had surfaced.

My platoon and I became baptized with the unholy waters of combat. I was overjoyed that contact had paid us a visit. There would be more dances to follow. It was a good engagement to learn of combat. For my veterans, they re-lit the candle of war in their hearts. For my privates and me; it was our first time embracing the Sirens. I will never forget my first touches of battle, or any of them for that matter. I wonder if any of us ever do.

I would later visit this village where the attack had occurred and spoke to the villagers. It was my first experience in meeting with the population there. The villagers "seemed" not to know anything, although some of them were, in fact, ANP. It appeared that they might have equated survival with not knowing anything. That initial visit did not provide me much in terms of information.

However, it did provide me with more insights into the gracious Pashtun-Wali code. As we patrolled the area, the villagers gave us bread, onions, and some sort of sweet milky yogurt. We ate heartily as we walked around the village. This was such a simple place here. Eating the bread and onions made me feel as if it was the 9th century. You learned to appreciate the temporary peace while you could.

The Pesh River Valley continued to be a great paradox of intense beauty and death with the two elements coexisting with one another. I soon learned to smell the beautiful flowers of Afghanistan intermingled with the scent of death. I began to see both dread and breathtaking beauty in every moment. One was never without the other.

JULY 2009

The Afghan summer matured and with it came the oppressive heat and more fighting. My men and I became ever more familiar with the faces and the terrain in our area of operation. I knew that our lives depended on the knowledge of the ground and its people. My platoon concentrated on maintaining freedom of maneuver on the Pesh River road, training the ANP, developing work projects in the local economy, and developing relationships with local village elders. It seemed that each day was joined with new and challenging lessons in warfare. My platoon added a TOW missile and ITAS system to its arsenal. I had this weapon system mounted on my vehicle, it provided me with a critical asset for command and control as well as the ability to mass fire power on the enemy. At first the TOW did not give us success, but it soon developed into one of our platoon's most devastating combat multipliers.

The surrounding terrain was daunting and powerfully rugged. The mountains were stunning and beautiful. The mountains stood as silent memorials to the thousands of warriors who fulfilled their destinies there. They were always there watching us. We conducted our toils of war in the shadows of death cast from their majestic peaks.

MEMORIAL – BATTLE SALUTE

We honored our fallen warriors at the front with memorials under arms. We paid homage to them and sent our prayers to God in honor of Steven Drees. On this solemn day we traveled west to my company headquarters and my first proper home in Afghanistan, COP Michigan. Our company formed up with mixed emotions. I was overjoyed to clasp arms with men like LT Gabriel Dearman, LT Alex Armstrong, LT John Cumbie, LT Tom Halverson, LT Mike Luth, LT Mark Zambarda, and SFC Travis Platt. However, this reunion of heroes was called for by a less than happy occasion.

We formed up as a company in the center of COP Michigan as a Western phalanx in this barbarous ground. The soldiers formed up shoulder to shoulder, with the officers in the rear. The *Star Spangled Banner* played and as always I felt chills run up and down my spine. Amazing Grace was played by bagpipes. It was inspiring. As we paid homage to this fallen hero, I prayed that contact would not take any more of our men.

We were a formation amidst these rocks. We stood shoulder to shoulder. Apache helicopters guarded our memorial. These archangels flew over us, keeping watch as we paused to mourn. We paid for freedom with our country's most valuable resource – life. It was a solemn day, fully demonstrating the cost of freedom. I prayed that God would speed his soul to the heavens.

Following this heart-wrenching memorial, we mounted up and returned to Honaker Miracle. As soon as we entered our gates, our COP began taking indirect (mortars) and small arms fire. It was exhilarating to enter our COP as the ground shook from incoming mortar fire. Although we were all a bit disheartened after the memorial earlier in the day, the sound of battle quickly boiled our blood and made us eager to return steel upon our enemies.

Our MRAPs fell into our battle positions. We began firing our M2 .50 cal and MK19 onto the mountains. I scanned and finally identified the enemy's position. I called in my first fire mission in combat. I acquired the grid and spoke the coordinates over the radio. It is one thing to request a fire mission in training, but to do it in battle with gunfire and incoming fire is entirely different. Soon, after a few whispers of my voice, I heard our 120mm mortars thunder. I watched as the 35-pound rounds splashed into the mountains. I smiled as I felt the shock of the explosions and heard their terror sound. The engagement was soon over. We had defended our small outpost with honor and American steel.

We were soon called to battle again that day. My friend, Tom Goodman, came under enemy contact as his platoon was leaving the village of Ludam. My platoon was called to arms and we manned the walls to provide cover fire as Tom and his platoon moved back toward our outpost. We again hammered the highlands and sprayed a wonderful assortment of fire upon the enemy. Kiowa helicopters arrived and aided us in our attack. My TOW missile was ready. We had not fired a TOW missile up to that point in the tour. We were anxious to put it into action. My gunner acquired a target.

TOW MISSILE AND THE 4TH OF JULY

I was given clearance to fire the missile. I gave the order and felt the exhilaration of the upcoming kill. I smiled, as I knew the enemy would soon receive a world of pain. The TOW missile launched with might, but I did not hear or attain visual on an impact. Unfortunately, the TOW did not arm and fell short. The missile misfired and bounced a few hundred meters south of our COP.

We continued the battle, utilizing our machine guns and mortars. Soon I was able to see my first bomb drops from American aircraft. The enemy was bombarded by three 500-pound bombs. Observing bomb drops is an incredible sight to behold. There are times in combat in Afghanistan that you don't feel like a superpower. Rather, it feels like you are merely infantry interlocked with the enemy infantry, using mostly machine guns. But when F-16's came to our aid, there was no doubting that the United States is a super power. From mere whispers of our voices, the power of all of hell's fury punished the enemy. Initially you see a cloud of smoke billow from the impact. A few seconds later the shockwave hits you and you embrace the true might of the exploding bomb. These bombs shook the very earth and my heart. Their gifts of unholy fire opened a bit of hell upon the earth.

Peace was again paved by overwhelming firepower. However, our misfired TOW missile lay just beyond our walls. We would have to blow it up at the coming dawn, the 4th of July. The following morning I rose early and with one squad from my platoon escorted EOD (Explosive Ordnance Disposal) to our unexploded TOW missile, on the south side of our COP. Luckily, the missile fell within 300 meters of the COP and did not cross the Pesh River.

Goodman's platoon had marked the misfired missile the previous night with an IR flash beacon. We found the missile within a twenty-minute walk through the terraces to the south. Our dog, Duke, accompanied us on the patrol. Duke was a brown mutt that looked somewhat like a Labrador. He loved us and joined my men and Goodman's men on patrols. EOD began their work and we cordoned the missile site.

My interpreter and I ensured that the local villagers remained at a safe distance. Several children were curious of our business. We warned them to keep away. The missile was prepped for detonation within minutes. It was laden with plenty of C4 (explosives). We hastily made our way to the western wall of the COP and awaited the explosion. The noise and shock wave was massive. Many of the soldiers on the base thought that we were under attack.

ANP

I continued my visits with the ANP as I attempted to build rapport. Solar street lights were installed along certain parts of the Pesh River road. In other areas the Taliban destroyed them. I stressed to the ANPs the importance of guarding them. The ANP listened and nodded.

I spoke to the Shege West commander, Nadir. Nadir was lean but seemed powerfully built. My interpreters did not seem to be very fond of the ANPs. The ANPs looked at us like we were a bastion of supplies. At each visit, they almost begged for fuel, Hescos, or other supplies. I would attempt to change the subject. Their insatiable hunger for supplies indicated the little support that their local government provided them. This repeated behavior of begging also indicated the amount of effort it would take to make this force into a competent body.

Amongst minor bickering, the ANP would at times offer me some food or tea. I usually accepted and broke bread with them. I enjoyed breaking bread with these Eastern warriors. All their lives they have known hardship, loss, and war. The more time that I spent with them, the more I realized how different these men were from Western forces. In the West we look to making our country strong and united. It appeared that to many of the Afghans the idea of strength and unity did not extend far beyond the walls of their checkpoint or village.

Elements of the Pasthun Wali code always surfaced in these meetings. On one occasion I was offered watermelon. There would be no tea following this treat. They told me that drinking tea with watermelon causes appendicitis. Chatting with these men made me feel as I was speaking to tribesmen in centuries long ago.

I began to invite the ANP on patrols with me. I watched the ANPs as they carried only a rifle and a few magazines on patrol. They were not bothered with wearing body armor. We seemed bulky and ungraceful moving amongst these jagged rocks as compared to our unarmored allies. I continued visiting them on my daily patrols and invited them to hold vehicle checkpoints with us. It was apparent that they were happy spending the hot summer days in the shaded shelter of their checkpoints rather than patrolling their areas. I was determined to teach the Afghans some initiative and military skills.

Patrols with the ANP.

COMBAT REFLECTIONS

Afghanistan is such an ancient land. Her rocks have withstood the crashing of constant waves of conquest. Her lands have played witness to the countless men at arms that have taken their march there. The ageless mountains breed very tough men. The martial culture of the Pashtuns seems to combine the best elements of the Samurai and the Apache Indians (assisted with RPGs, IEDs, mortars, and machine guns). These Pashtuns possessed a perseverance and ruggedness that I had never known before. This land and its people were not kind to those who come uninvited. I often wondered who these tribesmen were that faced us in battle. Who were these ghosts that we hunted? They traveled from the remote places of the earth to wage Jihad upon us.

They disappeared and re-appeared with cracks of PKM fire and RPGs. We heard them as their rifles echoed off the high ground. We rarely found their dead, or any blood. They burrowed into the rocks and hid.

The Watapor valley was just to our north. I thought it was amazing that only a few kilometers away from our outpost lay a highly contested combat zone. Valleys such as these have always plagued professional armies, as they did the Romans in ancient Scotland. I once questioned why Rome could not hold Scotland and why they decided to build a wall across the mountainous frontier. My time in Kunar made me understand the intricate challenges that mountainous terrain provided to heavy forces. Conventional armies have always had a hard time in such terrain. I began to understand why Hadrian's Wall was built. Our wall in Afghanistan was not one merely made of stone. Our wall was made of combat outposts, airbases, artillery, men, and raw firepower. We attempted to build the Afghan Security Forces into a wall of men as well. Each day we manned our battlements and attempted to bring light into those dark valleys.

For one reason or another, Afghanistan has both captivated and attracted military commanders for centuries. The mountains know the sound of war. They have heard the trumpets of Alexander; they knew the rumbling from the hooves of the Mongol hordes. They have seen the serried squares of her Majesty's Union Jack. They have seen Soviet armor and the forces of NATO. The mountains stand as majestic memorials to the thousands of warriors that have passed there.

It was amazing to think that getting shot at was beginning to feel normal. The battlefield itself started to feel normal. The storm of violence was beginning to feel somewhat manageable. I wondered how to explain the intense slew of emotions that soldiers experience in combat. The beginning of the action starts with a tightening of your muscles. This is what soldiers commonly refer to as the "pucker factor." It is the feeling of anticipation, rage, excitement, and fear combined. One thinks of the possibility of death or injury for some moments. However, I would remind myself that this was my chosen station in life. With this, fear subsided and soon turned into a primordial hunger for combat.

A late afternoon patrol in the Pesh Valley. The mountains watched us like stone dragons that waited to breathe fire down upon us.

QAMCHI GIRL'S SCHOOL

In this type of warfare, developing the community is as important as destroying the enemy. We attempted to show the locals how an organized government could enhance their quality of life. My platoon sponsored dozens of projects that included wells, mosque repairs, district center repair, humanitarian aid, and bridges. My travels took me again to the Qamchi girl's school. My dismount team and I walked across the bridge to the school and the young girls scattered at our approach. Their eyes flashed like emeralds, composed of different colors and shades.

The headmaster of the school invited us in. I was led to their school office and was soon served chai. This time I waited a few minutes before drinking my tea. I told them about the furniture we planned to bring them. The Afghan teachers were happy to hear this news. We sat together and spoke for a bit. One of the teachers suggested that we should convert to Islam so that we could go to heaven when we die. I smiled and thanked the man for the advice.

Following the talk I offered our medical services. My medic, PVT Rojas, assessed a few teachers for their ailments and I think he rather enjoyed treating these Afghans. As Doc Rojas was conducting his medical assessments, I looked out the window and saw my men in buddy teams pulling security and scanning the highlands. My vehicles were just across the river, in case we needed heavy firepower. As light-hearted as this mission seemed, American lives were at risk. We were at risk every time we left the wire, and even as we slept inside the walls of our outpost. We attempted to bring some hope and order into this land ravaged by chaos. I hoped that my men realized these momentous acts that they were undertaking in the valley. We attempted to plant the seeds of liberty in a desolate place. To me, their efforts would never be forgotten.

Students at the Qamchi girl's school. A glimpse of innocence in this chaos.

Students. Flashes of hazel intermingled with amber.

Later, we returned to Qamchi and conducted a furniture drop at the Qamchi Girl's school. We delivered dozens of desks and chairs. The children watched us as we unloaded furniture and carried it into their school. I wondered what these children thought of us. Did we appear as the barbaric infidels in their eyes?

The teachers thanked us for helping and supported us in delivering the furniture. As I prepared to leave, I briefly discussed a few points. I told them that the coalition was attempting to improve their communities. I brought up the fact that wherever we were followed clinics, wells, and roads, whereas the Taliban only brought death and chaos with them. I told them that in the end, the people would have to choose whom to support. I prayed that my case was made.

DISABLED VEHICLE. A LONG RECOVERY

One evening we moved north into the Watapor valley. We were attempting to set up a TCP (traffic control point, a check point in which we questioned and searched those who travel on the road). The road was very hard on our large armored vehicles. One of our vehicles was severely damaged and unable to move. The sun was setting and I knew that we would be in for a long night.

We called back to Honaker Miracle and requested mechanics. I thought we would be attacked that night and set in security as best we could. We were not very far from our base, yet it somewhat felt as if we were cut off. These valleys have the ability of nullifying technology and firepower. I reminded myself that we had more than enough combat power to destroy whatever came our way. We maintained our perimeter and waited as I trooped the line throughout the night. Admittedly, I enjoyed being out there doing what I had always fantasized about. We scanned the shadows, waiting for an attack that I thought was inevitable.

During the night, 3rd Platoon, Charlie Company, under Tom Goodman, sent a patrol and brought mechanics to our position. Their arrival added a high amount of confidence to our situation. The mechanics could not fix the vehicle and the recovery was fast becoming a monstrosity. We would need a wrecker, which meant more time in the valley with a damaged vehicle. It was a full moon and the night was brilliantly illuminated. Duke, our COP dog, came along with 3rd Platoon. He brought a certain amount of comfort and cheer to our eyes and hearts. My sergeants and men performed with excellence. They looked to security and prepared to repel any attack. However, no such attack came.

At sunrise the wrecker arrived. After a couple of painful hours of maneuvering the MRAP, it was ready to be towed. Watching the large armored wheeled beasts struggle along the Watapor road almost seemed to represent Western armies struggling in this guerilla fighter haven. The going was very slow back to base. The vehicle almost tipped while in tow.

Finally, we left the Watapor road. The wrecker could not head west on the bridge toward our COP as the corner was too sharp to take. Our convoy would have to turn around. In this terrain, there were only a few places to turn these massive MRAPs around. There were even fewer for a wrecker towing an MRAP. We headed east with the intent of turning around near Qamchi village.

MEDEVAC BY CHANCE

We continued east toward Qamchi. I was in the lead and was happy that we successfully recovered our MRAP without incident. I was looking forward to returning to our outpost and putting my men to rest. As we headed east, we came across the lead elements of the Combat Logistics Patrol. They were halted and something did not seem right. We waved them to proceed on past us, but they did not move.

I dismounted and spoke with the lead vehicle commander. Something was definitely wrong. His voice was shaken and he was having radio communication issues and appeared very stressed. I soon found out that they had been in an ambush and had two casualties. I called over the radio and informed my men of the situation. We pushed up and set in additional security. The casualties both appeared to be stable. We immediately sent the MEDEVAC request to COP Honaker Miracle. SFC Staley took a section (two vehicles) and evacuated the casualties to Honaker Miracle where the MEDEVAC bird was already en-route to.

The damage to the MRAP was extensive, as it was hit with multiple RPGs. An explosion under the vehicle destroyed the air brake line as well. It would have to be towed out. To make matters worse, the original wrecker that towed my vehicle became damaged while towing. The towing mechanism was damaged and we would need additional recovery assets.

We radioed the situation and soon a crane from Honaker miracle and a wrecker from ABAD with an MP escort arrived. Kiowas arrived on the scene. I took control of them and provided them areas of interest to observe. Unfortunately, my birds of prey found no signs of the enemy. The ghosts had faded back into the darkness as quickly as they arrived.

It was my first time seeing battle damage and American casualties. It was a sight that continued to educate me in the true dangers of war. We were soon ready to move out. We returned to the security of our COP. The summer was getting hotter and the attacks were becoming more ferocious. I knew without a doubt that our engagements with the enemy would continue. I continued to pray to God for the courage and wisdom to meet the enemy with honor.

MATIN, FORESHADOWING

As the month progressed, we continued our patrols in our area and our battalion's area of operation. At times we provided additional escort to the Combat Logistics Patrol. On one instance we moved west through the village of Matin, based at the mouth of the Sheriak valley. Some unnerving signs welcomed us. As soon as we were in sight of the village, I saw several people seeking cover and placing their hands over their ears. I thought that an attack or an IED was imminent and we diligently scanned the high ground as we moved through Matin.

It is in the moments where contact seems imminent that I attempted to control my emotions and instead thought of what I would do should battle be offered. I took note of our grid and looked to see if there were any pre-registered mortar targets in our area. I checked the spacing of my vehicles and took note of our sectors of fire. We prepared, yet on that day, no battle would come to us. SFC Staley told me, "Its moments like that; that will give you grey hair." He was right.

Patrols continued as I increased my efforts in developing a mental map of the area that I was responsible for. I visited the small village of Shamir Kowtz, which rested at the mouth of the Watapor valley. OP Jojo was an ANP checkpoint that rested on the ridgeline overlooking the village. The climb was not nearly as rugged nor as long as OP Rocky. OP Jojo had twelve foot stone walls surrounding it and was actually somewhat of a formidable military position.

The ANP greeting us at OP Jojo.

At times I would bring candy or toys to give to the children that flanked our patrols. On this day I brought a stuffed polar bear with me, looking for the right child to give it to. Amongst the shops I found a female child no older than five years of age. Her father was a carpenter. She looked at me with those large brown eyes that told the story of the hardships of this land. I prayed that the bear could bring at least some joy to this tortured world of war. I told my RTO, SPC Jones, to grab my polar bear from my assault bag (back pack).

"Hey, Jones. Grab me my polar bear."

"Umm, what sir?" Jones said.

"My polar bear." I replied.

"Sir, what the hell is a polar bear?"

"It's a large mammal that lives in the arctic."

We both laughed. He thought it was my nickname for some special piece of equipment.

Afghan girl in the village of Shamir Kowtz.

A ROUTINE AMBUSH

At times we attempted to ambush the enemy that so often ambushed our forces. One day we awoke in the very dead of night and set up an ambush to the east. Moving in the dead of night adds a certain amount of excitement to military operations. Like warriors moving in the days of old, we moved in the silence of night toward our chosen location. We waited for these phantoms and their Soviet weaponry to reveal themselves to us. Today, no luck could be found. We returned to our COP, ate breakfast, and went to sleep.

I was awakened by the unforgiving alarm clock called gunfire. 3rd Platoon received contact in the Watapor and had incurred some wounded. Whenever one of our forces takes casualties, the primordial instincts take over. You want to join the fight as soon as you can. Your instinct tells you to throw forces in that direction as soon as possible. But patience is what is needed. We know this concept as battlefield patience. The eye of the storm comes to life.

Our wounded were swiftly MEDEVAC'd out of the Watapor. 2nd Platoon, A Co. and 1st Platoon, C Co. soon arrived and staged at Honaker Miracle to provide assistance. We had over a company of infantry combat power and prepared to move out. My platoon and the snipers were ordered to move up to OP Jojo to provide overwatch and provide a support by fire from our elevated position.

My platoon lead the march out of the gate. It was quite a sight to see so many infantrymen in battle gear walking behind me. During peacetime, one can see this same sight on a daily basis during morning P.T. ruck marches on any military base in the United States. Here, it was like seeing it for the first time. Men walk differently with loaded weapons. They walk differently when walking toward contact. They moved like a pack of timber wolves; their movements appeared ever so beautiful to me.

We made our way to OP Jojo. It was horribly hot and we sweated and labored under our armor as we ascended this small citadel of rock and elevation. I could see the heat's effects on my men. We made it up and set in. We watched our brothers on the low ground and scanned the high ground to protect them. American firepower sounded its trumpet of terror throughout the day. A-10 Warthog planes dropped bombs and made several gun runs toward the mountain. Kiowa Warriors and Apache helicopters continued to deliver their payload of death upon the enemy. We lit that mountain aflame with our firepower.

Over watch on OP Jojo.

I spoke with several ANP officers who assisted us in the overwatch. They offered me tea. I thought it was such a strange thing to be offered hospitality when we were amidst a battle. This is one of the puzzles of the Pashtun-Wali code. A code bound by revenge, respect, and manners. Some of them appeared to be very dedicated.

A few of them showed me horrific wounds that they acquired from fighting the Taliban. I wondered when they would be able to defend their country. Until then, we would do our part.

Our troops began to pull back south from the Watapor. We scanned the high ground to the north and covered their retrograde. It was such a hot day and many of the men were famished. Once our troops made it safely back to near our base, we pulled off OP Jojo and headed back to Honaker Miracle. CPT Conlin greeted us upon our return, shaking each of our hands. We were all parched and exhausted. Our company had sustained wounded and we were glad to be back within our walls. We took off our armor and were satisfied after a long fight which every man *thought* was over.

COUNTER ATTACK

Only minutes after returning to our fort, the enemy launched a massive counterattack. Indirect and small arms fire began to hammer our base. Immediately we were back in the thick of it. Our COP was receiving effective fire from a recoilless rifle that fired 107mm rockets from the southern draw near the village of Ludam. SPC Krueger, who was on tower guard, began engaging with his 240B.

More incoming rounds pounded the base and their hellacious fire hit several of our buildings. An incoming rocket hit one of my MRAPS, taking it out of action. Luckily, no one was in this truck. The ground was shaking and it appeared that all hell was breaking loose. When a 107mm rocket lands, it makes a sickening loud noise that sounds different than mortars. Upon exploding, it produces a sound like a "whang!"

For the first time, I actually feared for my life as I was running to the TOC. The ground beneath me shook violently. I was occupied with ensuring my platoon was moving to our vehicles to assume battle positions. We were all exhausted from the day's fight thus far. I ran to the TOC to aid my commander in rallying our defenses. SGT Casey McClure filled me in as to the most current update to our dire situation.

My guard tower needed help adjusting mortar rounds on the mountains just to the south of our fort. I took it upon myself to run there and began making adjustments. A107mm round landed on the COP as I ran to the tower. I saw the dust rise and felt the shock travel through my body. They were getting close. A few PKM rounds landed near me as well. I ran as fast as my legs would permit me to go in full armor. I knew I would have some time before the next rocket impacted. I ran faster and attempted to shed that fear and help my men. I sprinted and felt my lungs scream for air.

SPC Krueger, SGT Rich, and PVT James were in the tower. I was instantly happy to be with them and fight by their sides. I adjusted 120mm mortar fire as Krueger fired the machine gun and James fired his M-14. It felt amazing to adjust this curtain of death via 120mm mortars and I smiled as the mortars presented their promise of death upon the field of battle. Their power was amazing to behold. Every burst of the 240B machine gun filled me with invigorating chills. The noise echoed powerfully loud in our guard tower. My ears were ringing and I was in pure euphoria and ecstasy at that moment. I was thrilled to see our tracer rounds, combined with the impact of mortars, fall upon the enemy positions. To fight shoulder to shoulder with my men was simply wonderful. It was amazing to observe artillery and bring steel rain upon the enemy. Without a doubt we certainly ended some of them that day.

Soon our TOW-Missile MRAP and MK 19 MRAP were online. I ordered CPL Dement to engage. He soon fired two missiles at our foe, both found their mark. SGT Wade unleashed some volleys with the MK 19, a brilliant display of American firepower. I loved seeing my platoon online, delivering a payload of death and destruction. I wish you could hear what it sounded like. Explosions of artillery, theirs and ours, echoed all around. Machine gun fire was rattling our ears and made our ears sing with that horrible ringing that those of us in the infantry are so familiar with. It was as I had envisioned battle would look like for years.

Once I was done calling for fire, I took the opportunity to man the 240B machine gun, my first time firing a machine gun in combat. I can still see the image through my scope. The enemy would intermittingly display his position by his own muzzle flashes. They continued to fire although we threw unholy fire upon them. I smiled with each pull of the trigger as the power of the machine gun radiated through me. I loved watching my tracer rounds burn toward my enemy. I smiled, as it was everything I thought it would be.

The ANA employed their D30 artillery piece for the first time. They were using "direct lay" (this refers to pointing this massive artillery piece directly at the target and shooting it like a traditional cannon.)." The D30 was just as loud as a 155. It was unholy to both listen to and observe. The ANA artillery continued to pound the draw. Soon our blanket of firepower smothered the enemy and the battlefield fell silent. We continued scanning for any further signs of a counter attack, without incident. The battle was over and we retired to a well-earned rest.

Knowing that I ended life was a mind-blowing emotion. It kept me awake for a bit. I did not feel regret. However, I felt the reality of responsibility that an infantry officer has entrusted to him. Taking human life and destroying their will to fight is the ultimate goal of combat. I found that ending life is nothing that should be taken lightly. Once you take a life, you can never give it back. You rob them of their most sacred gift. That day I found out what it meant to manage violence. Perhaps all combat leaders go through this realization after a few battles. I enjoyed the exhilaration. So this is war, I thought. Each moment in it, you experienced an entire lifetime of emotions.

TOW ENGAGEMENTS

Battle seemed to appear out of nowhere in the Pesh Valley. One evening as I was merely relaxing following a day on patrol, we received small arms fire again from the mountains. I had my platoon man their positions and sprinted to the TOC to find out the situation. After gathering the initial report of where the enemy was, I ran to my vehicle. That day, SGT Richardson, a veteran from Iraq, was manning the TOW for me. We diligently scanned in an attempt to find our enemy.

SGT Richardson saw the enemy in the prone in the high ground. I could also see him through my command viewer (this is a monitor that displays the image of what the TOW gunner is observing). Our enemy had no idea that a missile was pointed toward him. I soon ordered his destruction. I watched through my command viewer with my own eyes as our TOW missile spiraled through the air toward our target. We watched the after burner of the TOW missile in silent admiration. We sent death and vengeance toward our enemies. The missile exploded with a brilliant glow, fire, and sparks.

TOW missile launch near Able Main.

CASEVAC

We continued our patrols throughout the Pesh valley. One mission took us to our battalion headquarters at FOB Blessing. We spent a good portion of the day at Blessing. It had been a few days since we had been in action. As we were preparing to leave Blessing, I heard the thuds of mortars in the distance, suggesting we would soon be in battle. As we drove near COP Michigan, 2nd Platoon, under LT John Cumbie and SSG Douglas Middleton, came under fire. We scanned the highlands but did not see any targets. 2nd Platoon broke contact without incident.

A new enemy surfaced – the heat. The temperature was roughly 105 degrees F. It took a severe toll on the men as the platoon maneuvered down the mountainside. I dismounted to gain better situational awareness. Somebody screamed, "We have a casualty over here!"

I did not hear of anyone being shot, but I could have been wrong. I sprinted to where I saw a fire team of soldiers. SPC Williams, a.k.a. Big Will, had collapsed due to heat exhaustion. I was the closest officer to him. I ordered that he be placed in my Humvee immediately. He was a large man and barely conscious.

Big Will was going in and out of consciousness. I did my best to keep him awake by squeezing his hand. I stared into his eyes; it was painful to see a soldier in such a state. The ride to Michigan was maybe one kilometer, yet it felt as if it took much more time. We drove into COP Michigan, moving directly to the aid-station. I helped to lift him. He was alive, but felt like a sack of potatoes. He would be okay.

HOG...

As the month continued, we aided 1st platoon under LT Harris, on a night mission. We used the cover of darkness to insert them on the south side of the Pesh River. We crossed the Dag bridge and drove on the South

Pesh river road, a road that we had not been on before. LT Harris assured me that the road was in good order. We moved cautiously to the insertion point. Inserting and picking up troops is always an intense experience. We returned to COP Able Main and set in for QRF. We passed the night without incident. Each man attempted to find a comfortable way to sleep in his chariot of war.

At dawn, an ANA patrol with its Marine ETT (embedded training team) was moving in the highlands near the Jubai ANP checkpoint. Shortly after first light, the sweet horrible symphony of battle clattered as the unmistakable sound of gunfire and RPG explosions echoed off the mountainsides. The trumpets of war sounded as I felt my primordial instincts become activated once again from deep within me.

Soon the Marines called us over the radio and requested immediate assistance. I could hear a bit of distress in War Hawk's (Marine ETT) voice. We moved in search of our kill, moving hurriedly to the sound of the guns. This feeling of driving into contact is an exhilarating experience as you wade into the unknown. However, you wade into this pool of uncertainty and violence with the best company possible – American patriots and firepower.

As we drove toward our brothers in harm's way, I quickly formulated my plan. I looked at potential grids to call for fire, checked my BFT (Blue Force Tracker) and searched for any air assets that were available. We were in luck. Kiowa Warriors and an A-10 Warthog were inbound. We would have enough firepower to slaughter our enemies.

We rolled in like heavy cavalry at the decisive moment and I heard a feeling of relief in the Marine's voice on the radio. Once there, we quickly established the disposition of our friendly forces and the enemy. The Kiowas appeared just as we did. We acquired the enemy and gave the order to fire. I again gave my men the right to take life. Soon that terribly beautiful noise of American firepower echoed through this ancient dance floor for battle. It was like being at the origin of thunder as we delivered hell upon our foe. We covered the draw with MK19 and .50 cal., ripping apart the enemy fighting positions. I enjoyed, as always, seeing my men hammer the enemy. I smiled as the effects of our munitions walked up and down the mountain. The enemy fire slowed as the first Kiowa gun runs began.

We were still trading rounds with the enemy when I heard the A-10 Warthog come over the net. I had never seen these planes in flight, let alone in battle. As with many things in combat, I did not know what to expect from them. We soon talked them on to the enemy. It first unleashed its arsenal of 30mm cannon in a gun run. Hearing an A-10 fire its gatling gun is one of the most devastating and punishing sounds I have ever beheld in my life. It sounded as if the very gates of hell had opened and demons sounded their trumpets to charge. On the next pass, the A-10 dropped its 500-pound bombs. Shock waves moved through our vehicles and bodies from the explosions. The power was awe-inspiring as the bombs were dropped within 600 meters of us. The battle was soon over. At that moment A-10 planes became the favorite aircraft we ever employed in battle.

Bomb drop from an A-10.

JUBAI

Jubai was toward the western portion of my district. This place witnessed battle several times during my tenure on the Pesh. It also had an ANP checkpoint, well within range of the highlands. It seemed that the ANP and the Taliban here had a de facto live and let live treaty. I would visit there from time to time and meet with the ANP post commander, Abrahime. As always, they seemed very hospitable. In the course of one conversation, after I was given tea, I met one villager who was a mujahedeen in "the time of the Russians" – (this is how the locals referred to the Soviet war here). The ANP, of course, claimed to have fought the Taliban before. Relationships with the ANP continued to be an interesting dynamic and at times made you question their fabric of trust.

BATTLE FOR QATAR KALA #2

Again we visited the village called Qatar Kala. Our entire company moved north to conduct a meeting with the village elders. We pushed north once again into this dark valley known as the Watapor. My friends, Tom Goodman and LT Harris, led their platoons in the dead of night to set in the highlands overlooking this village.

My platoon followed the ANA as the first rays of dawn touched the valley floor. The mist from the cool night was beginning to burn off as we moved into the valley. It was beautiful to my eyes. The corn was knee high and covered the valley floor with a deep emerald green. A few farmers were tending to their fields in the early dawn's light, attempting to take advantage of the daylight before the oppressive heat took over. It felt as if I was walking back in time, centuries ago.

I smiled as I watched men move under the weight of their equipment. The shadows from the leaves of trees dance upon them, flickering like the shadows cast from a campfire. I remained vigilant, scanning each fold of earth as we moved. I searched for our enemies, as I knew that battle would soon erupt. The trail was very rugged and led us into some thick foliage. We moved through the vegetation like armored beasts. We crashed through the ferns and continued north. We crossed a stream and walked into the farmland, leading into the village of Qatar Kala. There was a very questionable bridge, maybe a foot wide, across the stream, more of a plank than anything else. After watching an Afghan soldier fall five feet into the water, I opted to cross via the water. I was soaked up to my waist.

We moved into the village, leaving the commander and HQ element next to the mosque and the area that essentially was the town square. My platoon established security positions in the northwest sector of town. We set in and scanned the highlands. Livestock passed by us, grazing and did not pay any particular attention to us. It was amazing to set in with our sophisticated equipment next to such rustic houses and livestock. Like so many of our patrols here, it felt as if we had crossed a barrier of time and walked into a place long neglected by centuries and order.

Things were calm at first. With our meeting with the elders complete, we began moving south out of the valley. We took up overwatch positions near the village called Marshagul, and waited to for 1st and 3rd Platoons to make their way south. Things were almost too quiet.

1ST PLATOON PINNED DOWN

As many things are in warfare, the stress level went from zero to ten in a matter of seconds. A hail of RPGs and gunfire again sounded the call to battle. As 1st Platoon was attempting to leave, they came under fire and took up defensive positions in a streambed. My platoon and the ANA moved to establish support by fire positions. I ran to the ANA's position and informed GYSGT Ventura about the situation. We moved up cautiously toward the sound of the guns. Moving toward the sound of machine gun fire took some getting used to, perhaps like a fire fighter getting used to walking toward a burning house. We pressed on. We heard the echoes of the PKMs trade screams with American rifles and machine guns. From that moment, I knew that we would be interlocked in a tough fight. I kept close watch on our flanks, as I thought the enemy might try to hit us as we attempted to support our hard pressed brothers.

The ANA moved up to the high ground to support 1st Platoon, we covered the south and west. 1st Platoon was making slow progress through the streambed. We had reports that the enemy were attempting to surround us and prepared ourselves for a large battle.

It was difficult, as always, to pinpoint the location of the enemy. The helicopters continued to hammer the highlands. My element received effective fire near a stonewall that provided some cover to our position. We repositioned to the streambed and continued to cover our flanks. Our forces provided suppressive fire into the highlands. The crack of incoming rifle rounds fills the body with the adrenaline necessary for movement. CPT Conlin called for A Co. 2nd Platoon, mounted QRF out of Honaker Miracle, to move up the Watapor road.

Our battalion commander arrived on the scene and joined the HQ/4th Platoon element on the ground. 1st Platoon continued to make progress south. For a moment it seemed as if all elements would safely make it out of the valley.

MACHINE GUNS BURST… SCREAMING…

The Apache helicopters were making gun runs and their fire seemed effective on the enemy. In modern combat our technology can give us the supreme advantage. However, employing firepower close to your own position is always a dangerous thing to do. Ammunition and firepower will tear friendly flesh as easily as it does our enemy's.

I heard a burst of fire from the Apaches very close to our position, followed by mind sickening screaming over the radio. I will never forget it. I knew what had happened even before anyone said anything. The Apaches were called off following the misplaced gun run.

I could not decipher words, but it was obvious that Americans had been wounded. I did not know which element was hit, nor the status of the wounded. My heart sank as we waited for the report.

We had wounded on the Marine's and ANA's position. The Army combat photographer was severely wounded in his left leg, CPL Ski took a wound on his left side, and the ETT interpreter was wounded. Just an hour prior to this incident, the Army combat photographer photographed me speaking to some Afghans in the village of Marshagul. He performed his job with honor, bravery, and emotion. He had performed his duty flawlessly and calmly under fire. I felt sad for his wounds. I did my best to concentrate on the MEDEVAC.

The C.O. ordered my platoon to investigate the situation of the wounded and the approaching MRAPs. As we moved up, I received effective fire within feet of me. As accustomed to combat as I was becoming, seeing rounds impact the ground near me was still unnerving. We repositioned and found that the mounted QRF platoon had linked up near the casualties. We moved back to the streambed and defended the western sector of our perimeter.

The battalion commander asked if I had a VS-17 panel (an orange flag used for signaling to aircraft) and smoke. I replied yes, and was ordered to set up the HLZ.

At that point I was with the main HQ element with my platoon still covering the flank and was separated from my platoon by about forty meters. I looked up at the mixed HQ elements taking cover below a terrace with us. I asked, "Who can run fast?"

A sergeant from PSYOPS raised his hand. My RTO, the PSYOPs sergeant, and I took off, sprinting. We climbed over the terraces and ran toward the Qatar Kala School, where I had predetermined the link up point for the MRAPs and casualties. I could hear the whizzes of bullets overhead. Our element returned what fire it could as we ran. I saw only random muzzle flashes on the highlands. As we ran faster, I attempted to ignore the threat and concentrated on helping our wounded comrades. As I ran, I observed an open terrace near the school that could be a suitable HLZ. It would have to suffice. The road was approximately thirty meters from the terrace; we could do it.

I ran to the road and linked up with LT Bill Fiorito of A Co. We clasped arms and I thanked him for his help. I was overjoyed to see such a familiar face in this storm of chaos. We discussed our hasty plan to move the wounded. We locked eyes, knowing that this was a hell of a fight. They carried the wounded out of the MRAPs on stretchers. I saw the wounded American soldier, his leg was mangled, attached by perhaps only a few ligaments. I tried not to look at the wound. The situation became quite surreal for me, yet I forced myself to remain focused. I helped the wounded ETT interpreter down to the casualty collection point. The photographer, Eros Hoagland, who had joined us on the patrol, assisted some of the wounded to the HLZ as well. I thanked him for his help. For some reason the presence of this civilian seemed to bring some peace to this moment of chaos. We collected the casualties at the edge of our soon to be HLZ. Additional men from the QRF came and assisted in establishing a perimeter for the HLZ. Men in the area stared at the horrific wounds. I screamed as loud as I could for the men not actively treating the casualty to face out and provide security.

Seeing such a severe wound initially brought feelings of intense fear. I thought of the possibility of being wounded myself, but the lives of the wounded were now in our hands. Rounds still flew close. My friend, LT Eric Bruns, arrived on the scene and offered his assistance.

My first real HLZ. I was screaming for the men to keep watch on the perimeter. (Photo courtesy of Eros Hoagland)

I popped a smoke grenade and the bird landed. The rotor wash was violent and kicked up dirt everywhere. Dirt entered my mouth and nostrils and the war entered me as I breathed. The medic ran toward the casualties and began prepping them. The wounded were not screaming, instead they appeared calm. I yelled as loud as I could to start moving our wounded men. We carried them to the safety of the bird. We ran back to the perimeter to cover the ascending helicopter.

By the time the MEDEVAC was complete, 1st Platoon had safely made it out of the streambed. Fixed wing bomb drops had soon silenced the enemy. The battle appeared to be over. Our elements began moving south. I saw the ANA platoon leader and said, "*Mectab te larsha!* (Go to the school!)" and pointed. He understood and moved his infantry. We all linked up near the school. The fighting was over and we began moving south.

The day was terribly hot and most of the men were out of water. Amazingly, I had a little bit left and shared it with the men. The temperature was over 105F, we were wearing close to eighty pounds of kit and weapons, and the heat was just overly oppressive. After crossing the Marshagul stream, several of the men nearly succumbed to heat exhaustion. As we set in hasty security, men were taking off their helmets. I constantly trooped the line with the little energy that I had left to ensure we were ready to defeat any attack. We pressed on.

Men walk like they are seeing into the unknown when they are well into the effects of heat exhaustion. I helped a few of the men walk as they were succumbing to the effects. As we neared base, I loaded some of the men with minor heat exhaustion on the ANA vehicles.

We waited for the remainder of our company and held overwatch in Marshagul. What remained of my platoon set in security around a mud brick house. My men, including me, were at our limits. SFC Roger brought a patrol from Honaker Miracle to link up with us and brought ice cold Gatorade with him. It was some of the best drink I have ever tasted in my life. SFC Roger, Tom's platoon sergeant, was another experienced warrior. He looked at me in my exhausted state and smiled. He asked, "How do you like it, sir?"

I simply smiled back at him. We trudged back to our outpost. We ended some of our enemy that day, but we were bloodied as well. I thanked God for helping us and prayed for the wounded. As we entered our COP, it was nearly the most exhausted I have ever been in my life. I was thankful that we all made it out of there.

COMBAT INFANTRYMAN'S BADGES

A day following our second battle in Qatar Kala, a general from the 82nd Airborne Division visited our COP. We formed up behind the walls of our barracks. Then the general came to us and awarded us with the badge sought by all infantrymen – the Combat Infantryman's Badge (CIB). It was a proud day and a day I would never forget.

Summer in the Pesh River Valley was in full swing. It seemed that the hotter the days became, the fiercer the fights were. My men and I certainly had experienced our fair share of combat in the little time that we spent in Afghanistan. The Afghan summer taught me the cost of combat and of the nature of war in Afghanistan itself. Our engagements thus far demonstrated the immense challenges that the terrain, combined with our tenacious enemy, presented us with. The enemy in the Pesh River Valley and much of Kunar were not to be under estimated. They were not these feeble untrained creatures that I imagined would attack us. Instead, they were determined and seemingly well equipped. We continued to collide with them several times a week. I knew my platoon would continue to meet them in battle.

Combat Infantryman's Badge.

AUGUST 2009

STORM APPROACHING

Two imposing events were on my mind as the summer continued: Ramadan and the Afghan National Elections. Each of these events presented my platoon with some of our most challenging tests of combat during our tour in Afghanistan. I made frequent visits to the neighboring district center and spoke with the ANP district commander. We spent hours discussing future joint operations and preparing for the upcoming elections. The anticipation of violence associated with these elections was apparent on the faces of the ANP. I could sense their stress grow as the election drew near.

There was a definite lull in combat in the weeks leading up to the Afghan elections. The enemy used the majority of the month to reserve their combat power. I spent several days mentoring the ANP and ANA who were tasked with providing security at several polling sites in our district. We discussed their various defensive plans to be implemented during elections. Their plans, though haphazard, seemed adequate. The ANPs appeared to have a decent plan with entry and exit points, areas to be cordoned with C-wire (concertina wire), as well as staging points for traffic.

SIREN'S SONG

You could easily sense the tension, energy, and excitement surrounding the election. In villages, large pictures displayed candidates and their chosen icons hung with flamboyant colors. These security forces were still in their nascent stages of development. I hoped to enhance their skills quite a bit during my year there.

The valley waits for us

calls to us

It tries to shut us in

It tries to stop the light of order

ABLE MAIN... CONTACT

On one occasion I happened to be near COP Able Main when we heard the unmistakable noise of battle. The enemy had attacked the ANA outpost near Able Main. We moved to the sound of the guns.

COP Able Main suppressed the target area with mortars. We moved our convoy parallel to the engagement area and began sending suppressive fire into the highlands. SPC Krueger engaged the enemy with the ASV (Armored Support Vehicle that has both .50 cal and MK 19). The rest of my trucks began to open fire, slamming a wave of destruction upon the mountain. I loved giving the order to fire as much as my men loved engaging. We were restrained by the very tight rules of engagement, which were necessary since our battlefields were so close to villages. Giving them the order to fire was like taking the chains off my pack of wolves and allowing them to charge their prey and tear them into shreds with their razor sharp fangs. They were trained for war and had volunteered for the infantry and for battle.

I was overjoyed to grant them the honor of delivering death to those that wished it upon us. The TIC (troops in contact) was over in a few moments.

Combat was becoming almost too routine. It was quite strange when a traumatic event such as a firefight becomes your reality and normal. Engaging in firefights felt as normal as eating a meal or taking a shower. Without a doubt, warfare takes a toll upon the mind.

SEMATAN

The village of Sematan was just to the west of our COP. On my first visit there I conducted a joint patrol with the ANA. We walked through a corridor of mud brick walls and a small stream flanked the path as it led into the village center. Each time I walked into a village, it felt nothing short of walking into a world centuries forgotten. I spoke to the elders and the village mullah (Islamic holy man). We offered help to repair some of their primitive structures, including their mosque. This aid would also help put men in their village to work. We continued to inject life within the valley. In many ways it was like planting flowers on your battlefields. I shook hands with the mullah and he said, "*Deera Manana* (thank you very much)."

A good deal of my visits in villages ended in the manner above. Successes in the valley were measured one day at a time. I said my goodbyes to the villagers and continued to our outpost. This was life as a platoon in the valley. Although no battles came that day, American life was taken less than two miles from here only a few weeks previously and my men and I had fought for our lives close to here as well. This coexistence of life and death was the way of the Pesh Valley.

DONKEYS

We again moved up our mountain citadel at OP Rocky. This time we moved as ancient infantry, utilizing donkeys to carry extra water, ammunition, and food. Departing in the early evening, it was incredible to see my infantry platoon moving with pack animals. This movement symbolized the millennia-old problem of infantry, moving weight with only the power of muscle and sinew. Perhaps, for just a moment, we resembled an ancient column of Alexander making its way through this remarkably rugged terrain. I loved this scene of my platoon flanked by these beasts carrying our supplies for war. I never thought I would ever see such a site – 21st century infantry moving sophisticated equipment, utilizing donkeys. I gazed upon my ancient column of infantry and smiled.

We ascended the height and established over-watch. We sought to intercept any enemy that was unlucky enough to cross our sights. The ANP offered us food and we broke bread with them and had chai. Khan, the ANP commander, and I spoke for some time. We shared some of our cultural differences and spoke of war. One of his men recently acquired a second wife. I congratulated this eastern warrior.

Nightfall set in, and we kept watch over our perimeter. Illumination was more than adequate and we could see quite well through our NVGs (night vision goggles), as well as our PAS-13 thermal scopes. No attack would come against us. I spent the night trooping the line and talking to the men. There is just something beautiful about being outside the wire overnight, peering through the darkness and searching for enemy. The remainder of the company occupied the high ground near the mountain called Punzar and the deserted village of Maidon. The Afghans told us that a nomadic tribe called *Kuchers* inhabited Maidon at times. I would never lay my eyes upon these nomads; they were just another thread in the mysterious tapestry of Afghanistan.

Utilizing donkeys on patrol.

After an hour of sleep, I awoke before first light and put my men at stand-to (100% alert). We watched as the blanket of dawn slowly rolled across the valley floor. The heat soon followed and my men were nearly out of water. 3rd platoon and 1st platoon made contact as they were climbing down the highlands on the opposite side of the Watapor valley. Shortly afterward, 1st platoon began their movement as well. We assisted with what we could by calling for fire on the enemy. The Kiowas, as well as a 2,000-pound bomb, made short work of the enemy forces.

During the battle, Khan, the OP Rocky ANP commander, came by my side to watch the battle. This man and his leathery face had known warfare all of his life. Looking into his eyes was like looking into decades of combat. He was a living witness to this land scarred by continuous warfare. All one must do to learn of warfare is to stare into his deep dark eyes. It has been said that the eyes are the windows of the soul. In Afghanistan, they are the portals to this land of unending war.

Khan.

We began our movement back to our fort, the extreme heat pounding us as we walked. Most of us were at the very limits of our endurance upon reaching Honaker Miracle. I felt the extreme effects of fatigue, as

I had been without water for a few hours. I had stopped sweating and was stumbling a bit as we walked down the mountain. At the base of the mountain I saw some children near a well getting water. I moved to the well and filled my helmet with water and splashed it on me. It helped put some life back into me. I was very happy to get back to our COP. Many of the men, including myself, took I.V.s to help rehydrate.

STORM CLOUDS APPROACH

As the Election Day approached, I sensed the storm clouds gathering in the distance. A tension seemed to dominate the air and I felt the upcoming battles to be fought in the coming days. My RTO (radio man/ assistant), SPC Jones, noticed that the tone of my voice was changing during mission briefs. He asked me if something was wrong. RTO's develop close relationships with platoon leaders. Always with you, they watch you and get to know all of your moods. Even though I knew he could see through me, I, of course, just said I was getting sick, and that I was not worried at all.

Nothing could be further from the truth, as I knew what awaited us in the coming days. I knew that with the approaching Election Day and season of Ramadan that the next few weeks would encompass some of the most challenging tests of our deployment.

In these beautifully forsaken valleys we would risk our lives to spread freedom and deny sanctuary to the enemies of our country. I found it overwhelming that we were attempting to transplant this idea of democracy founded by the Greeks and which formed the roots of American liberty. I sensed the large battles were only a few days away. Every ancient instinct and bone in my body knew it would be soon. I prayed for the wisdom and courage to lead my men out of this fray.

Kunar was a war zone without distinct front lines. Rather, the front line encompassed everything. It was in the hot air we breathed, in the rocks we walked upon, and in the dust that entered our nostrils. It existed in the dark eyes of the Afghans I saw every day. It was solidified in the wrinkles of the elders and in the sun as she pounded us with her heat. It was in the Pesh River and in our sweat. The war was all around us.

EVE OF BATTLE AND FORESHADOWING

One more day remained until the much-anticipated elections. My final day prior to the elections was spent inspecting the preparation of the ANP defenses at the polling sites. I learned that the ANP were planning on waiting for the Election Day to set in the defenses. I was somewhat shocked to find this, but such is the nature of this land.

We proceeded to the village of Qamchi where I linked up with Muhamed, the Qamchi ANP commander. He showed me his plan for securing the Qamchi High School as well as the location for the female polling site. At the conclusion of this quick assessment, we made our way back across the Pesh River to link up with my vehicles. I clasped arms with Muhamed and wished him luck for what undoubtedly would be a most trying day. His eyes met mine and he offered me thanks. Within his eyes I detected a deep sense of worry. I am sure I reciprocated this worry within my eyes.

Following our security assessments, we returned to our COP. SFC Staley and I dismounted while the MRAPs refueled. We walked back toward the TOC, discussing our plan for the following day. I was looking at the mountains as we walked, wondering what awaited us on the next day. Suddenly, I was greeted by those mind sickening whizzes and cracks of incoming bullets. Dust kicked up only a few feet from us as incoming rounds impacted around us. I could not believe it at first. We broke into a dead sprint and traced the line of Hescos, seeking cover. Adrenaline carried us to safety within seconds. I informed the TOC of the situation. The small attack ceased. It seemed a lone gunman was trying his luck. Fortunately, it seemed that luck was on our side.

We spent the final hours of the day conducting our last minute preparations of water, ammo, ammo, ammo, food, and batteries. I spoke with my friend, Chris, about the coming day. He said, "It's sure to be a sporting good day." He was right.

ELECTION DAY

I awoke in the dead of night. The air was cool and kissed me gently as I prepared myself for the day ahead. As I walked outside my barracks to shave, I stared at the stars and wondered what perils my men and I would experience. I prayed to God to deliver us from this storm of violence that was sure to come.

The first task of the day was to link up our pack donkeys with the ANP. The Afghans were simply better at handling our donkeys than we were. This was truly a test in terms of trust with our newly acquired allies. I called them the previous night and told them to link up with us well before sunrise. However, timeliness with the Afghans was not their strength and we did not link up until after dawn. The ANP were in civilian clothes and brought the donkeys up OP Rocky. I had hoped to use some of the pre-dawn darkness to cover our movement. By the time we began, the sun was already smiling upon us. My plan was to move my platoon and our commo team up OP Rocky, bypassing the cornfields. The corn was over five feet high in some places and offered the enemy several positions from which to assail us.

We began our movement as the eastern dawn began to dance upon the Pesh valley floor. The bazaar of Jumma Gundai was dead silent. The fields were empty of farmers and not a soul could be seen, not even a dog. An eerie silence filled the air. The only sounds were of a gentle breeze, our footsteps, and the creaking of our gear. The calm told of the storm that was soon to come. It was beautiful to my ears and eyes, one of those moments that looked exactly like what I thought war would look like.

We began our climb up our beloved OP Rocky. The ascent up the mountain with its endless moments of shale, loose rock, and elevation was not a favorite of my men and me. Your quads burned with great intensity as you hiked. Your lungs burned for air and begged you to stop. Sweat began to pour from under your helmet. However, if conducted with a smart pace, the effects were somewhat manageable. While resting on the ascent, I looked back upon the floor of the Pesh River Valley. The early morning light seemed to sparkle beautifully upon the Pesh river. The wind flew over the green corn fields, like waves on a lake. The greenery and peacefulness were rather deceiving.

We pressed on and soon made it to the top of our mountain citadel. We set in our security positions and I positioned our commo team consisting of Juan Herrera, SPC Johnston and SGT Aldeiv about 200 meters outside our perimeter. The entire company postured for a day of battle. 1st PLT, under LT Harris, was staged at Able Main for QRF. We held Rocky; 3rd PLT, under LT Tom Goodman, held the eastern gate of the Watapor, so to speak. A section of the ANA was stationed at OP Jojo and the Marines and ANA under LT Evan Johnson, were at Qamchi. It was quiet at first. It always was. We set in and waited.

WHIZZES AND DISHKA

Out of the quiet relative calm of morning we began to hear gunfire and explosions to our east. Soon we heard them to the west. The thuds of mortars and RPG explosions sprang out. It had begun. We would defend this experiment of democracy. My anticipation for battle increased. I scanned our line and looked upon my men. They were ready for the hell that awaited them. I was confident in both my men and in our position.

Soon contact, our dear friend, paid us a visit. Shots rang out and the sounds of whizzes pierced the air over our heads. Without any order, 1st section under SGT Richardson took positions along the northern wall and we began answering the call of battle. It was truly an awe inspiring sight to see my men, shoulder to shoulder, replying with their murderous fire. They fired their M4 rifles into the highlands. The 240B under SPC Warner and PVT Cortez began to reply with lethal fire.

It was the first time that I saw my men on line in battle. I love seeing the infantry on line, sending death toward the enemy. I loved it. It was a remarkable sight as they began to undertake the task for which they were trained; taking human life. For a moment, I wanted to ditch my radio, map, protractor, and take the line as a rifleman once again. However, I had an element cut off from my perimeter and we were taking fire from at least three different positions. I knew I had to get artillery assets and air support as soon as possible.

We began calling for fire. Our mortars began landing within 700 meters of us. The ground shook under the earthquake of our creation. However, our rounds did not find the enemy and we continued to receive direct fire. Khan, the ANP commander, soon appeared on the scene. This ancient Mujahedeen began employing the Dishka against the enemy. It was an inspiring sight to see Afghans fighting shoulder to shoulder with Americans against a common enemy. Each of those rounds fired from the Dishka shocked both the surrounding earth and air. Our bullets flew toward the enemy together. For a few moments this union of Afghan Security Forces with our men provided glimpses of hope for Afghanistan. I smiled at this beautiful site and communion amongst warriors. Shared danger and fighting for common survival is one of the best methods to unite warriors from different cultures.

Finally our Kiowa helicopters arrived. It spurred our morale and confidence. We directed them onto the enemy positions as best as we could. My commo element was almost back to our perimeter. I ordered suppressive fire, which kept the enemy's heads down. It was a rather stressful moment for me to have an element in the open moving under fire. We continued to pour 120mm mortars into the highlands. In order to obscure the commo team's movement, I ordered an eight round fire for effect with white phosphorus. The white smoke provided a smoke screen to hide my men from the rifle sights of the enemy. It worked.

The commo team soon returned to our perimeter and I was deeply relieved. This heavy exchange of fire kept up until well into the morning hours. I was impressed to see my men take shifts on the northern wall of OP Rocky. I was still bent upon sending additional artillery into the highlands. However, there were several battles on the field this day and support was delayed. After a period of time, I was granted a 155 mission from ABAD. It is astonishing to witness 155's in battle. You can hear the rounds break the air about them as they deliver their promise of death. They sounded like what you would imagine a crashing plane to sound like. It was a sweet song indeed.

At certain moments I would look upon my men and see soldiers such as James, Stacey, or Jones moving from the bunker to the Northern wall on our perimeter. I looked upon them and into their eyes. One could sense the pride as they delivered rounds against the enemy. The hours of boot camp, monotonous time spent in formations, details, and physical training finally paid off. They were maturing as dealers of death. CPL Dement and PVT James continued to deliver precision fire with their M-14's on the enemy. A lull in fire came just before noon. The enemy had paused, undoubtedly to eat and to pray. We reconsolidated what little ammunition remained and rested while we could.

VALLEY FLOOR AND RESUPPLY

In the early afternoon we began taking fire again, not only from the high ground but also from the valley floor. We spotted fighters moving through the cornfields and streambed just to the northeast of our position. They were bounding toward us. I could not believe my eyes. They set up a position that was very close to a small white mosque.

My men replied with their arms, yet we would need mortars to halt the enemy. I called the grid up to prepare a fire mission. The enemy's position was dangerously close to houses and a mosque, but my men were threatened. I ensured that I had acquired an accurate grid for the enemy's position. I called the grid up and waited for the mortar. In order to minimize collateral damage I utilized an 81mm. I held my breath for a moment as I awaited the impact. It landed with the desired effects and, thankfully, without collateral damage. We halted the enemy advance on the valley floor.

Sergeants Moffet, Krueger, and PVT Cofflin repositioned on the south side of OP Rocky. They had received effective fire at their previous position. The firefight continued in bursts and we continued to trade indirect fire and a storm of bullets with the enemy. We were running dangerously low on ammunition. At the time, I did not know how long this battle would last and I knew we had to hold this ground. We would not surrender it to the enemy. We needed a resupply of ammo and water, especially, if we were to hold this position into the night. I requested a resupply drop (speed ball) from Honaker Miracle.

Resupply drop at OP Rocky during the Election Day firefight.

Soon a Blackhawk helicopter and Kiowa warriors were inbound with our resupply. The Kiowas arrived and executed a gun run, sending rounds with the potential to tear flesh pounding into the mountain. This gun run provided covering fire for our resupply drop. The massive Blackhawk came low and dropped off our supplies near the northern wall of our perimeter. As the bird lowered to the ground, it released a very violent rotor wash. The sight looked very intense. To the north, the mountain was smoking from recent gun runs and mortars. Dust created a small cloud around us. It was a perfect image of war. The sight will forever be burned into the chapters of my mind and heart. Ironically, our unit used body bags for these hasty resupply missions. I watched as these body bags and duffel bags full of water and ammunition fell onto our position. In the early afternoon we had another small lull in the battle. We reconsolidated ammo and waited for the enemy again. We held. They would not cross our line.

FIRE FOR EFFECT... SILENCE...

Rounds came dangerously close to us. I had placed a Gatorade bottle just above me on a wall. A bullet whizzed by my head and caused the Gatorade bottle to explode upon my armor. At first, I thought I was hit as I noticed my armor covered in red. I began to search my body for wounds and even pulled out my 9-line Medevac card. However, that day I was lucky. I was relieved to find that the red liquid was not blood. My interpreter locked eyes with me and saw the dread in my eyes as I thought I was wounded. I was somewhat embarrassed at that moment, a peculiar feeling in battle. I smiled and attempted to dismiss my fear.

We were in a hail of gunfire and traded lead again. I was thankful that we had received a resupply of ammunition. Our 240B screamed upon the enemy, holding them at bay. My men acted with valor upon the field. We made adjustments for the final fire mission with the help of SGT Rich, who held the north wall.

We fired one last fire for effect. Ten 120mm rounds impacted the high ground. This rain of steel successfully fell upon the enemy's main position. We found our mark and had ended the enemy. Their comrades most likely lost heart in the attack when we destroyed their main element in the highlands above us. The attack was over. Incoming fire had ceased on our position in the early evening.

We continued to over-watch the Watapor valley. As the heat of the day was cooling off, the battles of the Pesh River Valley had died down as well. The echoes of battle throughout the valley were reduced to nothing. As the sun was beginning to set, we moved off the mountain. We had done our duty and defended democracy with American firepower.

The march back from OP Rocky was very pleasant. I thanked God that he spared my men this day. I went outside my quarters and, although a non-smoker, found it comforting to share a cigarette with my men. To the infantry, few things are more sacred than a good smoke following battle. I watched my men inhale their cigarettes, with sweat caked dirt upon their faces. It was in their eyes that you could see what they had just lived through. There was something about watching soldiers exhale cigarette smoke following an action. They truly savored each puff. The taste of tobacco let you know that you were still alive. Life is such a fragile and sacred thing. War reinforced some of the most important lessons in life. Life is truly a gift.

AN EARLY MORNING

Although exhausted from the action on Election Day, I found it difficult to sleep. I was fully amped by the day's engagement. Eventually I was able to sleep. Shortly after dawn a loud knocking upon my door awakened me. It was my friend, LT Brandon Fridia, the company XO. He moved next to SFC Staley's quarters. SFC Staley, who was typically an early riser, was already awake and alert. He received the mission brief.

We were informed that A Co. had taken some severe casualties from an IED in Chapadara, to the west of Blessing. We were to go to ABAD, pick up a crane and escort it to the IED site. I had only heard bad things about the Chapadara region. I prepared myself for one hell of a fight. We moved to ABAD and linked up with the crane. On the way back west, I linked up with my battalion commander, who provided me with a Chapadara district artillery target map. We made a quick stop at Honaker Miracle to switch out a Humvee for an MRAP and then proceeded west toward Blessing.

We arrived at Blessing and received the reality of the situation. 3rd Platoon, D Co., under Mike Luth, had been hit. One MRAP and her crew had been devastated. SGT Ingram of our company had fallen in battle and PVT Adams was severely wounded. Another MRAP lay on its side in the river. It was a costly day.

The battalion put my platoon on standby until they could finalize planning for the recovery of the downed vehicle. The casualties had been MEDEVAC'd long ago. We sent our platoon to the transient barracks near the HLZ so that they could rest before rolling out in battle yet again.

I ate lunch and sat next to SFC Staley, SGT Wade, and SGT Rich. After we ate, we all sat there in silence. Perhaps each man, like myself, pondered his own mortality. My squad leaders had fought alongside SGT Ingram in Iraq. News of his death struck all of the Dagger company veterans especially hard.

The Chaplain came by to visit our men and talk about our fallen comrade. He was consoling us for our loss. The men were singing his praises and brought up pleasant memories about SGT Ingram. We were interrupted as SPC Troxel, formerly one of my men, ran up to our area and shouted, "Where's your PL?"

I quickly stood up and he informed us that we were to be QRF for Dagger Company that was engaged near the village of Matin. We mounted up and sped east. I knew that men of my company had already been wounded. I was desperate to see that no others would fall in battle.

We soon arrived near Matin village. Men from my company were in the process of moving down the Sheriak valley and began taking fire. My company commander, CPT Gianoulakis, came on the radio and reported the friendly and enemy dispositions. Instantly, we identified the enemy positions and sent hell upon the mountainside. Our company successfully finished their climb under an umbrella of our .50 cal, MK19, and TOW missiles. We provided over-watch for our company as they traveled back to COP Michigan. I shared dinner with my friends, LT Cumbie, LT Halverson, and LT Zambarda. Although it had been a somber day, we drew comfort from our brother's in arms.

MEMORIAL

Again, we paid homage to a fallen hero of our company and nation. We traveled to COP Michigan, our company HQ, to honor our fallen comrade. SGT Matt Ingram of Mississippi. It was a very solemn event, which displayed freedom's cost. The sadness of the day reverberated throughout all of our bodies. Standing in formation, I had a large lump in my throat.

As we do in all memorial services, we conducted a roll call. As our 1SG (First Sergeant) called out the name of our fallen comrade, it cut through me with the sharpness of a katana. I prayed that no more of our men would fall. I prayed that we would destroy the enemies that were responsible for this. I prayed that God would give this man a hero's welcome and rest.

REFLECTION

This Afghanistan, with her rugged terrain, can seep the strength out of a man. The sheer rocks can cut into you. Each step taxed your strength and breath. This was a brutal land of extremes. These rugged peaks surrounded us on all fronts and served as bunkers for both sides. I prayed they would become the graves of the enemy.

Here warriors learn to savor each cup of tea, each cigarette, and every moment not kissed by combat. These Afghans have been at war for decades. After so many firefights and casualties, I wondered what would become of this place. I wondered what would become of places such as Qamchi village and I prayed that our efforts and sacrifices would be remembered.

I gazed upon OP Rocky. On any given day the primitive fortifications on OP Rocky looked like an ancient and lazy farmhouse. It was strange to think that rounds flew all over that position, mortars exploded, and Kiowas strafed the highlands. However, at that moment, all was quiet. Not a shot was fired and not a bullet tore the air. I heard only the breeze and the cawing of a few birds. I knew that the peacefulness of this place could explode into violence in mere moments. It changed like the course of the wind.

Coming close to death was becoming an all too common occurrence. Each day I prepared myself for this fate. In many respects, I was beginning to walk each day with one foot in the river Styx. Living on the banks of life and death places you in a different state of mind. In some aspects, many things in your life slow down. I asked my men to live on this cusp of the next world on a daily basis. I asked so much of them. They never faltered.

NEW ARRIVALS

New men arrived at our battalion headquarters and were distributed to the various outposts. Following a patrol to FOB Blessing, we transported a few of them to our outpost. The senior ranking SGT out of these new men approached me as my platoon prepared to head out east. He was a veteran and had seen combat before, yet he was accompanied by some untested PVTs. I could see the hypersensitivity in the eyes of the PVTs. It was an indicative characteristic of men newly arriving on the lines. They looked at the surrounding terrain in awe, much as I did when I first arrived in country. The men loaded up in our vehicles and we continued east.

I had only been at war for three months, yet I felt that I had experienced more in those months than I had in the past decade of my life. Each engagement that I participated in matured me and drove in hard lessons. In combat, you became tempered and educated into the horrors of mankind. War teaches of a deep hatred and

I felt it several times a week as the enemy attempted to slaughter us on the plains of battle.

War teaches you that the world is not entirely made of up of those peaceful small towns and suburbs that many of my men and I came from. Instead, this is a world whose freedoms and liberties must be earned with blood and sacrifice. It is a world where the walls of freedom must continually be manned. It is a world where the enemy wanted nothing more than to slaughter our countrymen, children, and families in our cities. The enemy hated us. It was this hatred that led them to clash shields with us on a near daily basis. For the time being, we fought them there in their mountains. I preferred meeting the enemy in combat in those valleys rather than our own streets. I kept a picture of the smoldering ruins of the Twin Towers upon my desk in my quarters. I stared at this picture whenever I questioned why we were in that God-forsaken valley. We held the lines of freedom.

SEPTEMBER 2009

RAMADAN

RAMADAN AND JANAT

Ramadan had begun. Ramadan is the Islamic month of prayer and fasting. In villages and throughout the valley one could hear the Koran being read aloud throughout the day. This holy book is read aloud in Arabic over the radio and in loudspeakers in villages. This sound reminded me that I was in a land far away from home. There was no doubt that we were the foreigners here. It is also in this month fighters, in the name of Jihad, come searching for paradise.

My interpreters told me that the fighters here considered it an honor to die fighting during Ramadan, as their passage to heaven would be guaranteed. The intensity and frequency of the attacks during this holy season confirmed that there were many Taliban who came in search of this road to *Janat*, "paradise."

CONTACT AT JUBAI

I was on patrol working with the ANP. We were conducting a traffic checkpoint, searching vehicles. The day was hot and the valley seemed asleep. Out of the quiet day came the distant singing of war as a faint sound of machine gun fire echoed over the mountains. Over the radio I heard the call for assistance. 1st Platoon was in contact near COP Able Main. My platoon mounted up and moved to the sound of the guns.

By the time we arrived on the scene, the contact had ceased, or so we thought. We thought perhaps it was only harassing fire. Just to be safe, we set up in an over watch posture in the vicinity of the Jubai Draw. We scanned the highlands and did not detect any enemy movement. 1st Platoon continued their movement toward Able Main. All was calm, which was always a bad sign.

1st Platoon again began taking contact from the Jubai Draw. We aggressively moved into position and began unleashing lethal firepower into the draw as I adjusted 120mm mortars on to the highlands. I loved using mortars in combat. The mere shock of their impacts seemed to intimidate the enemy. SFC Staley, SPC Kruger, and SGT Wade directed .50 cal and MK 19 onto the enemy. The enemy returned fire and again we began this ancient dance of trading fire. In the midst of battle I looked at the impacts of the enemy rounds kicking up dust around our positions. It was in those moments where time stood still. I think all warriors take moments such as these with them throughout their lives. I heard a few rounds impact our vehicle. Each smack upon our armor was a constant reminder of the potential for danger that always exists in battle. I stared through the heat and watched the highlands wave back and forth in the heat's convection. The action was soon over and 1st Platoon arrived safely back at COP Able Main.

Kiowas arrived on scene. We directed them as best as we could, yet the ghosts returned to the shadows from which they came.

A LONG DAY... CASUALTIES

Although the temperatures of the summer began to slacken, the fighting season was far from over. We began this day thinking it would be easy and uneventful. As I later found, that is when things came at us the hardest. We began our morning by heading to COP Able Main and dropped off one vehicle with SPC Krueger, SSG Wade, SGT Rich, SPC Jones, and the snipers. They were going to FOB Blessing for a variety of reasons, from fixing their SGLIs (life insurance), to SPC Krueger attending the SGT selection board. It was to be an easy day for them.

My platoon, along with a few men from 3rd Platoon, moved east to ABAD to drop off a few civilian contractors. I was not going to eat breakfast that morning, but SFC Staley advised that I should. I was glad he did. We broke our fast at ABAD, which was always a treat, as this base was far more built up than our small outpost. We returned to Honaker Miracle and prepared for a short mission to check on a project at the beginning of the Watapor road. While preparing for the mission, we heard that the convoy traveling from Able Main to Blessing had been in a firefight. I heard that QRF had already arrived on the site and that the battle was over. Grave news also accompanied this report of battle. I heard that a man from 1st platoon, SGT Loney, fell in battle. I prayed and wished his soul to heaven. I briefed my men with a heavy heart for what I thought would be our last patrol of the day.

My platoon moved toward the village of Shamir Kowtz, stopping first at the district center. The ANP chief informed me of a potential IED on the Watapor road.

The idea of an IED made my senses come alive. Up to this point in our tour, we had not encountered any IEDs in my area of operation. It seemed as if warfare there was finally moving into a worse chapter of insurgency. A new chapter of our war began.

I told the ANP chief that I would speak to him after my quick assessment of the entrance of the Watapor road. We had recently commissioned a work project there and it appeared that efforts were underway to improve the road. I felt a tension in the air as we moved through the village. My interpreter, Nanji, felt it as well. We moved back to the District Center and attained further information on the IED. SFC Staley, a veteran of the IED strewn roads of Iraq, was particularly helpful in discussing this threat. With this newly acquired information, we moved back to our COP and informed CPT Conlin.

Within 45 minutes, we were ready to march. My platoon headed out with a sniper team to OP Jojo. We sat in overwatch of 3rd Platoon and the ANA's movement to the IED site. To make things worse, a large funeral procession gathered near the IED site. It was concerning to have this sea of civilians so close to our chaos. Hundreds of people were there, thus the potential for civilian casualties was very high. The ANA tried drastically to keep them away from the IED.

An EOD team soon arrived on site and cleared the IED with speed and efficiency. My platoon and our snipers continued to scan the highlands for any enemy. There would be no action and our elements left the Watapor valley and made our way back to Honaker Miracle.

We soon departed for Able Main, taking CPT Conlin and the 1SG there to console 1st platoon over their loss. Upon arrival at Able Main, I learned that our platoon had incurred its first wounded earlier that morning. Our MRAP that accompanied the patrol to Blessing had taken an RPG round on its left side. SPC Jones received some shrapnel in his back, as well as ruptured his eardrum. SGT Rich received some burns to his hands and a sniper had received shrapnel to his face. By the grace of God, and the strength of our armor, all of them would return to duty.

We remained at Able Main for a while. Our forces had lost one man today and several wounded. I visited LT Harris and offered my condolences for the loss of SGT Loney. I returned back to my platoon. We were staged to leave Able Main and our gunners over watched the highlands. I looked upon my men differently for the first time. I saw Jones smile. I saw Rich and Wade bullshitting and Krueger laughing. I cherished seeing them in this light. Dark clouds seemed to move away as the evening set in. A few minutes later a rainbow appeared in the clouds, indicating perhaps hope would prevail in all of this chaos.

Thank you father, for sparing them. These are men of value... Deliver them...

They were as sons to me and I swore that I would do what I could to destroy the enemy and deliver my men from the war. We all sat on the HLZ, waiting for CPT Colin. Strangely we were all at peace. SPC Jones reflecting on the ambush said, "Everything just went red and black when the RPG exploded."

Chance is such an important part of warfare. Mars spared his bloody tax on my men. I hoped that it would remain the same for the remainder of our tour.

Rainbows at Able Main. A sign of hope.

NIGHT AND SUNRISE OF FIRE

One night we headed east toward the city of Asadabad. I was ordered to link up with a large ASG (Afghan Security Group) convoy and escort them to FOB Blessing. We pushed east and came upon this large convoy of unarmored vehicles. I dismounted with my RTO and my interpreter, Nanji.

I would forever miss these exciting night link ups. I was given a simple mission to meet our allies and escort them to FOB Blessing, without any further coordination. They were simple orders, my kind of orders. I approached this foreign convoy in the darkness. Afghan warriors carrying automatic weapons were staring at me with dark eyes. The convoy commander was an imposing site, around 6'3", and spoke excellent English. He informed me that his trucks were unarmored and only lightly armed. He agreed to follow us and in a few moments we were on our way west. The ASG convoy was an interesting site to see. It was a mixture of pickup trucks with men armed with AK's and PKMs. These late night rendezvous brought excitement into our patrols.

I THINK I SEE A ...

We moved west on the Pesh river road. Up to this point in the deployment, the enemy rarely staged attacks at night. I thought my convoy would make it to FOB Blessing and back under the cover of darkness without incident. I would be incorrect in this assumption. Instead, the next eight hours would encompass our longest mounted engagements up to this point. We rolled west into the darkness.

We were moving near the Shege East ANP checkpoint when I heard a rather unusual transmission from my lead vehicle.

SSG Wade stated, "I think I see a truck or something on fire up ahead."

At first I questioned if I had heard correctly. As we pressed on, I could see some glowing light, like that of a large campfire. Into my line of sight came this hulk of a pickup truck, completely engulfed by flames. Like many things in combat, it did not seem real. A truck was burning. We could not stop and assess it because of the large numbers of soft skinned trucks in our convoy.

We received some small arms fire as we passed. I watched the red tracers of the enemy rounds fly overhead. We returned fire with a roaring fury, unloading with a wave of steel from our .50 cal and 7.62. We punished the aggressors. We provided enough suppressive fire so the ASG convoy could safely make it through the ambush site. I could not stop and offer battle because of the importance of safely escorting the ASG convoy to FOB Blessing. We pushed to Honaker Miracle and staged the unarmored convoy there.

We cautiously moved back toward the site of the burning pickup truck. We moved silently under the cover of darkness and scanned the highlands, finding no signs of the enemy. We moved east to speak with the Shege East ANP checkpoint and to investigate the situation at hand. We were informed that a small ASG convoy composed of two pickup trucks escorting a flatbed truck had been attacked. The burned out hulk on the road was one of the escort trucks that received one RPG round. The Afghans had moved their wounded to Asadabad, followed by the flatbed truck.

I moved east into Asadabad to track down the survivors. After a good amount of confusion, I finally linked up with the second ASG vehicle, on the bridge in Asadabad. The Afghan Security Guards informed me of the situation. They told me that they had taken their wounded to the hospital. My nerves were alive with the excitement of the moment. I remember urinating in the river as I was talking to the Afghans. I did not have the chance to piss before the mission or since the last small engagement. My interpreter, Nanji, was pissing next to me. Admittedly it must have been a very humorous sight to behold.

With some help from ABAD's observation blimp (this blimp had a long range camera and was used for surveillance) I finally found the flatbed truck that the ASG was escorting. ABAD informed me that they would maintain over watch of the truck. I was relieved to have finally finished this first debacle of the evening.

My platoon moved back toward Honaker Miracle where we reestablished linkup with the ASG convoy. We did not have much time left before sunrise. We were ready to push west. We traveled the length of our battalion's battle space and arrived at FOB Blessing without a shot fired.

Soon after our arrival at FOB Blessing, the east was illuminated with a beautiful sunrise. I knew this beautiful sight would not be taken in without paying a toll. The dawn promised battle as well. I prepared myself. We made our movement east on the Pesh river road and passed the area near Tantil village where in recent days an ambush had occurred. On the side of the road was the burned out hulk of a civilian truck that had been let aflame by RPGs on that fateful day. Passing its charred remains invoked rather intense emotions. The hulk resembled a charred skeleton and stood there as a silent reminder to the destructiveness of our enemies.

We continued east and approached the Sheriak valley with caution. The air around us ignited as we began taking small arms fire and RPGs. Slowly rolling though the engagement area, we returned fire and punished the mountainside with our firepower. I found that my friend, LT Luth, was in contact near Able Main. Our platoon continued moving away from the Sheriak valley toward the sound of the guns to assist my brother in arms. The echoes of battle sounded just over the mountains to our east, telling of the action that awaited us.

We soon came upon the battlefield where 3rd Platoon, Dagger Company, under LT Luth, was locked in the grips of combat. They were pouring fire onto the highlands with the enemy returning fire. Our armored beasts maneuvered into position and started laying hell onto the enemy. It was pleasing to join another Dagger Platoon in mounted combat. Both of our forces pounded the high ground with .50 cal and MK 19. CPL Dement attained visual on the enemy and engaged with two TOW missiles. COP Able Main finished the engagement with 120mm mortars. This storm of steel soon silenced the enemy.

We pressed on east and although we were all weary from battle, we took contact one last time while rolling through Mulkhana. We stopped and returned fire. The small firefight was soon over. We happily returned to base and rested for the remainder of the day, allowing both our minds and bodies to rest.

RAMADAN REFLECTIONS

Before the first week of the holy month of Ramadan had ended, we averaged a firefight a day. It truly felt as if the Pesh valley was on fire. The valley sounded like a rumbling volcano as the echoes of firefights rumbled through it. The echoes of battle told of the true state of chaos that made up our world in the Pesh valley. My senses for combat were heightened and so was my hunger for battle. Our enemy continued their attacks against us. In a way, I welcomed combat with them. It was very difficult to find these ghosts that hid amongst the rocks. Yet, they revealed their positions when they attacked us. It gave us a chance to end them. At times it seemed that only violence could provide resolution in the Pesh Valley.

VIEWING AMBUSH POSITIONS

One afternoon we conducted a patrol to both Shege East and Qamchi. Upon our arrival at Shege East, I linked up with the ANP who then accompanied us. We went to the location where the ASG pickup truck had recently been ambushed. I met some locals who lived nearby and they showed us a trail that led to the high ground. The ANPs were very motivated and patrolled with much gusto. We found enemy fighting positions and promptly destroyed them. It was strange to look upon the road from these positions. They offered excellent fields of fire. It was eerie to look upon the road from the same point of view that the enemy had done only a few days prior. We marked the positions in our minds; we would never be ambushed from there again. In future patrols when we passed this position, our senses heightened, and our gunners scanned more diligently.

ANP TRAINING MEETING

I prepared an ANP training curriculum that would commence following Ramadan and met with the ANP district chief to discuss my intentions. It was a good meeting adorned with all the charm that one could expect in the heat, while drinking chai. I looked forward to teaching military skills to these tribesmen. He seemed very enthusiastic about the program that I presented. We spoke of a great range of subjects, from TCPs and partnered patrols, to overwatches. I attempted to institute weekly leadership meetings and a district-wide training program. I was extremely enthusiastic about the training, yet the reality of Afghan military energy made me realize the limited effect of western charisma.

PEACEFUL CONVERSATIONS

Talking to reporters on the battlefield almost made you feel like you were not at war. A team of Italian reporters spent a few days with my platoon. One day on an uneventful patrol, I spent a good portion of the afternoon chatting with a reporter named Mario. We had a great conversation and it reminded me of those philosophical conversations I had while still at college. It made me feel as if I was not surrounded by hundreds of fighters who would like nothing more than to take my life and the lives of my men.

Mario joined us on a patrol to the village of Dag. On that visit I hiked up to the Dag ANP checkpoint and was greeted in the Pashtun manner with smiles, hugs, and tea. After some brief small talk, two of the ANP accompanied my patrol across the Dag footbridge and spoke with the villagers. It was clear they were unaccustomed to U.S. presence in the village. We spoke with some of the shopkeepers and sensed that atmospherics in that village were less than hospitable and I could feel tension in the air. Perhaps fighters were amongst the villagers; perhaps fighters had been there only moments before I was. It was hard to tell. Soon our time at Dag was over and we picked up and returned to Honaker Miracle.

A ROUTINE PATROL

One fateful evening we entered our outpost, having completed our patrols for the day. My men and I were looking forward to dinner and the next day of rest and maintenance. We had no further missions planned for the night and the coming day. We were to only eat our dinners and call it a night. Yet, combat does not always work in conjunction with your rest schedules.

CPT Conlin called me into the TOC a few minutes prior to our nightly meeting. He informed me that a civilian supply convoy would be making its way through our AO soon. We were ordered to patrol the road and ensure it was clear of any enemy threat.

We departed east in the early evening and kept a keen watch on the¬ highlands. We scanned them diligently, but found nothing. We pulled into the field that my men called the "shooting range" in Qamchi and set in overwatch. The sun had set and the heat of the day dissipated into the dark folds of the ground. We scanned the highlands with our optics and found nothing. It was quiet, like it always was before hell paid us a visit.

As the night progressed I called back to CPT Conlin and reported that we did not detect any activity. I requested to pull my platoon back to base and was granted permission. After the overwatch we were all eager to call it a night. We approached the mountain draw near the Qamchi High School.

BULL'S EYE...

We proceeded west and the night exploded with the horrible booms that are only made by RPGs. The sky lit up in a display of tracer rounds and explosions. A few nights previously I heard SGT Richardson describe RPGs floating by him at night in Iraq; he called them, "the bull's eye." I saw them for myself that night. The RPGs appeared initially as slow moving tracer rounds. I thought that they were only bullets, until I heard the unmistakable thunder clap of the RPG explosions.

We thundered back with our own compliments of death, trading a wave of lead with the enemy. I ordered my gunner to "spray the fuck out of them" and watched in awe as the night air erupted around me into a concert of violence. The Armored Support Vehicle (my third vehicle) had sustained damage to its tires and armor. SFC Staley's vehicle had sustained severe damage to its brakes and steering. One round drove deep into the windshield, only inches from SPC Stacey's face.

We called in immediate suppression (quick mortar support) on the Qamchi Draw. 120mm mortars began to crash near our enemy's position, slowing their rate of fire and spurning our confidence in the fight. I had prayed that some of those rounds ended a few of the enemy, giving us precious seconds to organize. Much to my surprise, the ANP began to trade bullets with the enemy as well. I finally received a green status from all of my vehicles, meaning everyone was okay. With the damage we sustained to our convoy, we would have to break contact for the time being. We limped back to our base at a very slow pace. We pulled into the gate of our fort and began work on our damaged vehicles. SFC

Staley and I made our way to the TOC and gave the report to CPT Conlin.

My TOW MRAP conducted overwatch to the north as we prepared for a counter attack in the Qamchi Draw. PFC Cortez spotted enemy near OP Jojo. He gave me the grid and I cleared him to fire. He delivered the missile effectively onto target. 1st Platoon, from Able Main, was soon called in to offer assistance. I took command of the combined platoons and would control the fire assets. Again, some fear passed through my body, but the fear quickly turned to rage as I desired to kill the enemy that had attacked us. The rage provided me with the courage I needed. 1st Platoon was staged at the front gate waiting for us. Together we pushed east again, into the formidable darkness.

ARE THERE FRIENDLIES HERE?

We moved east back toward the contact with enough firepower to overwhelm our enemies. We returned to the ambush site slowly and stealthily, utilizing our night vision instead of headlights. We moved like panthers stalking their prey in the dark night. I had F-15 fighter jets, helicopters, and mortar assets at my disposal. We soon arrived where, shortly before, my platoon was ambushed. We set up in the darkness and scanned for our prey. Within two minutes, PFC Cortez asked me a question that I think I will never forget, "Sir, do we have friendlies (friendly forces) here?"

I replied with a, "No."

I was a bit confused at first as to why he would ask such a question. There was an ANP checkpoint nearby, but it was unlikely that they would be on the mountain.

One look at my command monitor, and I knew why PFC Cortez asked me this.

I saw them, the phantoms we hunted. These ghosts materialized from the darkness and took human form. These ancient folds of mountain and rock no longer hid them. They were walking toward the high ground in the draw, carrying the same weapons which they used to ambush my men. They must not have had heard us roll up. They were hiking nonchalantly with their weapons over their shoulders. I clearly saw their RPG launchers and other weapons. Our enemy would receive the very death they had attempted to send to us. Instantly, a feeling of intense anger overcame me. I found the bastards that tried to kill my men. A difference of a few feet and the ambush could have been different for my men. I would have been spending the next day writing letters to the families of my fallen. But their rounds did not find their mark. However, I knew our rounds would find their targets. We would take revenge upon them. We were eager to destroy the enemy, which we plainly saw that night.

SGTs Rich, Maudlin and I all shouted to Cortez, "Take them! Take them!"

At the thunder of the missile, I saw one of the enemy take a quick glance back in our direction. It would be his final breath. I watched the glow of the missile's after burner as it spiraled with its package of death toward the enemy. The shot was approximately 600 meters. In seconds, we returned the death that came so close to our armor. The missile detonated with a loud explosion that brought light into this darkness.

We all shared in the reverberating exhilaration of the kill. It awoke those ancient feelings of the hunt. Our vehicles suppressed the area with a roar of machine gun fire. We switched gunners for a few moments. SGT Rich found additional enemy and we fired another missile at them.

SFC Staley was back on the COP helping to control the air assets with the JTACs (Joint Tactical Air Controllers, Air Force). We soon had F-15s on station, circling, looking for their kill, like steel sharks in the ocean of sky. Kiowa helicopters arrived and hunted for prey as well. We fired the TOW again and marked the target area for the F-15s. We received no return fire. It was likely the enemy had exhausted all their ammunition on the attack earlier. We scanned and hunted.

Soon the F-15s came in for the kill. They dropped two GBU-38s, 500 pound bombs. Their explosions shook our vehicles and sent shock waves through our bodies. Soon afterwards, a 155 mm Excalibur GPS guided round delivered its promise of death onto the enemy. We shook that valley with the power and might of God. The ground shook beneath us.

We scanned, thinking nothing could be alive in that draw. But, Afghanistan, with its multiple boulders and folds of ground, offers protection to both our enemy and friendly forces. We continued scanning and PFC Cortez saw an additional two enemy figures. We loosed yet another missile and showered the highlands with machine gun fire. Alas, we would find no further movement. Our time with the Kiowas was almost over. We moved our patrol east of Qamchi and turned around. We moved west and scanned. The battle was over. Nothing was left alive there. We had defended ourselves with honor. We moved back, under the cover of the Kiowas. We burned that mountain draw with unholy fire that night. We would never receive an attack from that place again. We denied the enemy that terrain through superior firepower.

I felt alive with passion and was in euphoria. I loved destroying the enemy, yet I came close to losing men this night as well. The night could have ended differently for me. I was thankful that my men reacted to the attack with violence. I thanked God for not taking my men from me. This battle was another intense lesson into this education of combat and added another memory to my nights that I would never forget.

REST, MAINTENANCE, AND CLASS

The following morning we repaired our vehicles from the firefight in Qamchi. In the daylight I was able to see full well the impact of the battle damage. The windshield from SFC Staley's truck had a round impact deep within its glass. It was an unnerving sight to witness. I observed the damage to my ASV – deep cuts from battle on the previous night. Your armor on your vehicles feels so strong when you lay your hands upon them. It is only when they are scarred or torched by enemy armament when you see just how strong armor is.

Following maintenance, I took the opportunity to teach PFCs Brenton, Cortez, and Martinez how to call for fire utilizing our 120mm mortars. Although all soldiers receive this training in preparation for war, one does not truly learn how to call for fire until doing so with live rounds. I was able to teach a man to perform this vital skill in about twenty minutes. After a brief lecture and some practice with a compass, we met with LT Eric Bruns, our Fire Support Officer. He gave the men the finishing touches of our crash course in calling for fire. He reminded the men, that artillery and mortars are "area weapons" (having the ability to destroy a massive area at one time). The men called in the strike and had 120mm rounds pounding the mountains soon after. Their voices sounded unsure during the initial calls and the adjustments, but they sounded confident when they called for the fire for effect. I saw them smile as the echoes of the mortars rolled down the mountain toward us. It was a lovely sight and I loved this part of war – teaching soldiers. Calling for fire was an integral part of warfare in the Pesh River Valley. I ensured that each of my men had the skills to do so.

I DID NOT HEAR AN OUTGOING...

Reporters and photographers continued to join us on our outposts from time to time. These men came in search of finding war, yet they carried no weapons. It seemed that the Siren's call rang in the ears of non-warriors as well. I eventually agreed to a taped video interview with Mario.

He interviewed me one afternoon following an early morning patrol. He had just begun the interview, seeking my opinions regarding the war, when all of a sudden I heard an explosion. It was an artillery impact. Initially I thought it was our mortars conducting a training mission. However, I quickly realized that I did not hear an outgoing fire from our COP – it was incoming fire. Dement, Martinez, Phelps, and I sought cover for just a few minutes. With indirect fire, you never know in Afghanistan, it may just be an artillery attack. However, in these remote outposts, indirect fire is known to precede enemy ground assaults. You never knew when a simple artillery attack could turn into a fight to hold your perimeter.

After a few moments, my fire team and I sprinted to our quarters and to the TOC. I geared up and mounted my TOW MRAP. The day was powerfully hot and a few more mortar rounds landed on our COP. We soon found the enemy and promptly dispatched them with a missile.

During the editing of this book I read the above paragraph. I noticed that I described destroying the enemy in only three sentences. When I first arrived to Afghanistan, such an event would have been forever burned into my mind. War had become normal to me. Death was a part of my everyday life. Three sentences described the destruction of the enemy. It is interesting how this mortal act became normal to us.

MEMORIAL

We attended the memorial service of SGT Loney of 1st Platoon, C Company. It was a very moving ceremony, bringing forth tears from many a warrior. These memorials served as a constant reminder to the brutality and viciousness of this valley. These sullen times told us of the cost of freedom. As much as I loved being at war, I feared losing one of my men. These soldiers sacrificed so many of their freedoms so that their families and friends could live freely without fear. Each day they embarked on our patrols under the shroud of death.

INTERPRETER QUITS

Interpreters for me seemed to come and go. My first interpreter was named Nanji. He was my best interpreter and seemingly had a good heart. He was but 20 years old and being with my platoon was his first experience away from home. He was horribly shaken up after the close ambush in Qamchi. I did my best to console the young man and told him that his country needed brave men like himself, but he chose to return home. He left this valley of chaos for a more peaceful life in Jalalabad. I couldn't blame him to want to leave this hell and return to a place where death would not come to visit on a daily basis.

At the same time, I wondered how many Afghans were truly inspired to risk their lives for the ultimate goal of freedom. I wondered how many true Afghan patriots there were. Unfortunately, the ranks did not seem to swell of patriots that would remind me of Lexington and Concord in the American Revolutionary War.

SEMATAN

I loved visiting this village because of the warm welcome we always received. I always made sure that I brought a great deal of candy or pens for the horde of children that would flock to us. Sematan was a like a breath of fresh air each time we visited. I am uncertain as to why we were so welcomed in this village, but took it for what it was. The mosque repair project that I had commissioned there was going quite well. Since I was Christian, I was forbidden to enter the mosque to check on the progress. Instead, my interpreter entered it and took photos of the various repairs being conducted. I waited with my men outside and spoke with the elders and the mullah. The Koran was being read aloud on the small speaker from the mosque. The Koran was recited in Arabic, and it made some of the men uneasy. However, I found the recital relaxing.

FAR AMBUSH

We began the day with a march at first light up to our beloved OP Rocky. I enjoyed moving infantry in the dull light of pre-dawn darkness. If you tried, you could hear the soft sound of our armor as we walked. Our ammo and equipment quietly creaking, like that of the pitter-patter of a spring rain. This sound has not changed through the millennia of western heavy infantry formations. It was the essence of death on the move. I loved moments such as these.

We made excellent time up OP Rocky and arrived fatigued. We set in security and began our silent hunt overlooking the Watapor valley. The morning was cool and pleasant, as it always was before the sun crested over the eastern highlands. I loved trooping the line on mornings such as these. As I moved from position to position, I would stop and scan with my binoculars and chat with my men. It was quiet, the deceiving innocent peace that blankets this land before it erupts into violence.

"SIR, DO WE HAVE ANA DOWN THERE?"

We saw them first. SPC Maudlin was scanning the valley, staring through the scope of his M-14. He asked me, "Sir, do we have ANA down there?"

At first I wondered why he would ask me such a question. As I looked down onto the valley, I saw an enemy squad conducting a patrol in the Watapor valley. They were carrying AK-47s, a PKM, and RPGs. Just to be safe, I confirmed that we did not have an ANA patrol in the valley.

We initiated. Initiating contact on the enemy was such a beautiful thing. Few things in the life of a warrior are sweeter. My men were poised and ready to take them. I gave them the signal to commence firing. We began the contact with the M-14 and 240 B. My other men replied with their M4s, adding lead to the attack. SPC Jones was spotting for SPC Maudlin. SPC Warner of Pennsylvania, arguably pound for pound my strongest man, worked his delivery of death with the 240B machine gun, utilizing the machine gun as an artist would a paintbrush. The site was breathtaking. I looked upon my men with great pride as they brought death to our enemy.

The psychological shock of this ambush was tremendous to the enemy and these fighters were apparently unaccustomed to reacting to contact. They immediately broke into an undisciplined run. They returned not a single round as they fled to a tree line just north of them. We continued to deliver our payload of death – 7.62mm and 5.56mm showered the tree line. I smiled as I was again afforded the opportunity to shower the enemy with rounds from my rifle. I took aim at the enemy position, attained a good aim, and smiled as I pulled the trigger. Each shot rang out loud and pierced my ears. The ringing played that sweet tune of battle that I enjoyed so much.

The enemy held up in the tree line and prayed for safety. I looked upon my men. We all enjoyed utilizing the shock of initiating contact upon them. We smiled as we were filled with the urge to kill. This euphoria seemed to be enhanced by watching the enemy run away like prey. These jackals ran from the lions today. The valley stood witness as we shook the mountains with our roaring fire. SSG Wade and the men continued their fire. I was proud of them. We later found that our fire met the enemy with the desired effects.

The survivors and their wounded moved to a tree line about 1200 meters from our position. I requested both mortar and air support to finish them. I was given F-15s, whose firepower is awesome, but with houses so close, their power was nullified. I was denied mortar support as well. If we had been taking fire, it would be another story. But, the enemy did not reply with a single round.

I expected a counter-attack. I received reports indicating that the enemy was preparing themselves. We scanned, waited, and continued to pound that position intermittently with machine gun fire. The remaining enemy squad did not fire a shot. They slipped away with their wounded, utilizing the nearby villages as their shield. This battle ended for the time being. We denied the enemy the valley that they thought was theirs. We took them. I wondered what they had planned on doing before running into our ambush. I supposed they were moving to the road to conduct an ambush of their own. I was overjoyed that we stopped them.

We held our position and postured for any further enemy contact. Later in the morning, we heard enemy outgoing artillery fire from across the Watapor valley.

For a moment I thought my position was being targeted with artillery fire, and we braced ourselves to react to such a threat. We radioed Honaker Miracle and warned them. Four rounds impacted on the COP. It was hurtful to watch those rounds land on our fort. We scanned diligently for the point of origin. SPC Smite, my forward observer for the day, spotted it and we brought fire to them, sending death back to them. From Honaker Miracle, we responded with counter battery fire. We requested air assets and soon F-16's were flying overhead. We called in the grid and they dropped a 2,000 bomb on the site. We ended them.

Mountainside patrol.

The rest of the day had become quiet. We watched and waited for the counter-attack that would never come. By evening I was ready to prepare my troops for the hike down. This day was a bit warmer than the rest of

September and we were ready to call it a day. We retired from our position as the sun was setting, each man full of pride for having ended some of the enemy that day.

INCOMING FIRE

As Ramadan continued, our COP came under an increasing number of artillery attacks. We returned fire with 120mm mortars and, at times, helicopters arrived to help us search for our enemies. The ghosts we faced in battle knew they only have to be lucky once to cause horrific casualties. My TOW truck, with its ability to touch the enemy at long range, was constantly called into battle. Our mortar tubes replied with a ferocious counter-battery fire. On one occasion the FSO (fire support officer), LT Bruns, was almost hit by an incoming round. We maintained watch on the highlands near our base. At times my men found the enemy who were responsible for the attack. We replied with our TOW missile and silenced them.

LIFE IN THE CHAOS

It was during Ramadan when the true chaos of this place came to bear. I wondered what it must be like to be born into a world ruled by war and violence. Kunar was a savage and dangerous place. It was truly one of those dark, uncivilized places left in the world. I wondered if freedom could ever truly penetrate that deep canopy of violence and archaic customs.

One afternoon a house was destroyed in the fighting. With it, a woman and five others were killed. A man brought in his wounded child from the mountain. He had lost nearly his entire family. The look upon him embodied sadness. Yet it almost seemed as if these people have an amazing capacity to handle tremendous catastrophe. They were somewhat like the herbivores on the African savannah; they must live their lives knowing that death could be waiting for them in the next creek or thicket. They lived their entire lives within view of the crocodiles and lions. These Afghans lived in the fires of chaos itself.

CORN

The Afghans grew corn in the Pesh River Valley. This crop grew well over seven feet tall and provided a great deal of food and money for the valley. At the same time it provided excellent concealment for the enemy. The enemy attempted ambushes very close to the road, utilizing this crop as concealment. Occasionally we received reports of these ambushes prior to a large convoy passing through our area. We patrolled near the fields and hunted these beasts.

I recall one mission in particular. We moved west, ready to bring death on the enemy. We crawled slowly along the road, seemingly to invite contact. We received reports that the enemy wanted to attack but knew they would be out-gunned. My interpreter would occasionally hear the Taliban on his "walkie-talkie." The Taliban used icoms or "walkie-talkies" as a cheap and effective way for them to communicate. It was quite unsettling at times to hear them speak. Although I was not nearly fluent in Pashtun, hearing enemy voices certainly had an unnerving effect on me.

The enemy was afraid to attack us on this occasion, as we had helicopters in support. We searched for them.

It felt like we were hunting monsters in the fields, as we scanned the highlands and the corn for the enemy. It oddly reminded me of hunting boar while I was a second lieutenant on Ft. Benning. I remember searching for these beasts in the wilderness. While on a boar hunt, my friend mentioned to me, "It feels like we are hunting Grendel." That's what it felt like.

On this occasion we ran this gauntlet a few times. The enemy chose not to engage. I was certain we would make contact, but it would not come to us that day.

Describing the emotions of my own psyche during a hunt for them is truly difficult. Imagine, if you can, what it is like to drive slowly on a road, 20 meters from a thick cornfield that is sure to hide fighters. We drove hunting our enemy, with our hair standing on our necks. SFC Staley commonly referred to that as our "Spidy Senses." We rolled and searched for them. Undoubtedly we would have won the fight, but the first five seconds of the engagement would have stood witness to the embodiment of violence.

FUEL TRUCK. BLACK SMOKE

Ramadan continually provided me with new stimuli for my education at war. This holy season was fast becoming sensory overload, even for wartime. One afternoon we received word about a burning fuel truck in the village of Mulkhana. It was a civilian truck and apparently the Taliban had kidnapped the driver. Upon hearing the report I stepped out of the TOC and observed black smoke slowly billowing into the sky. The rising smoke, darker than any that I had ever seen in my life, seemed to tell of the current state of affairs in this region. I found this smoke to be very symbolic. As it rose, it represented the chaos, death, and danger that loomed around each corner there in the Pesh River Valley. It was a fitting symbol for my experience of Ramadan.

Black smoke rising from Mulkhana.

My platoon escorted a crane to the site of the burning truck. By the time we arrived, the majority of the fire had burned out. CPL Dement and I dismounted and assessed the area with the ANPs. The fuel tanker looked like some large charred carcass of an animal left for dead. The fire had only burned the outside of the truck, leaving the fuel tank intact and full of fuel. A few flames continued to smolder on the road.

The crane moved the tanker, on its side, off the road, clearing it for traffic. Fuel began to leak, with some scattered flames burning about five meters from the tanker. At that moment a multitude of children ran to the truck with buckets to collect the leaking fuel. I told the ANP that it was not safe, but he did nothing to keep the kids away. CPL Dement and I stomped the flames out with our boots. An ANP offered to shoot the tanker and make more holes for the people to collect fuel. I angrily told him to leave the scene.

Civilian fuel truck. Children came to collect fuel when it was tipped on its side.

Sights such as this were normal in the Pesh valley and such things were normal to these children, as was war, death, and extreme violence. It was sad to watch the children collecting fuel from this burned hulk. I could not imagine seeing such a sight as a mere child. This may not even be a memory for them. I wondered.

THE AIR STARTED TO BREAK...

Toward the end of Ramadan, I had my first ANP district commander meeting, with all the post commanders in attendance. The meeting went well and was received with much enthusiasm. I was very surprised at the level of energy present as we discussed the training that I had planned for them. I left the meeting feeling very motivated and hopeful about the future of the valley.

At the conclusion of the meeting, the Qamchi ANP commander accompanied me back to the base. He informed me that the enemy sent a messenger to his checkpoint in regards to the battle in early September. The enemy wanted to know why the ANP shot at them. I was getting to the bottom of the story when I was interrupted by a most disturbing sound.

I heard the sound of air breaking. The air was breaking before an incoming artillery round. It sounded like a plane diving through the air over your head. I had heard this noise only once before, on OP Rocky on Election Day. On that day, it was from my own hand. I remember the air breaking from the 155s that I called in on the enemy.

This time the air was breaking from an incoming enemy artillery round. It smacked the ground about thirty meters from me. The shock wave of the strike startled me and the noise was horrible. At that moment I wondered if I should find cover or run to the TOC to rally our defenses. I decided to make a run for it and sprinted in full armor to the TOC with adrenaline pumping into my muscles. Being killed by an incoming round was not in my plan. Another round landed about 100 meters behind me as I ran. I would make it.

Safely in the TOC, and after updating CPT Conlin of the situation, I sent my TOW MRAP to scan the highlands. Only two rounds impacted our base. Within thirty minutes, our TOW sighted the enemy to the northeast of the base. I gave the order to take their lives, returning the very death that the enemy attempted to deliver upon us. I smiled.

REFLECTION

So this was combat. It was an intense mixture of confusion, anger, fear, and adrenaline. I was honored to be in this amazing profession that my men at arms and I chose. We as guardians of freedom were determined to protect the light of the world. There were still moments where I looked upon the land, forgot about the war, and permitted myself to be lost in the savage beauty there. Those sites were breathtaking. It was such an honor to serve as an officer there, shoulder to shoulder with these patriots. I would forever be inspired by their bravery and sacrifice. I told myself that I would ensure that their sacrifices, perils, and acts of honor will not be forgotten.

Meeting and fighting these Sirens of war continued to be an unforgettable experience. I found her and learned to sense her coming. At times she would make me feel excitement, fear, exhilaration, stress, anger, and euphoria – all in a single second. I felt this combination of emotions a number of times during Ramadan. There certainly was no shortage of firefights this month.

As I was writing at war I wondered who would actually read this. "To you, my reader, I wonder who you will be. Will you be a child of mine or a part of my family? Will you be a student of some sort attempting to understand this experience called war?"

The constant ambushes, artillery attacks, and counter-attacks that occurred during Ramadan certainly tried my faith at times. I never lost faith in our skill at arms or abilities. Rather, I thought of the prospects of laying a foundation for peace and liberty in the Pesh Valley. I did my best to remain positive and entrench my faith in our mission in Afghanistan.

I knew it was my duty as an officer to execute my mission to the best of my ability. Each day my men and I put our lives on the line to deny our enemy a base of operations in Afghanistan. However, freedom is not a gift than can be given to those who do not want it. Making a democratic or even a centralized government presence in these valleys was very challenging. These valleys have been ruled by tribal dynamics for centuries. A centralized government would not work flawlessly overnight; it was going to take time.

At times I likened this process to planting grass in the desert. Even though grass does not naturally grow in a climate such as a desert, it is possible with support such as irrigation and fertilizer. Freedom and democracy is possible, but it would take time, effort, money, and lives. Our patrols and our incessant efforts continued in our attempts in cultivating this liberty and promise of freedom.

OCTOBER 2009

US AND THEM

We wear and move in heavy armor. Our weapons and munitions cost thousands of dollars. We can see in the dark, seeing humans in the form of heat signatures many kilometers away under the cover of darkness. We can call for an array of air support, ranging from unmanned aerial vehicles, F-16s, A-10s, to Apaches, and Kiowas. We can drop 2,000-pound laser guided bombs. Our 155's can hit targets, accurately, from miles away using GPS. We can MEDEVAC the wounded and save life. We can air assault supplies and ammo within minutes of a request. We have satellite imagery and can communicate instantly with our comrades utilizing state of the art communication equipment. We are loud, menacing, and, most of all we are ungodly powerful.

Our opponents wear no armor. They wear linen and carry just a few magazines or a few RPG rounds. They have no laser sights on their weapons, any air support, or satellite imagery. They do not have platoons of men waiting to be a Quick Reaction Force. They can't call for fire on the move, nor see in the dark. They cannot MEDEVAC their wounded. However, they have the heart to persevere. They fight against overwhelming odds and do amazingly well.

This Afghanistan, with her mountains of stone and heat, hides the fighters within her folds of stone and jagged rocks. These guerillas move like shadows in the forest and attack from relative safety. The mountains are their armor; they serve as their air support, and as their reconnaissance platforms. The mountains are theirs. They can blend into the rocks as well as the populace that surrounds us.

This is our war. This is what we did. I only hope that I have painted an accurate picture of warfare for you, my reader. I often wonder. I can only hope that these pages and thought survive to my loved ones and perhaps future students of war. There can never be a single work that accurately describes all aspects of war. This is but one story of the plethora of experiences, as seen through my eyes. It is not the entire truth, but merely one perspective.

COP KEATING

October provided further lessons into the dark nature of war in Afghanistan. I awoke one morning to frantic knocking on my door. I was told to head to the TOC and to see CPT Conlin. I rolled out of bed, quickly grabbed my rifle and my notebook, and made for the TOC. Hearing no gunfire or explosions, I wondered what this could be about. The day was dreary and a light rain covered the earth. CPT Conlin informed me that COP Keating, in 3-61 CAV's (another battalion or more appropriately a squadron in 4th Brigade) area, had been hit very hard and its perimeter breached. We heard that the battle was fierce and that there were American and ANA casualties.

I was given a map of COP Keating and the surrounding area and stared at the austere terrain. For most of the day my platoon was on standby for a quick reaction force. We prepared to air assault in and prepped for it with plenty of ammunition, water, and food in our packs. We waited but the order did not come. Ground forces and air assets successfully reinforced COP Keating. That battle would go down as one of the fiercest battles for our brigade and for US forces in Afghanistan.

I prayed to God for the fallen and wounded. The news of this came at a time when we were immersed into this world of daily battle and bloodshed. We were becoming fatigued as the battles increased. My close friend, Kyle Whipple, was in A Troop, 3-61 CAV. Kyle had served in the Marines and attended ROTC at Eastern Michigan University with me. He was a good man, a good Marine, a good warrior, and an excellent officer. I prayed for the safety of him and the soldiers in his squadron.

The attack on COP Keating demonstrated the true savagery of this land. The enemy in Afghanistan, unfortunately, were not poor substitutes for fighters. Instead, they were highly motivated and believed in their cause, without question. The death they brought to this fortified outpost demonstrated that we were not the omni-powerful gods that we thought we were. We had our weaknesses, as does any force. This attack was a reminder that we were in one of the most dangerous places on earth. We prepared with even greater vigilance than before to face our enemies and to hold our ground.

ANP TRAINING

We began an ANP training program on my small rustic outpost. It was another attempt to instill some western military skills into these tribesmen that were given uniforms and weapons with minimal to no formalized training. We began by separating the ANP patrolmen from their post commanders. My men trained the ANP patrolmen on various military skills that included patrolling, shooting positions, and searches. I trained the commanders and taught them various leadership principles and fundamentals. In the first training session I tutored the Jubai commander in some of the fundamentals of military leadership such as troop-leading procedures. We practiced a scenario utilizing the latrines as an objective. The training went well and in a small way we helped to develop this place that resided on the fringes of order and civilization.

KIDNAPPING

It seemed there was a negative action born to counter every positive action that we embarked on in the valley. One day a kidnapping occurred in the village of Shege. The villagers told us that the Taliban were dressed in military uniforms and had a checkpoint on the road. They kidnapped a young man whose family owned a cell-phone store in Asadabad.

We conducted a patrol in Shege and, as chance would have it, we arrived at the site as the man's brother was there. I told them that I would do what I could to help.

These kidnappings seemed to be a way of life for the people of the Pesh. The family was not heard from again. I was sure they paid the ransom, and steered clear of the coalition.

REFLECTION: FEELING COMBAT

When I first started writing, I set a goal to explain what it "feels" like to be in contact with the enemy. I began to realize that this would be a very difficult concept to describe with my pen.

In those initial heartbeats of contact, emotions fall upon you like a waterfall. Your muscles tense and your stomach tightens. Your heart rate increases, as you attempt to control your breathing and remain calm. This transformation awakens the predator within you. Instantly you are transformed into a different state of mind. You exist very close to death itself. The feeling cannot be replicated, your sinuses clear, your eyes are wide open – you are ready.

It can be compared to the initial feeling when you almost get into a car accident while traveling at 80 mph on the expressway. In that instance as you slam on your brakes and gasp for air; you are relieved to find that you are still alive although you came inches from death or serious injury. You might stare at the vehicle in front of you and picture the consequences had your reflexes failed. You might imagine what affect the mangled steel and plastic would have had on your soft flesh. You look at your flesh and you are unharmed – at least for the moment. In the civilian world that feeling of intensity may go away in a few seconds. However, in battle, that feeling can linger, at times for hours.

As the action begins, you desperately want several things in the same moment. You want to know where the enemy is and to destroy him. You want air and indirect fire assets. You want to know the status of your men and vehicles. You want all these things in the same second. All this you want and attempt to communicate with others who are just as amped up as you are. It can be a little like communicating with a bunch of guys who just drank eight cups of coffee.

In moments such as these, the "fog of war" began to roll in. I studied the concept known as the "fog of war" for years, by authors such as Clausewitz and Moltke. I imagined this concept of confusion and misinformation that occurs in battle while I was in the confines of a comfortable university library or a coffee house. However, I never completely grasped this concept until I experienced combat first hand. When the moist mists of the Siren's touched me, I truly understood the meaning of the "fog of war." This lesson of fully grasping this fog, like so many others in combat, can only be truly learned while in contact with the enemy.

The intensity of the moment is quite heavy as a slew of emotions run through you. Even writing about it awakens the ancient hunter instincts. It is dangerous to revisit the primordial self. It is this beast within us that perhaps keeps men in this bloody profession.

I have talked to many warriors about my wishes to accurately describe the feeling of battle. Many warriors simply gave the response, "they will never understand." Perhaps they were right. I wonder if you, my reader will understand. However, I wanted to share this tale with others that have not heard nor smelled the field of battle.

I wanted to tell the tale of combat; at least, my tale of combat as seen through my eyes.

The greatest difference between the battlefield and the training ground for me was that in combat you knew that both death and danger were real. The threat of death pulled upon your most basic tenets of self-preservation. To do your duty, you had to suppress some of your instincts. In training scenarios, I would tell my men to do something without a second thought. However, on the battlefield it was not as easy to send my men into the jaws of the beast. I am quite sure that, on the training ground, one cannot replicate the fear of being killed. One can replicate stress, fatigue, and even confusion, but the fear of death cannot be replicated.

DEFENDING THE COP

Indirect fire attacks continued to hammer our small combat outpost throughout the fall season. On one occasion, we were preparing to conduct a joint patrol to Shege village with the ANA. My platoon was just about done conducting their test fires. I was at the front gate, making my final coordination with the ANA officers, when I heard a large boom. In my heart I knew it was not the explosion of a MK 19 from my platoon's test fires. The incoming alarm soon sounded, as we were being shelled again.

My platoon assumed mounted defensive positions overlooking the walls of our fortress. I mounted up in my TOW truck and scanned the northern highlands. We stood as an armored line of steel and death, scanning diligently, searching for our enemy. The enemy continued to hammer us with mortars that shook the earth.

SIREN'S SONG

A mortar landed within fifty meters of my vehicle, in the field just to the north of our base. It was unnerving to see the impact so close; I watched the dust rise. We held our ground. It was like staring death in the face; the very face that I asked my men to stare into on a daily basis. My men did this for their country, for freedom, and for each other.

As we continued scanning for the enemy's position, the eagle-eyed vision of our TOW found them, as they sought cover near a few boulders. My heart rate intensified as I reported the position over the radio to our headquarters. I gave the order to fire two missiles at the enemy position. Although we were sending the promise of death through the sky, it was a beautiful site watching a TOW missile fly toward its target. The glow of the after-burner gives you confidence and instills fear in the enemy. Our missile found its mark, and paradise welcomed more of our opponents.

We continued to unleash hell onto the highlands. I called in a fire mission using ten white phosphorus 120mm mortar rounds, along with an Excalibur 155 round. Soon the engagement was over. Calling for artillery after a missile strike was fast becoming a favorite tactic of mine.

FALSE SENSES

At times in combat your ability to sense contact betrayed you. This day we conducted a short patrol to ABAD and were on our way back toward Honaker Miracle. The day was growing very dark as storm clouds gathered in the skies. For some reason, the storm seemed to awaken the primordial self in all of us. The hair on the back of my neck was standing upright. No one said anything, but it felt like we were about to roll through an ambush. We all sensed that something was amiss. To make things even more bizarre, SFC Staley said over the radio, "Be ready for anything."

We crept along the Pesh River road, diligently scanning our known ambush areas. Nothing came out of this psychological mist and not a shot would be fired. Who knows, maybe an ambush was being set on us, but never came to fruition. Perhaps we were all just hypersensitive after the near constant fighting during Ramadan. We would never know.

SHURA

We continued partaking in the ancient meetings with the Afghans at the nearby district center. A shura is actually a good example of how to gauge coalition frustrations in Afghanistan. American officers, including myself, attend a shura with a positive attitude and with a meeting outline created from years of training concentrating upon public speaking, organizational theory, and from our own countless meetings in the Army. Initially in the shura, an officer may be able to pass on a clear and concise plan. Then, without a doubt, an Afghan may get offended. The officer will apologize, and an Afghan will bring up an off-topic point. There will then be a large unguided conversation, very little of which will be concerned with the initial plan of action. Then we will all partake of tea, with little of what we had planned accomplished. Our western plan prepared for the shura is like a beautifully cooked steak dinner. Once introduced to the Afghans, our steak dinner is thrown into a blender and splattered onto a wall.

I did not blame the elders that we met with; they were the ancient fathers of the land. They knew war, suffering, foreign occupation, and, most of all they knew how to survive. These men were like cacti; they have existed in the most desolate of environments plagued by constant war for generations. They have adapted to life here. Perhaps they knew that the democracy or the semblance of a democracy that we were attempting to transplant would take a great deal of time, and lives. They were patient; they waited like cacti in the desert for what little sustenance would come their way.

QRF AT ABLE MAIN

Since COP Keating, every attack injected a renewed sense of urgency, especially those at the smaller outpost of Able Main. One night, Able Main received several RPGs and small arms fire, leaving a small building on the COP severely damaged. We were soon ordered to respond as QRF. My men and I were all sure that our dear friend contact would pay us a visit.

The platoon moved west at a very rapid pace under the cover of darkness toward Able Main. In my gut, I sensed contact. We moved, and I prepared myself for whatever fate that awaited us. Fire from our 120mm mortars covered us as we moved. I loved seeing explosions under the cover of darkness; fireballs in the night were thrilling and placed a great smile upon my face. We arrived at COP Able Main and set in over-watch – we found no signs of the phantoms we hunted that time.

LUNCH AT THE DISTRICT CENTER

Like a shura, formal meals with the Afghans were conducted in a circle. You are typically seated on cushions or the ground. The Afghans begin the meal by having a young man walk along the circle with a kettle full of water, a washbasin, and a rag. You wash your hands and await the meal to be served. I could not help but smile at such times, when I was seated in my armor with my rifle at my side. As I became more comfortable with my allies, I would at times take my armor off. I was sharing an ancient custom with these tribesmen. Centuries and very well millennia of thought and culture came together in our small meetings. It was an amazing picture to see myself clad in armor, my NVGs, and radio tied to my cuirass. We spoke to these ancient seeming tribesmen draped in scarves and with linen wrapped round their bodies. It was another example of different centuries breathing upon one another.

The food was always served with a hearty portion of bread. It was followed by meat stew, goat, vegetables, and, at times, fruit. The Pashtun-Wali code demanded that hosts be very gracious in meals. We did not discuss business during meals; we smiled at one another and exchanged pleasantries. Our Afghan host always ensured that you had just a bit more than your fill, always an enjoyable experience.

BOMB DROP

3rd Platoon was patrolling in the Watapor Valley one afternoon near the Qatar Kala school. Goodman's platoon would not receive contact. Instead, our beloved Kiowas received fire from a Dishka in the highlands.

Their attack had no effects on our forces. However, their harassing fire would turn to be a grave mistake for the enemy who would pay a high price for their harassment fire. F-16s soon came on station and hunted our enemy.

In the early evening, the birds of prey found their mark and employed a lethal dose of firepower, killing a large number of enemy fighters. We gained much satisfaction upon learning about this recent victory. The locals told us that this was one of the most successful attacks on the enemy in years. This coalition victory afforded us some peace, at least for a few days.

However, our peace was short lived. Killing the enemy in Afghanistan is, in many ways, like stomping on dozens of ants. You may kill a dozen of them or more in one day, but in just a short amount of time they will be back. We were continually reminded that the enemy was back, as they serenaded us with their indirect fire a few times a week. As always, we returned the fire. The valley echoed with our dance and our calls to battle.

KIOWA PATROLS

Air power in this type of warfare provided key confidence and the firepower necessary to combat this tenacious enemy. At times, we would employ a Kiowa helicopter escort on our patrols throughout the valley. It felt like I commanded a rolling machine of death with our pseudo armored column and the angels of death hovering upon our shoulders. It felt remarkable to have such power at my fingertips. We rolled through the valley feeling mighty, but I never forgot the power of our formidable opponents.

ECHOES

At times, the call for QRF did not require a radio transmission to have us prepare for combat. Sometimes you could clearly hear the echoes of battle bouncing off the sides of the valley. On this occasion I was walking to our rustic gym to blow off some steam. During my walk I heard the distinct thuds of battle and the slight crackle of machine gun fire coming from the west. Upon arriving at the TOC, I found out that Able Main had received indirect as well as some small arms fire. My platoon jumped into action and prepared to move west.

It was in such moments that tensions were very high. There was a deep sense of urgency as my platoon prepared themselves for Quick Reaction Force missions. Again we moved toward the sound of the guns. My muscles tensed as we were wading into a potential storm of lead.

We arrived and were eager to engage in battle. We wanted to end them and destroy their will. We began hunting. The enemy briefly offered us battle and traded lead with us. Able Main was providing accurate 120mm support and the enemy quit their fight. We detected some enemy personnel attempting to flee the area. Seeing the enemy running with weapons always ignited our killer instinct. With a whisper, I gave the order to end them. I signed the warrant of firepower onto our foe. We pounded their positions with TOW missiles, M2 and MK19 fire, destroying them.

Following the battle, smoke slowly rose from the mountains. The valley had just erupted in a volcano of violence. With the battle finished, the valley was calm once again; only the wind could be heard as it slowly caressed the highlands.

INCOMING AND CRATER ANALYSIS

Artillery attacks against our outpost came so frequently that we grew to expect them several times a week. These incoming attacks, while they did not injure any personnel; continually grinded and frustrated us. I went to Infantry Mortar Leaders Course while I was a 2nd LT at Ft. Benning, GA. I am amazed at the amount of mathematics involved in attaining accurate mortar fire. The fact that they were able to hit on or near our base with precision was impressive.

At times we were called upon to conduct crater analysis on the impacts from the artillery rounds. We would depart our fortress and embark on short mounted patrols near our outpost. On this occasion we moved to the district center and picked up a couple of ANP. We then moved just to the north of our base. It was beautiful to look at my full platoon adorned with their heavy armor and weapons moving dismounted on the recently harvested cornfield terraces. We set in security behind the terrace's rolling terrain.

The harvested crops and the cooler temperatures marked the passage of time for us in that deadly valley. The temperature was perfect and a slight breeze graced the lands – a perfect scene. I wish you could see it through my eyes; there was an overcast, but it was one of those pleasant cloudy days of early fall, many of the nearby trees had begun to shed their leaves. I was overjoyed that the days of extreme heat had passed. I thought that perhaps the fighting season was nearly over. I would be mistaken.

FROM PROJECT ASSESSMENTS TO DIFFICULT DECISIONS...

We moved into Sematan and inspected the progress of a well that we commissioned there; providing clean water and jobs to the village. It was within a day of completion and I sat and spoke with the old men of the village. About thirty kids, ranging from the age of 4-17, surrounded us. If Afghanistan was short of anything, it was not children. The villagers seemed happy about their new well. In the course of my conversations, I saw a young boy who had cut his finger. I offered medical assistance and he followed us back to the road.

As I dismounted, my medic, PFC Rojas, took care of the boy's cut. Kiowas engaged the mountains to our northwest. We were uncertain as to what they engaged. My heart pumped with adrenaline and prepared me for a potential battle. I bid my farewell to the villagers and we mounted up. 1st platoon was searching houses in Dag. We moved west to provide over watch and secure the dismounted element. Reports had indicated that the enemy might try an attack. We waited for them upon the field of battle.

By the time we arrived on the scene, the small firefight had ceased. 1st Platoon reported they had seen men with weapons walking to the north of us. We scanned, and the ITAS acquired two men walking up the mountain. I had to decide whether or not to take life. I had the power to rob them of life by merely whispering the command in my microphone. If I wished, I could have sent a missile designed to destroy tanks hurling toward these men and shattered their bodies into mist and bone. I thought about this decision for only a few seconds that seemed to last hours. We were not in contact, not a single round was fired, and I could not positively see weapons.

A well we commissioned in Sematan.

There were a few villages only a couple of hundred meters from their position. This is one of the challenges of fighting the enemy so close to the population. Were the men that we saw enemy? Or were they men collecting firewood? I was not certain; therefore I could not take their lives. I prayed that I made the right decision. We continued observing them until they crested the mountain. They were soon out of view.

Those men, whether they were enemy or not, were alive. They had no idea that our crosshairs were on them for several minutes. They had air in their lungs for yet another day. Such decisions were a part of being a combat leader in Afghanistan. Had we accidentally killed innocent civilians, the ramifications of the act would have had grave consequences. The population that we attempted to win over would have lost faith in us. We would have lost a great deal of moral ground gained in the past months. I prayed for weeks that I had made the right decision.

ROLLOVER

One evening my platoon was called upon to transfer a soldier to FOB Blessing. We thought it would be a quick trip. While moving to the test fire area, I experienced my first rollover in an MRAP. I felt the ground give way under our vehicle. The workers on the base had been using some of the area adjacent where we drove to fill sand bags. A portion of the driving path was left unstable which led to this unfortunate occurrence.

My MRAP rolled 90 degrees. I hit my head, but my helmet absorbed much of the shock. After being somewhat disoriented for a few moments I called to my men, SPC Sanderson and CPL Dement. They indicated they were able to get out of the MRAP. We were all treated for minor injuries, luckily everyone was okay.

IED

One evening as we were returning from patrol, I received a report that the Combat Logistics Patrol encountered an IED near the Sematan ANP checkpoint. The very word IED immediately sent images of horrific injuries and damage into my mind. We had only encountered one IED in our district up to that point in the deployment. I was upset that warfare there continued to evolve, apparently for the worse. In that instance that did not matter, I knew that my brothers in arms were in harm's way. I cleared my head of the dreadful images and prepared myself for battle.

We moved west again into the darkness. I conducted a hasty link-up with the F Co. element. Thankfully, the IED did not damage any vehicles or cause injuries. We took command of the IED site and the F Co. element continued on their mission. We established a cordon of the area and searched for any signs of the enemy. Unsurprisingly, we found nothing. Contact would not pay us a visit again that night.

I walked upon the IED site. The crater was a large gaping hole, horrid in appearance. The IED had been placed inside a culvert and devastated half the road. We held our positions and waited for the EOD element that was coming from ABAD. We continued scanning the highlands, thinking that the enemy may try an attack. I spent the night wondering if my area of operation was heading into a new and more dangerous era of warfare.

When EOD arrived on the scene, I dismounted with PFC Cortez and linked up with the team leader. EOD investigated the IED site initially with a robot and then on foot. I was angry to see such an attack in my area. Looking at the destroyed slabs of road, I recalled the many stories of Iraq, as told by my combat veterans.

The following day I continued my investigation of the IED blast site and spoke to the ANP who occupied the Sematan checkpoint near the site. They indicated they did not hear or see any enemy movement. They patrolled with me and we looked for the potential trigger points used in the attack. We continued our patrol and talked to some men that lived in the houses to the west of the checkpoint. They did not offer any helpful information. As always, they were gracious and I was offered tea by one of the elders. However, that day I did not have time, as we had to move west to FOB Blessing.

For what it was worth, I thought the ANP were concerned about this IED and would improve their security efforts. We shook hands and they assured me they would be careful. I finished my business at the Sematan checkpoint and we continued our patrol toward FOB Blessing. It was the last time that sunlight would shine upon the walls of the checkpoint.

A DISTANT FLASH. IED?

Following our business at FOB Blessing, we moved east toward our COP, tired and ready for the day to be over. As we moved, I thought I saw a flash of light in the highlands far off to the east. I asked if anyone else had seen or heard anything, no one did. I thought I was mistaken. We soon entered the Honaker Miracle AO and switched over our radio frequency. We were immediately contacted by another patrol on the Pesh River Road.

A patrol was heading west toward Blessing when they heard and saw an explosion. They reported they saw burning objects on the road just to the east of the previous night's IED site. Initially everyone thought that another IED detonated. My platoon was ordered to ABAD to link up with EOD. 1st Platoon out of Able Main moved to secure the west of what was thought to be another IED site.

We linked up with EOD and sped back into the Pesh valley and soon arrived at what we thought was the IED site. By the time we arrived there was quite an assortment of forces. Governor Zalmay (the Afghan district governor) and ANP from the district center were at the scene. It was actually quite humorous to see the Governor walking around wielding his handgun. CPL Dement and I dismounted with the EOD team.

1st Platoon, under LT Harris, was sent to link up with the ANP that were thought to be close by at the nearby checkpoint. Within a few moments, we learned that there was no IED that night. LT Harris reported that the checkpoint was no longer there. At first I questioned if I heard correctly. We climbed up the small hill to investigate the scene.

The ANP Sematan checkpoint was completely destroyed. It took a few moments for this to settle in my mind. It was leveled; all that was left was mangled reinforced concrete that reminded me of the leveled clinic in the Watapor. I was very upset that such a thing occurred to the ANP I had trained – another coalition creation flattened by our enemy.

The ANP and Afghans around me did not appear to be too upset. They reminded me of gazelles that continue to graze on grass only a few hundred meters away from lions eating some of their own kind. The Afghans appeared so apathetic at times, but their lack of emotions was undoubtedly engendered by decades of chaos, violence, and strife.

Amidst the ruins of this former emplaced outpost, built with western money, I looked around in disgust. The ANP had not fired a single shot in defense. EOD said they would have to come back in the morning and investigate the site by the light of day. Goodman's platoon would escort them back shortly after dawn.

ANPs

After a sleepless night, I took a fire-team and went to the district center to speak about the recent events. We learned that the police officers from the ANP Sematan checkpoint had been kidnapped during the attack. We spoke to Governor Zalmay as well as the ANP chief. We spoke for a couple of hours and were interrupted as Honaker Miracle was attacked by mortar fire. We sought cover with our ANP allies and watched the engagement unfold. We waited out the attack in the district center while our mortars counter-attacked and pounded the enemy positions.

Later in the afternoon, the ANP who had been manning the Sematan checkpoint were found. They miraculously arrived at the district center and claimed that they attempted to fight off the Taliban, but were overcome. However, neither Able Main nor my COP reported any gunfire. These peasants in ANP uniforms claimed that the Taliban held them at gunpoint and they begged the Taliban not to kill them since they were Muslims as well. The Taliban agreed to spare their lives.

I assumed that the ANP were probably all asleep and did not post any sentries. I am sure the Taliban most likely just walked into their checkpoint. This failure was a slap in the face to my training program that I thought was going so well. The ANPs claimed that the Taliban took them into the mountains and then later released them. Their story was full of holes and was almost hilarious to listen to. It definitely taught me a lesson regarding the amount of effort that it was going to take to build a competent defense force out of them.

The former ANP chief was relieved and that afternoon I met with the new district ANP chief. He seemed a great deal more charismatic and intelligent than his predecessor. I hoped that he could spark energy into that wounded ANP organization.

NIGHT ATTACK

I spent that evening attempting to figure out how to improve my methods of instruction to the ANP. I was a bit demoralized about the loss of the checkpoint. I was both embarrassed and frustrated as the vast amount of time my men and I sacrificed to train them appeared wasted. At the same time, I knew that I could not appear to be too distraught while in front of my men. I was sharing a cigarette with a few of my soldiers and I attempted to tell them how we should not lose faith in our allies.

My attempt to motivate them was interrupted when I heard the call to battle. Our outpost received small arms and RPG fire. The booms of RPGs never failed to invigorate you. The whizzes and cracks of incoming rounds whistled once again over my head. Another evening began with war's serenade.

My men and I sprinted into our rustic barracks, dressed in our armor, and mounted our vehicles. We began pounding the mountainside with .50 cal, 7.62 and MK 19 fire, trading rounds with our enemy as we did countless times before. As mortars and artillery pounded the mountain, the enemy fire died down. The mountain glowed in the darkness from the smoldering remnants of our fire. Once again quiet rolled across the land. There was something about fighting a battle at night. Defending our walls at night almost seemed to bring more urgency to the moment. We again held the enemy at bay.

BUILDING ALLIES

The fall of the Sematan ANP checkpoint further solidified the inherent challenges involved in training the ANSF (Afghan National security forces). It forced me to look at the nature of the men that I attempted to build a legitimate force out of. I was trying to build a fortress of home grown Afghan-patriots, strong as stone. I wanted to build a castle and battlements to guard Afghanistan and its populace. I found that the hopes of my stone citadel were instead being made with mud. However, in time such structures can become as strong as stone. Several houses and walls were made of mud, but mud brick structures take a long time to fortify and stand. The tribesmen would take a long time to strengthen.

The Afghans simply knew survival. I was uncertain if they wanted our promises of liberty. At times it was overwhelmingly apparent that these forces were created overnight. I wondered how one motivates these men. The British seemed to build regular units of Indians, but the Brits were in India for over a century. I had auxiliaries, the ANP, who lost a checkpoint without firing a single round. The loss of the checkpoint certainly affected my energy toward the ANP. Ultimate victory in Afghanistan would have to come from the hands of the ANP and their Army. I prayed for the patience in training them and continued my duty as a US Army officer on the fringes of civilization. I continued my efforts to build a wall of men out of the ANSF.

FLASHES OF BATTLE

One evening we conducted a patrol to ABAD. We picked up mail as well as the executive officer, LT Brandon Fridia, from leave. As we were traveling to our outpost for the night, we received word that Honaker Miracle had received indirect fire.

Attacks at night affected us differently. Although we had the technological upper hand, attacks under the shroud of darkness seemed to invoke more fear than usual. As always, I felt the physiological transformation from within my body. I knew we had to make it back quickly and reinforce our COP's defenses. I was angry and eager to destroy the enemy as we moved quietly in the night, cutting through the darkness. I radioed Honaker Miracle and told them we were en route. I peered west through my NVGs and saw flashes illuminate the night sky as our forces and the enemy exchanged artillery and gunfire. The flashes in the sky reminded me of the description of the front lines as described in the books I read about WWI. We quickened our pace toward the sound of the guns as the sky continued to flash with the explosions of battle.

We pulled into our fort and immediately moved to our battle positions. I rushed into the TOC and received the situation report. We were still in the thick of battle and another rocket detonated on our base. Once again we provided suppressive fire into the highlands. Our 120mm mortars lit the mountain aflame and ended the fight. We continued to scan after the small engagement; the battle was over for the time being.

REFLECTION

The mountains were perpetual sponges for our devastating ordinance. We pounded these rocks with bullets, bombs, missiles, and more bombs. They did not melt, although we poured fire on them. The mountains represented the very nature of the enemy we were locked in combat with. The mountains persevered and were constant, like our enemies. The mountains wore a man down, much like how this type of war has a way of wearing down an army.

I have read, studied, analyzed, and written about warfare for all of my adult life, this has been my only true profession. Upon studying guerilla warfare, I had always looked at the losers, such as the French and the Russians, as not having the guts to fight, or as simply being weak. As a student not yet touched by combat, it was easy to think of guerillas as an undisciplined mob in the mountains and nothing more.

My time spent living on the frontier and leading men into the jaws of combat shattered my misconceptions concerning the enemy in Afghanistan. What I did not account for was that these fighters were perhaps some of the most motivated warriors of our era. They incessantly harassed our organized formations and fortified outposts and fought as if they did not fear death. Rather, they fought as if they welcomed it. These were not the weak feeble creatures that I imagined. Instead, they were a formidable foe. They have laid waste to armies before and have fought outgunned before.

In the Western tradition we pray to settle this affair known as war in a single afternoon or season. Yet, our battalions have marched upon these mountains for nearly a decade. I wondered how much longer it would take to find this victory that we all prayed for. I listened to my men speak their mind over the status of the valley. They saw battle several times a week and knew that they had ended the lives of many of the enemy. However, these constant artillery barrages, ambushes, and fallen comrades had an effect on morale at times. I did my best not to become demoralized and continued to remind my men of the importance of defeating the enemy.

A good deal of literature has called Afghanistan the limit of superpowers. If there is anything true about war, it is that the outcome of violence is unpredictable. Only time would tell and judge us for both our actions as well as our efforts here. I believed and still believe to this day that we fought to keep our homeland safe. We fought hard against an enemy who spilled thousands of innocent lives in our homeland.

ACCEPTING CHAOS

As my time in the Pesh River Valley continued, I was amazed at what you could get used to. I began to understand how the Afghans seemed to handle death and chaos so well. Chaos was normal in the Pesh valley. I remembered the children collecting fuel from the burned out fuel truck while the road was lit with flames. If that were all you knew of Afghanistan, you would think the people there were unaware of the possibility of dying. The truth was, they were all too aware of the possibility of death. Combat was as normal to the children of the valley as running through water sprinklers was to my childhood. The people of the Pesh valley were simply desensitized to horror, explosions, and death. War was normal to them.

I became more and more desensitized to our acts with every engagement. Combat was becoming almost too routine. Incoming fire, bullets, RPGs, artillery, and TOW missiles became natural every day stimuli. Of the many things that become normal in a man's life, war and killing should not be one of them. Yet, in the Pesh valley, they were. War became normal to me.

NOVEMBER 2009

MOVING TOWARD CONTACT...

In the 21st century, with our state of the art technology, we at times have an idea of when we are about to move into the storm. Our technology gives us the instinct to sense the coming of a storm, much like the beasts of the field can. This typically begins with a radio call. Sometimes, you can hear the sounds of a firefight echoing only a few kilometers away. These echoes usually come to you when you least expect it.

When a firefight commences, I am called into the TOC where I receive a warning order from my commander. The information is always extremely limited, and the span of the unknown is great. Although I feel the beast coming alive and the ancient self awakening, I try to appear calm, relaxed, and methodical as I receive the information. My breathing and heartbeat quicken as I keep direct eye contact with my commander. I try to appear brave and confident in my demeanor, regardless of how bad or limited the information is. Usually there is no time for questions or enough information about the situation.

After receiving the information, I move across the courtyard to my barracks. I will soon give my own warning order to prepare my men. The storm intensifies deep within my body. In that short walk from the TOC to SFC Staley's room I try to harness those primordial feelings and block any look of worry from my face, speech, or posture. I feel the storm, first in the pits of my stomach and then my throat. At the same time, I attempt to develop a tactical picture and tentative plan of how best to deal with the situation. I quickly analyze where the superior ground in the fight will be, what artillery targets are in the area, the position of any friendly elements, and the location of any historic ambush sites that we will pass moving toward the fight.

I walk into my barracks and breathe deeply in an effort to gain control of my breathing and slow my heart rate. I wipe the sweat from my hands and attempt to transform any fear into anger and hunger to destroy the enemy. I make myself the officer that I was trained to be. I knock on SFC Staley's door and give my own warning order to him. SFC Staley receives the report calmly, as always. He smiles and says, "Alright." His face had the ability to calm me, even in the most dire of circumstances. After delivering this 40-60 second snapshot of the battle to come, I head to my quarters to dress in my armor.

Here, alone for a few minutes, I again diligently try to harness the storm within. All at once the intense feelings of anger, exhilaration, anticipation, and a bit of fear are mixing within the grog that has become my stomach. Within ten minutes I would have to brief my men about the storm of violence that I will lead them into. As I dress, my mind drifts back to the storm that waits outside. I first put on my kneepads, then wrap my journal in a bag, with a note on it labeled, "to my family."

I place this package, which I hope is never delivered by anyone besides me, in the center of my desk. I take a few moments to pray and give myself to God, so that I may fight like a lion and not worry about the potential of death. Once my prayers are complete, I draw the RHO KAI on my hand.

In hoc signes vinces (in this sign you will conquer).

I am ready for the darkness. I dress in the rest of my armor, grab my map, notebook, and my rifle. As I turn the light off in my quarters, I look at my journal neatly set in the middle of my desk. I hope I am the one to see it next. I close my door and breathe out sharply, convincing myself that I am brave. I feed the storm with anger and move to brief my men. I wade into the darkness.

I brief my platoon in our "war room." Our vehicles are staged and running outside. My men are seated in their full armor with their eyes on me as I give them the mission brief. It was a version of the OPORD (operation order) that you learned, practiced, and rehearsed as a student for months on end. I attempt to sound confident and sure about the situation at hand. I prepare my men for battle, with as much information that is possible in this fog of war. I dismiss them.

WADING INTO THE DARKNESS

The platoon moves to conduct test fires with their big guns prior to heading out on the road. At this juncture I walk toward the front gate, alone. I walk under the premise of preparing my interpreter. In all reality, I could just call him on his cell phone or radio the guard tower to prepare an interpreter for me. I walk these few moments to be alone and clear my mind – before wading into the darkness. I utilize these final moments to gaze upon the mountains and set my mind at peace.

This walk can be either quiet or greeted by the sound of gunfire in the distance. Sometimes you hear the thuds of the battle that you will soon join. These sounds play havoc with your psyche. The sounds of the firefight add further anxiety as you realize your brothers-in-arms may be hard pressed by the enemy. My stomach, throat, and other muscles begin to tighten. My breath and heart beat quicken for the fight to come. I remind myself of the level of firepower that my platoon is capable of breathing into the ranks of the enemy. I remind myself of the artillery and aircraft that I can call into the fight. My breathing returns to normal, I am brave again, as I must be for my men. My men deserve to be led with honor and bravery.

I tell my interpreter, "We have mission right now!" (spoken brokenly on purpose). He smiles and says, "Okay."

My trucks soon appear. To me, this was always a very sacred moment. They appeared, with rising dust from the road, like a column of Alexander's Companion cavalry from days long forgotten. Seeing them rolling slowly towards me sent shivers down my spine every time, reminding me of the power my platoon was capable of slamming into these god-forsaken rocks. It was an awesome sight. I saw this sight every time we rolled out of the wire, yet it struck me differently when we rolled toward contact.

As we move into the darkness, my stomach clenches again, and my breathing quickens a bit. I remind myself to relax. I attempt to bullshit with my soldiers and add humor to the situation. The men and I were sometimes relaxed by telling jokes. Sometimes it works and we all laugh, other times, the ever-approaching thuds of battle do not permit for such humor to spread. We move toward contact, uncertain what perils awaited us in the next mountain draw. We scan the highlands in search of our date.

The contact erupts with a noise that sounds like every trumpet in hell is being sounded. Your senses come alive. It is those first seconds of contact that were the most critical. The gunfire and explosions sound as if you are near the source of thunder in a storm. You experience a lifetime of emotions in those few seconds of contact, every time. Your emotions become lit aflame. The very onset of battle seemed to last a lifetime.

MULKHANA

The enemy favored many of the same ambush areas repeatedly. On this occasion my friend, LT Alex Armstrong, came into contact near Mulkhana. Alex was a strong and competent officer. I knew he would be okay in a firefight, but I wanted to assist him. We prepared our vehicles under the veil of the unmistakable echoes of battle to our west. I entered the TOC to gather a picture of the unveiling violence.

An additional unit of MPs arrived at the battlefield and joined the chaos. Sometimes, additional forces, especially those that you are not familiar with, can add more havoc than value to the fight. The troops in contact had some trouble calling for fire onto the highlands. From the TOC and the courtyard, SFC Staley and I were able to help our comrades in contact. We pushed our TOW MRAP to the western wall of the COP. SGT Richardson observed the impacts of the .50 cal in the engagement area. We were able to attain a grid on the mountainside and called in a grid mission with 120mm mortars and achieved good effects on target.

There was a slight lull in the battle. We took this time to mount up and move toward Mulkhana, firing mortars into the highlands, lighting the mountains on fire as we pushed west. The sight of fire balls of ordinance exploding, covering our movement, filled us with confidence and prepared our palate for the taste of oncoming battle.

A long line of civilian traffic was halted on the road as we pushed west. These civilians were not huddling under cover, as you might expect, but were standing outside their vehicles, looking bored as they waited. They looked as if they were civilians merely stuck in Memorial Day traffic. So accustomed to battle were these people that they merely waited for this slight inconvenience in their day to be over. We moved pass them and continued toward contact.

Our patrol halted in the engagement area where three patrols were now postured – my platoon, Alex's platoon, and an MP platoon. It was quiet as we scanned the highlands for movement. Our bodies were tensed as we waited for the thunderclap of contact to present itself to us. It soon would.

Contact erupted as the enemy's tracer bullets came over and landed around our armored column. I was surprised that the enemy chose to give battle with all the firepower we had assembled on the road. All the American vehicles answered with our own devastating display of firepower, sending a storm of lead and destruction into the mountain. It was simply awesome, an intense feeling of euphoria coursed throughout my body. It looked like a wave of steel tracers was sent unto the mountains. I smiled – as strange as it might sound – I was happy.

We continued sending volleys of fire into the highlands. SGT Richardson soon shouted, "I see them! I see them!"

We spotted the enemy in the high ground to the south with our TOW missile and needed to move to gain a clear shot. Children darted onto the road during the engagement to pick up the expelled brass from our machine guns. I was angry at them for risking their lives and for stalling my counter attack. We shouted to them to move out of the way, so that the back blast of the missile would not harm them. I opened my door and screamed, "*Za! Za!* (Go away!)" and "*Kore Za!* (Go home!)" at the top of my lungs.

They finally listened and SGT Richardson employed the TOW missile. The sun was beginning to set as I watched the bright red afterburner of the missile spiral toward our enemy, smacking onto the mountain with a beautiful explosion. I called in the grid to Honaker Miracle and prepared an immediate suppression mission for our 120 mm mortars.

It was a simple and lovely beauty to watch the mountain burn in the early evening as the smoke from the white phosphorus mortars crept across the mountainside. It looked like death himself, slowly rolling his blanket over the mountain. The sounds of death's clamors were soon silenced, the sun was setting, and the battle was over. The valley returned to its deceivingly calm setting.

SHAMIR KOWTZ

We visited the mouth of the Watapor valley in the village of Shamir Kowtz from time to time. It is much more enjoyable to walk on the Watapor road than it is to drive on it. I truly enjoyed this little walk. The Watapor road, as I have described before, is a stream for the first kilometer or so, as deep as four inches in some places. We were constantly flanked by children who hoped and begged for anything and everything we might give them, from candy to pens. At times we obliged them.

Sergeants Moffet and Richardson in Shamir Kowtz. Chris and I are speaking to an ANP in the background.

I never forgot about the threat that surrounded us in this place, but for a brief few seconds I lost myself on this small walk. Stepping into this stream in my uniform and armor and watching my men splash through was beautiful to my eyes. From time to time we set up traffic control points on the road and questioned the people as they drove past us. I smiled as I looked up at my men setting in over-watch. It was a wonderful time of my life; I would always miss leading this small group of brave men. This has been the greatest honor and responsibility of my life and I will forever miss my days on the line.

ANP TRAINING

I realized that even with the shortcomings of our auxiliary forces, I could not be discouraged. I compared training the Afghans with the patience required when you plant a tree; training these forces was going to take years. I decided to do what I could to strengthen them. I felt it was my duty and that I was sent to this frontier of earth for a reason.

We continued our weekly training sessions with the ANP. On one occasion I taught a series of weapon disarming techniques, as well as armed retention. The ANP seemed to enjoy it. I was filled by a deep sense of euphoria that took over whenever I taught classes. It was a welcomed emotion in such a time of uncertainty. Teaching made me feel alive. It was amazing to think that these martial arts techniques that I learned in the fields and mountains of Camp Pendleton, CA were being taught to these peasants turned police officers in this rustic land. I hoped our efforts would make a difference.

A WALK

We continued patrols up to our high citadel, OP Rocky. I loved watching my warriors as they moved with loaded weapons at the ready. They moved so differently on patrol. Each time they moved like lions on the prowl, searching for their prey, it was a beautiful sight to my eyes. The sky to the east was just beginning to give birth to a new day, still hiding our movement, but lighting the path ahead. It is another one of those moments that I would forever carry with me.

We moved through the still deserted mud brick stalls of the bazaar of Jumma Gundai, which would not be open for business for a few hours. Just before the butcher's shop was a trail that led into the infamous Watapor valley. In the daytime, one could see hanging carcasses of cattle or goat for sale, with their fresh blood dripping onto the pavement.

We moved north on this rugged trail. Not far from the butcher's shop was a small waterfall cascading from the highlands. I found both the sight and the sound of this falling water soothing. It was almost as if God had placed one last piece of heaven for you to see before you crossed into this hell. That beautiful site was like so many others here, simply out of place. The path was not wide, it was just enough for two men to stand side by side in some places. Moving north, we had a full view of a terraced farmland that looked as though it had changed very little in preceding centuries.

Moving further along, the trail raised about three meters forcing you to climb through a very small streambed. Depending on the time of year, the water may be only a few inches deep. At that juncture, the trail squeezed our men between the highlands strewed with a few houses and a stream over-looking the biblical farmlands. Further north, the ground opened a bit so the troops could actually spread back out in the semblance of a tactical formation. The trail collapsed again, and we began our climb.

Moving up this ground could easily sap the strength of a man. We could see the sand bag bunker atop Rocky as we continued our climb. Our FOB dog, Shadow, happily accompanied us on the trail. Dogs brought smiles to us as they patrolled and they never let any of the Afghans get close to us. They kept us safe and considered us as their pack.

Making the summit on Rocky gave you command of the valley for as far as your weapon system could reach. I enjoyed this piece of ground, which my men had defended with honor and precise fire on more than one occasion. We set in security.

The ancient and rugged Mujahedeen Khan greeted me. I enjoyed studying the face of this ancient warrior. His wrinkles upon his face told the story of the many engagements he had been in. I was given hot tea and a type of corn bread. The over-watch was completed, with no enemy movement detected that day. We moved down the southern face of OP Rocky, back to our COP.

WINTER APPROACHES

The initial signs of winter arrived and the skies were covered with a blanket of dark clouds. Rains moistened the lands and produced a great deal of mud. The lower highlands were covered with clouds and mist. The weather seemed to suck the energy out of the locals, as well as the fighters.

Winter approaches.

The cooler temperatures in November brought snow to the northern highlands. Snow would soon block many of the mountain trails and bring fighting season nearly to an end, but the enemy continued to fight with us as long as they could. Artillery battles continued on our COP. We received incoming rounds, and again partook of this ancient dance known as combat, returning their fire.

FROM A VISIT TO COMBAT

On a daily basis I asked my men to go from gentle smiling puppies to teeth baring wolves, ready to tear flesh from the bones of our enemies, all on a moment's notice. In this type of warfare, I had to tell myself to change from pseudo-diplomat to a manager of violence in seconds. Such was an occasion during a visit to my favorite village of Sematan. We were speaking to villagers about the violence in the valley. The talk was going very well and I was enjoying the beautiful morning and temporary peace that was afforded to us thus far that day. I loved spending time in this tranquil town square, for a few moments it seemed that peace might actually have a chance in this valley.

Then, I heard a few thuds just to the east. They were the unmistakable thuds of incoming fire. Our fort, our haven, and our bastion of safety came under attack. Instantly, I felt the beast from within me come to the surface. My emotions changed and I prepared myself for the fight to come.

Incoming fire attacks may be only a few incoming rounds. However, incoming fire could, and sometimes did, mark the beginning of an aggressive attack. We always had to be ready to meet death on the field with honor, to defend each other and our outpost. We had to hold our ground. I was angry that they were attacking and we were not there to defend Honaker Miracle.

I promptly ended our visit and rapidly proceeded east toward our COP. My nerves were clinched as mortar rounds continued to fall near our COP as we entered the gates. Once inside the walls, my chariots of war assumed their defensive battle positions. Our two optically enhanced vehicles, the CROW (a remote control machine gun; the gunner operates the gun from within the vehicle) and the TOW held their stations on the north wall, scanning for any targets. In almost no time, our ITAS detected an enemy position. We fired two missiles and peppered the area with M2 from our .50 cal., raining fire upon the enemy. We ended the fight by sending a few volleys of 120mm at the target site – an awesome display of power and violence.

PROJECTS

Besides hunting and killing the enemy, a good amount of our time was spent on project development in the small villages near our fort. At times I went on patrols with personnel from our civil affairs unit. On this occasion I met with the ANP District commander as the civil affairs personnel met with Sub Governor Zalmay's semblance of a staff. My meeting with the ANP chief was short and productive. Following my meeting I moved over to the government building and linked up with civil affairs. I was given tea and conversed with the Afghans, utilizing my limited vocabulary of Pashtun.

We moved west, directly to the Shenigam bridge (the Indiana Jones Bridge), to the southwest of Honaker Miracle. Crossing this bridge was always a humorous experience. Civil affairs conducted a site survey as well as spoke with some local elders to discuss funding for a new bridge. We concluded our meeting and continued through the village.

Once through the village the ground opened to a seemingly peaceful path along the river. Anywhere else in the world this path would have been a nature trail, providing the visitor scenes of delicate and primitive beauty as it traced the Pesh river. It would make a great place to visit on a sunny afternoon, if it was anywhere else in the world. Here, however, it was but a path to move supplies from farm to market. On my way to the bridge, I passed some shepherds and their gigantic water buffalo that were grazing on the harvested fields. I had never seen these large beasts so close before. I wondered how they were brought here and how long they had been in the region.

Path near Shenigam.

The PSYOPs team, led by SSG Kingsbury, began to join our patrols. I enjoyed their company and the extra manpower they provided. We continued on our journey to the Shenigam mosque. We sat with the elders and spoke for a while before moving north and crossing the open fields to the north of Shenigam. We attempted to develop the very lands that presented us with battle. We continued to plant flowers on our battlefields.

We moved into the bazaar of Jumma Gundai, where the civil affairs and PSYOPS personnel again conducted a site survey. Civil Affairs and I went into a small building that was the village's tiny flourmill. Walking into the dark room, with the wood-burning furnace, looked like something out of a living exhibit at a museum. An ancient feeling surrounded that place. Each time the boots of my men left the walls of our COP, we walked back in time.

ANDERSILLE VILLAGE: TEA AND WAR

Even after months of patrolling, I continued to come across new experiences. On one occasion, we made a visit to the village of Andersille, to the east of Honaker Miracle. It was there I received the warmest welcome I had ever known in an Afghan village. I dismounted and asked the villagers, "*Cherta Malek?*" (Where is the elder?) An old man soon came out of his house and bid me welcome.

The elder brought us into the guest room of his house and served us tea. The room was plain, adorned with white walls with a large carpet on the floor. We sat in our armor on the cushions. The elder had piercing green eyes, flanked by leathery wrinkles. He fought during the "time of the Russians." The look upon his face was that of war – the face of Afghanistan.

It was a pleasant conversation. I enjoyed these moments of primitive simplicity where we exchanged pleasantries and talked of future cooperation. In an attempt to create a more human and friendly atmosphere, we took off our helmets in such meetings with the locals. It helped, but you cannot hide your armor adorned with magazines, grenades, and your rifle. We brought a message of peace and security, while my platoon, armed with enough firepower to destroy a great multitude of life, scanned the highlands outside his door. The locals knew war and her warriors. They looked deep into my eyes when I spoke. I felt them searching into the depths of my soul. They appreciated the talk of projects and the benefits that were sure to come. But they have seen foreign armor before. They knew warriors. They stared upon our weapons, and although they smiled with us, they knew what we were capable of.

The same can be said of them. I looked at the young males and appreciated their smiles and seemingly good manners. But I knew they were capable of a great deal more than just digging wells or making walls for the coalition's projects. These men were the descendents of the Mujahedeen that ousted our Soviet opponents only a few decades ago. I knew war and her warriors as well. I drank tea with our friends, as well as our enemies; such was the nature of that place. This civil and generous atmosphere of tea drinking and pleasantries were much like the very nature of the savage beauty that surrounded us there. Although we smiled with one another, we watched each other's every move. We both seemed to know that although we were at peace while drinking the hot tea, we could be opponents one day. That was the nature of this land and the reality we accepted.

SHERIAK VALLEY

One of the darkest places in our battalion's area was the Sheriak valley, a valley that has dealt a great deal of death and chaos for months. The valleys here, such as the Watapor, Sheriak, and Korengal, marked the frontiers for the coalition. The enemy held those god-forsaken folds of earth. These valleys are like the forest floor that offered more shadows than light.

We moved west one day, travelling to FOB Blessing. We diligently scanned the highlands as we approached the mouth of the Sheriak valley. Contact kept us waiting no longer as the world erupted around us in a hail of PKM and Dishka fire, but no RPGs this time. One is able to keep calmer a bit easier without the thunderclap of RPG explosions. I ordered my platoon to halt and fight it out. Our TOW began scanning the highlands for targets. I contacted COP Michigan, and prepared a fire mission.

I could see enemy rounds impact the ground and field next to our vehicles. We were locked in battle with our elusive enemy. A hail of radio traffic, noise, and rounds were exchanged. I selected a good artillery target to call fire on and began pounding the enemy positions with 120 mm mortars and 155 mm from FOB Blessing. At a whisper, we called for the destruction of the enemy. Steel rain fell upon the earth. I adjusted on the area where I saw enemy muzzle flashes. Seeing muzzle flashes can be an unnerving sight. They appeared to me only as sputtering sparks that reminded me of fireflies flying in the summertime in my native Michigan. I was quickly on top of the enemy positions with artillery and called for the fire for effect. I watched the magnificent display of American firepower cook the mountainside. The sheer power was astounding and I felt like a child watching fireworks in the summer. A few of the enemy emerged in new positions to our south.

Kiowa attack helicopters soon arrived on scene. I de-conflicted the artillery, ceased firing the mortars, and talked the Kiowas on to the enemy positions. They soon began employing rockets and machine gun fire on the enemy. I was still amazed and enthralled to command such terror in battle. Being in command of infantry here in this war-torn land was the true school of command. This was my school of war or, in Pashtun, my *Mectab di Jang*, where I learned the principles of war that were not taught in the manuals. There I learned war, to take life, and to become infantry.

The ANA vehicles that accompanied us attempted to break contact and ended up damaging one of their vehicles. The PSD (Personal Security Detachment) platoon arrived on the scene and we seemed to have defeated the enemy immediately to the south. The PSD platoon passed my position, continued east and reestablished contact with the enemy a few hundred meters east of my position. My platoon began suppressing the newly emerged enemy positions as our two mounted elements began pounding the mountainside. My TOW scanned the rocks and soon spotted the enemy. We cleared the Kiowas out of harm's way and engaged with a TOW missile, which smacked the mountainside with a tremendous noise and explosion. We had found our mark – the enemy fire ceased, the battle was over. We left the battlefield.

It was another splendid taste of combat. My men all performed with honor. Battles such as this did well to add to the euphoric feeling which combat can at times give you. You feel euphoria when you are the dominant force. It felt amazing during this fight. As we pounded them, I could see the allure to becoming a career infantry officer. Commanding such violence, by your voice, is an amazing experience.

FISH PONDS

One fall afternoon we traveled to the village of Dag. My men and I conducted a very short population engagement in the bazaar, then decided to patrol around the village where we discovered that Dag had a fish farm. It surprised me to see these small ponds about ten meters wide by thirty meters in length. It reminded me of my family's land in Michigan.

These newly discovered bodies of water filled me with peace. I would have loved to sit by these small ponds and write by the water, as memories from my youth bombarded my mind. This illusion of peace only lasted a few fleeting moments, as my eyes moved to the highlands less than 800 meters to the south of my position. These very highlands housed and may very well still house enemy fighters. Only a few weeks previously I remembered pounding that ground with both artillery and missiles. That is the paradox of this place, a beauty that may erupt into violence at any time.

ROLLOVER

Rain came more frequently as winter approached. The night prior to this occasion a cold rain kissed the earth and made road conditions very poor. The enemy rarely attacked in rain, especially when the rain was accompanied by the cold. This morning I blew off some steam in our rustic gym and was enjoying breakfast and a cup of coffee as I was writing in my journal. I enjoyed the peace that the weather seemed to guarantee.

SSG Telford, of the mortar section, ran into the dining hall and told me my platoon had to spin up. It would be about five seconds before I heard the rest of the situation, he did not want to tell me the entire situation in front of the Afghans who were employed to clean the dining hall. In that brief moment in time, a number of different scenarios raced through my mind. SSG Telford informed me that a convoy had rolled an MRAP and had incurred casualties. I asked if there had been contact, as I did not hear any indications of battle. He did not know.

I swiftly moved to my barracks to dress for battle. My men had already received their warning order from SSG Wade. As I dressed, SSG Wade told me that it was a non-combat related roll over. That filled me with some relief, yet I knew we had to be swift in our recovery efforts. We mounted up and brought our COP's crane operator with us.

It was always somewhat depressing to see one of our armored beasts lying on its side. My platoon set in security and we began recovery operations. I was relieved to find that the casualties were only the minor bruises that come with rolling over in a 40,000-pound vehicle. My men and I kept watch on the highlands throughout the recovery. The mountains always had a way to make you feel vulnerable when you had a disabled vehicle. No enemy attack came, and before long we recovered the vehicle. As we left the site, a horde of children ran to where the MRAP had been on its side. They searched for any remains we may have left, resembling a horde of seagulls swooping in.

THANKSGIVING

My first Thanksgiving at war was a very relaxed day, without combat. A general of the 82nd Airborne (under whose command we fell), visited our combat outpost and thanked us for our service. The camp's cooks prepared an amazing meal. Although fortunate enough to partake in a large dinner like this under arms, our minds drifted to our families and we felt the sacrifices that each of us made. However, we felt pride that our families were enjoying Thanksgiving under the shadow of the shield that we provided. We stood there at the edge of earth, the edge of civilization, and of freedom. We stood, we hunted, and we defended. As patriots we stood as torches against this darkness that threatened our homeland. We stood there and extended our lines of defense and our trenches far from our shores, homes, and families. We attempted to hold our enemies there.

EID dinner. From Left to right: SSG Kingsbury, me, LT Eric Bruns, and LT Tom Goodman.

EID

EID is the Islamic festival that marked the end of the Hajji in Mecca and ended the month of Ramadan. We conducted a patrol to FOB Blessing and expected heavy contact on the route on such a holy day. Instead of moving to contact, we passed through scenes of festivals that seemed unchanged for centuries. In each village we passed goats and cattle being slaughtered, quartered, and prepared at the river's edge. They were quite prolific sights indeed. Young girls lined the road, wearing bright shades of pink, green, and red. It was a sight quite contrary to the large battles that I expected to encounter.

In the afternoon, an Afghan contractor came to our fort to sign contracts and receive half the money for projects that we commissioned. Our meeting was interrupted by our old friend "incoming fire." We had not had incoming fire for some time. The first impact shattered the temporary peace we had enjoyed for a few days. It filled my body with aggression, energy, and anger as I ran to my quarters to rally our defenses

We received two more incoming rounds. I was angry for the break in peace and wanted to destroy the enemy. Our TOW soon spotted an enemy position and I ordered it destroyed. We finished the fight with 155's out of Asadabad; the fight was over and peace returned to the valley.

It seemed the fighting season was finally coming to an end. As the heat fell away from the land, so did most of the enemy's appetite for war. Even without the near daily occurrence of firefights in the valley, our patrols continued. Each day we set out in search of the enemy and met in the villages with the Afghans. As winter approached, I thanked God for helping me lead my men successfully throughout the peak of the fighting season. We looked forward to the fragile peace that winter seemed to promise.

DECEMBER
2009

AFGHANS NEVER GIVE UP

My education into the Pashtun way of war continued daily. These lessons were not only delivered in the auditorium of our valley battlefields. Lessons of war were taught to us even when the air was free from the screaming of bullets. Lectures were recited from the lips of the Pashtuns that we interacted with on a daily basis. Here, as in ancient times, the oral tradition of story-telling provided a wealth of information. The tales of war in Afghanistan could fill libraries with books. Yet, the majority of these stories will never be written. Instead, they exist in the minds of those who fought there. They echo off the mountainsides and in our memories.

One such lesson was delivered to us one afternoon during a visit to the district center. We sat in the ancient and timeless meeting circle and listened to the district governor. He was discussing some of the problems of inter-tribal/family warfare that is an inherent part of the culture in the Pesh valley. He was speaking in Pashtun and our interpreter repeated his words in English. He stated, "We have such problems, because Afghans never give up."

His words drove a lesson very deep into my mind. I felt that sentence: "Afghan's never give up" truly summarized the perseverance of the enemy. It embodied the very nature of the enemy that we faced in those mountains. Like many insurgents around the world, the Afghans knew that they did not have to win in the classical sense. Rather, they only had to keep fighting. I wondered if their back could ever be broken. Time would tell, I supposed.

ARTILLERY, LAUGHTER, AND DESENSITIZATION

One afternoon the enemy attacked the ANP at OP Rocky from the highlands near their outpost. I sent my TOW and CROW trucks to search for the enemy with their advanced thermal sights. My men soon began to engage the enemy with pinpoint M2 Fire. The CROW was a wonderful weapon system as it allowed for highly accurate fire. During the attack, I was talking to the ANP on my cell phone. They exclaimed with joy as we prevented the enemy's advance on their location. After the enemy was suppressed, we called for 120mm mortars to finish off the enemy. Eric Bruns, the company FSO, and I, observed the fires from the courtyard near our TOC.

It was certainly a novel moment in combat. We had a feeling of combat euphoria due to the recent air strikes deep in the Watapor. We laughed and joked as the mortars cooked the mountainside with their unholy fire. Watching the white phosphorus smoke slowly creep across the mountainside was like watching death itself crawl amongst the rocks in search of his prey. Eric and I remarked at our level of insensitivity as we were laughing at our enemies dying from our hand. We watched and smiled as the clouds of smoke from the white phosphorus rolled over the mountains as if we were young boys watching cumulus clouds roll across the summer sky.

Combat seemed to make killing normal. When you lived in a world dominated by war, taking life became normal. We had only lived in this environment for seven months and were already desensitized to death. I began to think of the Afghans and Taliban. This has been the only world they have ever known, a world where explosions and gunfire are as common place as seeing birds in flight. Afghanistan truly was a world deeply entrenched in war.

THE FALLEN

One of our brave men, SGT Nichols, formerly our company armorer, fell in battle. He was a good man and a fine soldier. I prayed that God sped his soul to a warrior's rest within the gates of heaven. I prayed for his family. We knew SGT Nichols quite well and his loss wounded all of us deeply. We continued our duty, even under the saddest of tidings.

ANP TRAINING

The ANP continued to visit our outpost on a weekly basis for training. For some of them, it was the most comprehensive training they had received in the short time they wore a uniform. On this day, I taught the ANP how to use their rifles as weapons, in both lethal and non-lethal methods. Teaching the bayonet class brought back several fond memories of teaching martial arts in the Marine Corps. I smiled to myself as I saw these tribesmen executing the techniques with Kalashnikov

AK-47s. I was amazed at thinking of the span of training ground where I had taught these classes, from the fields of Camp Pendleton, CA, to Selfridge ANGB in Michigan, to Damneck VA, and the now the Pesh River Valley.

I taught the following techniques: thrust, slash, horizontal butt stroke, vertical butt stroke, and the smash. Following these combative techniques I taught some riot control procedures and formations, teaching them how to deploy into riot line from marching into column:

1. Form line- "Landa Jorgkay."
2. Form Column- "Qatar Jorgkay,"
3. 10m run/charge "Las Meters manda."

I put these tribesmen on "line" during the drills. The line seems to be the essential foundation of the Western military tradition. To place men on line, shoulder to shoulder, still to this day inspires strength, power, lethality, and fear. As Westerners, we are intimately familiar of the very majesty and power that resides in a line of men. Seeing the ANP conducting shallow charges and practicing bayonet techniques with their Kalashnikovs made me very proud. I thought that perhaps one day they would embrace some of the principles of the Western military tradition.

I noticed that they were very unaccustomed to handling handcuffs. Obviously the crash course of an academy that they attended did not make them proficient. After a few turns each, they all began performing the techniques with fluidity and seemed to enjoy the training very much.

ANP Training.

Teaching martial arts always reminded me of the primitive nature that embodies warfare. As I was teaching, I saw an Apache with its sophisticated weapons and optics fly close overhead. My ANP were formed in their riot line, shoulder to shoulder, as the shadow of the Apache rolled over us. That moment, watching men on line shadowed by modern weaponry, was beautiful to my eyes. That piece of time embodied this ancient and perpetual drama known as warfare.

REFLECTION

Some early mornings and evenings my platoon stood up and scanned the highlands with our TOW. We searched the high ground and peered through the darkness with our advanced optics. We searched for prey, by scanning for heat signatures given off by the heat of their living bodies. When my platoon was postured in that manner, we attempted to be as the eagle that hunted for his prey beneath the surface of a lake. We wanted to find the enemy and rip his flesh with our talons; to snatch the life out of him before he knew what hit him. I wonder if such a thing sounds brutal or overly violent to you. Such is the nature of war, I suppose. Perhaps you can be a judge of that.

OVERWATCH AND MIGHT

We continued our marches up OP Rocky. The climb was much more enjoyable with the cooler weather than it had been in the summer months. The cool air felt refreshing as it blew upon our bodies. I embraced my fellow warrior, Khan, of Sematan. I felt a deep camaraderie with this man, the type that you can only get through the bonds of combat. We set in and began our overwatch.

I trooped the line throughout the day, reviewing our various defensive positions. I spent some time with PVT Brenton who asked for my binoculars. I smiled and gave them to the young warrior, who had a child on the way. The day was quiet and I ate a lunch of bread, rice, and tea with the ANP.

Whenever I climbed and observed this valley from OP Rocky, I continued to be amazed by its savage simplicity and beauty. The valley floor was carpeted with a beautiful green, provided by the freshly planted winter wheat. The wheat looked like grass indigenous to the peaceful suburbs of my homeland. This simple beauty of epic scale could almost fool a person into thinking that combat did not exist there, but distant booms of battle ongoing in Matin dispelled that small midday dream. Hearing the echoes of distant battles certainly refreshed the multitude of sites and emotions that I have weaved into this tapestry of my combat experiences.

We scanned the Watapor valley but found no signs of the enemy and climbed down around sunset. The men were happy to climb down the loose shale of OP Rocky while there was still daylight.

In the evening I was back within the walls of our COP and was walking to dinner with LT Evan Johnson when we heard distinctive booms in the northern highlands. Our air power had again conducted an air strike. I ran to my quarters and grabbed my night vision goggles. It was interesting to view the cloud of destruction from exploding ordnance in the early night. A small mushroom cloud rose quietly in the darkness, looking like death bringing souls to their rest.

It felt wonderful to see the true measure of our 21st century dominance in war technology displayed on the field of battle. We sent hellacious fire from our planes in the sky. As our enemies were often unseen in the midst of battle; we did the same – we attacked as phantoms. We shook our piece of the earth that night with our power and might.

MEMORIAL

We proceeded west. The valley was cold and wet from the previous night's rain, clouds hugged the peaks of the highlands. When we moved toward Matin or Blessing, I could feel the tension within my men. We were like beasts of the field; we could sense contact at times. Each of those battlefields that we crossed still carried the feel of battle and the air came alive whenever we passed. The ground seemed to whisper about the thousands of bullets that have been traded there.

Today, however, we were untouched by contact as we traveled to COP Michigan to honor our fallen comrade, SGT Kenneth Nichols. He gave his life for freedom and was remembered as a hero. We held a memorial at my first home in Afghanistan, COP Michigan. We honored SGT Nichols to the halls of Valhalla, with all military honors.

As we returned to our AO, we stopped at the village of Andersille, were given a warm welcome, and invited into the elder's house. We spoke as ironclad knights with seemingly friendly peasants. We drank tea and made small talk. At times such as these, I studied the local elders that I spoke with. I looked at their leathery faces, with deep imbedded wrinkles. I thought to myself, "So this is what a face that has never tasted the sweet nectar of freedom looks like."

I stared into the deep green eyes of this ancient Afghan, whose face was adorned with a long white beard. As I studied his eyes, one could almost see the Russian occupation that preceded me by thirty years. His face was concerned, even under all the smiles that he graciously sent my way. We finished our tea, hugged, and said our goodbyes.

ROCKY BY NIGHT

This night offered extremely poor illumination (natural light provided by the stars as well as the moon) as we waded into the darkness. A squad of ANA joined us on our march. I loved watching this scene of shadowy warriors moving through the darkness. I watched our shadows drift over the road as we took part in this seemingly eternal drama of war. The climb was quite challenging as we scaled the unforgiving terrain in this shroud of darkness. We completed our ascent and arrived, exhausted. After setting in security, the men and I put on warm clothes.

I spent the night trooping the line and talking to my warriors. I could not have asked for a more beautiful night; the stars were out and shimmered brilliantly throughout the darkness. I saw several shooting stars, which seemed to tell of hope following the war. As I stared into the cosmos I thought and felt how wonderful it was to be serving there with these great men. There was no other place on earth that I wished I could have been at that moment.

I wondered if I would miss nights and missions such as this as I walked from battle position to position. This was my first and last war as an infantry officer, my days of walking, driving, and leading my platoon would be over before I knew it. Reminiscing over this night will always bring a smile to my face.

The night's sky was beautiful and primitive, with the temperature hovering around 40 degrees F. It was a bit cold, especially as our bodies were laced in sweat following our long climb. It was very dark; I tried hard not to stumble as I trooped the line and spoke to my men manning various positions. I could see my breath as I exhaled the pure mountain air. It was as if I watched my spirit joining the Pesh River Valley. I would forever miss moments such as this and stayed awake throughout the night, eagerly waiting for the sun to shed both light and warmth on our position.

1st and 3rd platoon air assaulted on the opposite side of the valley. I watched them from the vantage point of my ancient stone citadel, following them from the blinking of their IR flashes. They cleared the area and climbed down the mountain without incident.

Daybreak came and the ancient mujahedeen, Khan, invited me for breakfast. I had warm tea and bread with him, the other ANP, and a few of the ANA that accompanied us. It was a fantastic scene to have our two warrior cultures side-by-side, exchanging pleasantries and stories of combat from summer. Before long, we bid our goodbyes and happily marched back to the walls of our COP.

HA-SISH

One afternoon I conducted a partnered traffic controlled point with the ANP. The day appeared to be going quite well with nothing out of the ordinary, but, as with many things in that environment, the mood quickly changed. The ANP became very aggressive with some locals they were searching who had been smoking "ha–sish", similar to marijuana. The ANP found a few pounds in the vehicle and handcuffed the men. I provided them with a zip-tie (tactical hand- cuffs) to help finish the job. The ANP hastily picked up the detainees and moved out to the district center where the men were placed in a holding cell. I was very proud to witness the ANP perform this task, another step in their long journey into becoming a legitimate police force would could promote and maintain law and order in this savage environment. This arrest both inspired and reenergized my efforts in helping to train and develop this nascent police force.

JOURNALISTS, PATROLS AND CHATTER

I began this day by meeting with LT Evan Johnson. We entered the quarters of the ANA officers and discussed our plan for our joint patrol. Following mission planning, the ANA bid us to eat with them. I obliged and broke bread with these eastern warriors.

In the afternoon, we moved out to the village of Qamchi. A journalist, Neil Shea, accompanied us on the march. It was interesting to see civilians amidst warriors. These writers, journalists, and photographers were certainly a different breed of man. They ventured here to the ends of the earth as we did, but they came without weapons. They wore light armor and attempted to capture this war and to bring this experience home.

I always enjoyed the conversation with a civilian in a war zone. They seemed to bring a fresh outlook on things. It felt almost like I was taking a hike with a buddy as we chatted along the way. The day was beautiful and the sun fell upon the lush green fields of winter wheat perfectly. Neil and I spoke about the biblical landscape that surrounded us. I truly enjoyed having him with us that day.

As we approached Qamchi, the ANA with LT Evan Johnson, established a dismounted over watch in the infamous Qamchi Draw. We crossed the Qamchi bridge and walked through the ancient mud brick alleys. The narrow alleys soon opened up to the lush green fields full of winter wheat. We walked along the narrow edges of the terraced fields. As we walked, Neil and I spoke of how long these fields must have existed. I thought this place must have looked the same for centuries, if not millennia.

Winter wheat in Qamchi (courtesy of Neil Shea).

As we approached Qamchi, the ANA with LT Evan Johnson, established a dismounted over watch in the infamous Qamchi Draw. We crossed the Qamchi bridge and walked through the ancient mud brick alleys. The narrow alleys soon opened up to the lush green fields full of winter wheat. We walked along the narrow edges of the terraced fields. As we walked, Neil and I spoke of how long these fields must have existed. I thought this place must have looked the same for centuries, if not millennia.

On the walk to the Qamchi boy's school, my interpreter picked up some icom (walkie-talkie) chatter concerning our presence. The enemy, as per usual, had eyes on us. I heard their voices. They noticed our large numbers and warned the other fighters to be careful. It was an amazing era of warfare that I experienced; sometimes we heard the voices of our enemy long before we locked shields with them. This chatter can be quite unnerving and this time we did not have the big guns of MRAPs or our TOW missile to support us. I passed the word to my men and we kept keen watch on the highlands. I dialed in coordinates for the mortars on the highlands, in case I had to call for fire. We moved through a few more clumps of houses and tight alleyways toward the school. No battle would come to us, and we completed our peaceful winter walk under the eyes of our enemies.

CHRISTMAS

My first Christmas at war was a beautiful and peaceful day. The weather was perfect, the air was crisp and clean, and the sky was a deep blue. I spent a good portion of the day at rest. The men passed time with softball, poker, and a video game tournament. Our battalion commander and CSM (Command Sergeant Major- the senior enlisted man in the battalion) visited our fort, and commended our company on a job well done. They reminded us to remain vigilant, even during the lull in fighting.

Care packages from home were a very important element of maintaining our morale, especially during the holiday season. Each package brought a piece of home and hope with it. I received many wonderful packages from my mother, sister, and my friend's mother Barbara

DaRonco. We all shared with one another whatever treats we were lucky enough to receive.

I gave my first oath of re-enlistment, to PFC Joshua James. He enlisted for an additional four years in exchange for a choice of duty station of Ft. Lewis, Washington. It felt amazing to swear a man into service:

> I, state your name,
>
> do solemnly swear to support and defend the constitution of the United States against all enemies, foreign and domestic, that I will bear true faith and allegiance to the same, that I will obey the orders of the President of the United States and the orders of the officers appointed over me, according to the regulations and the uniform code of military justice, so help me God.

I remembered when I first took my oath of enlistment in September of 1997 at the MEPS (military enlistment processing site) in Warren, Michigan. I felt deeply honored to be in the position to swear a warrior into the ranks.

DRAMA

On a visit to the village of Shege, I seemed to have walked into a land dispute amongst the Afghans. I spoke to a few farmers and then went to visit the elder, who was sick. My doc, Rojas, checked him out and prepped some medicine for him. I found that the village of Shege was having a land dispute with the village of Kiralah, located near Asadabad. The residents of Shege were told to leave their village by an apparent court order. In an attempt to resolve the situation, I invited them to our outpost on the following day. I had a Mr. Will Hall, from the U.S. State Department, aid me in this matter.

Speaking with Mr. Hall gave me hope for this Afghanistan. Measuring this war in terms of battle and conflict does not give one much room for optimism, but seeing it through the eyes of a trained diplomat, one is able to see the war in a positive manner. I believed we could accomplish our task at hand here.

We invited the elders from Shege into our fort. Mr. Hall, Chris, and I listened to their story. A man called Sha Ma Mood attained a court order from Kabul, mandating that the villagers of Shege must leave their land. The elders maintained that Sha Ma Mood's deed to the land was not legitimate, and that he bribed some very high-level judges. We listened to this story, a somewhat sad one. I studied the faces of these ancient men. Their leathery faces adorned with wrinkles served as the perfect media to explain this story of Shege and of Afghanistan itself. This village was on the border of the Afghan district and had little to no contact with any Afghan government body.

Mr. Hall and I stated we would do what we could. We then broke bread with the elders and engaged in some small talk. One of the elders overheard that either Will or I did not have any children. He gave some sound advice. He stated a man should not wait too long (he made a limp gesture with one finger). He said that once a man loses youth, he could never regain it – humorous but sound advice.

Mountains near Shege.

DRIVING WEST...

" 42 redcon1/ duke up, (we say redcon1 meaning we are ready to move out and duke up: meaning that our counter IED mechanism is on) 46 redcon1/ duke up, 45 redcon 1/ duke up, 47 redcon1/ duke up."

"Roger, we are good to push." We left our outpost and passed through our gate, briefly facing north into the dark Watapor valley and the mountains beyond, whose peaks were sprinkled with snow. We turned west upon the road and moved under OP Rocky and through the bazaar of Jumma Gundai.

In the bazaar, I saw the dark eyes of the Afghans, mostly glaring at us, but with a few smiles shining through. I watched the butcher as he did his work upon a carcass. Goats crossed the road and a dog lay in the sun. We continued west, entering the village of Sematan. The people smiled there. Scores of children ran to the road in hopes of receiving candy. A few of my men tossed candy or MREs out of their gunner's turrets. It was ironic that the children found such hope for treats from the turrets of our devastating heavy weapons.

We moved past the ruins of the Sematan ANP checkpoint. I remembered the night when it was taken and destroyed. A few meters more, we drove past the site of the IED attack. We continued west.

We moved to the town of Mulkhana. The ground to our north opened to a large draw, leading into the highlands. It was here where I felt and first experienced combat with my platoon. It served as a canvas for more than a few battles. Each time we crossed this ground each man braced himself for a fight. That day we passed without incident and continued west.

We moved near the village of Dag and its ANP checkpoint. This Dag footbridge was one of my favorite sites here, its beauty almost out of place. We continued and passed the Dag Vehicle Bridge that leads a way south of the Pesh River. We moved near Able Main; we had previously exchanged our share of volleys in defense of this smaller outpost. We moved on to Jubai and her draws that seemed to spawn contact. I recalled the great fires we pounded this ground with; many fine days of battle.

We pushed west and headed toward the Sheriak valley. The road became a long curve before opening up into the highlands south of Matin. This place often echoed to the sound of intense gunfire and RPG explosions. Each time you pass the mouth of the Sheriak valley, your body tensed and you prepared for combat. No rounds came that day. We continued west and traveled through the village of Bar Kanday. There we saw the remnants of the solar lights that the enemy destroyed in early June. They remained as skeletons to coalition efforts in this part of the valley. We continued our move toward the fortified outpost of COP Michigan, the place where I first heard the whiz of a bullet fly past my head, and my first home here.

Dag footbridge.

We moved toward FOB Blessing and passed the villages of Tantil and Sundray. These areas were some of the most dangerous and costly battlefields for men of my platoon, company, and battalion. We scanned the highlands in preparation for battle, nothing came. We continued west and soon entered the somewhat built-up city of Nangalam, with its many blocks and stores.

We were soon through the city and could see the walls of Blessing.

CONTACT AT MICHIGAN, MORE CHOICES

We finished our business at battalion headquarters and headed home for the day. As we passed COP Michigan, the small outpost began taking small arms fire. The action began with the unmistakable crackle of automatic gunfire. It had been some time since I last saw or heard these Sirens of war. I saw their beautiful seductive eyes in the form of muzzle flashes upon the mountainside. SGT Krueger spotted the flashes and engaged. I embraced her and replied to her kisses with the embrace of 120 mm on the highlands east of COP Michigan and watched the impacts of the mortars on the mountainside.

PFC Cortez soon spotted four men in the highlands. It had been some time since we last fired a missile toward our foe. I called the grid to COP Michigan and watched the men move through my command viewer. We did not see any weapons on these men, so we continued watching them. They were moving and would stop and observe the firefight from time to time. Our crosshairs stayed on them, waiting for a sign of a weapon or a hostile threat. We saw none. They may have been civilians fleeing, or they may have been the enemy who set their weapons on the ground seconds ago. However, on this battlefield we must be certain; we did not fire.

PEACE? PLATOON LEADER TIME. TRANSITION

On a visit to COP Michigan, I spoke to CPT Eastman and he informed me that my time as a Platoon leader was soon coming to an end. I had been with my platoon for well over a year now and it was soon time for me to pass the reins. I was informed that I would give up my platoon at the end of January. I sighed at the thought, but I knew that I could not be a platoon leader forever.

After serving with 4th platoon in battle, it was going to be difficult to entrust the lives of the men who I had lived, trained, and fought with for sixteen months, into the hands of another officer. To me, they were all brave patriots and men of value. Some of them had braved hostile fire in both Iraq, and now in Afghanistan. They sacrificed so much for freedom and for this opportunity to serve on the lines.

I did not hear or see the echoes of battle for a good number of days in December and enjoyed the peace and time to relax my soul. I wondered if I had seen my last battles as the head of 4th platoon. I certainly had mixed feelings in regard to this. A part of me still longed to command volleys of TOW missiles and .50 cal into the faces of our enemies, yet there was a part of me that looked forward to my time of peace that was sure to accompany me with my new position working in battalion headquarters.

For freedom we were there. For revenge, we were there. For honor, we were there. I shall never forget heading this small unit. It seemed to mean more and more as my days in that position became less and less. This experience was the pinnacle of my military career up to that point.

Each evening that I was not on patrol, I wrote in my journal. I enjoyed writing the memoirs of my Afghan war experience by candlelight. It made me feel as if I was sharing the experience of writing with other officers throughout history. I thought of officers centuries ago that scribbled on journals of their own by candlelight on a rustic desk, perhaps in a tent of sorts. For me, it only felt fitting that I wrote of war on the fringes of the civilized world to the glow of a solitary flame. Surely we were there to bring light into the world's dark places.

JANUARY 2010

REFLECTIONS OF WAR: NOISE

Noise is an integral element of combat. Typically, it initiates your experience within the grasp of battle. The Sirens sing and you come to find it is not the sweet song of bravery or romance that you once envisioned as a boy. The song is violently loud and you feel it within your bones and in your guts. The legendary Greeks that followed the Siren's song heard warnings as they neared the island home of the Sirens. They heard the waves crash upon the rocks. The same was for me as I approached firefights or took part in artillery engagements. The Siren's song told the Greeks about the impending danger. The horrible noise in modern combat provides a similar warning. The explosions, if they miss you, tell you of the potential danger that has spared you by perhaps just a few meters. The impacts of bullets or mortars tell you that Death, although close, decided not to take you.

Contact always presented her face with a large unmistakable noise. It was a noise that you came to know both immediately and without question. This noise took on several different forms. At times it was the ungodly loud explosion of an RPG. Sometimes it was the explosion and thud of indirect fire. At other times it was the whizzes and the cracks of incoming bullets. There was no mistaking that whatever caused these noises was trying to kill you, burn your vehicles, and destroy your men.

Noise and her power shocks through you. One can feel the force of impact of an RPG, a rocket, or a mortar. The explosion's power rattles your body and spills fear into your blood. I recalled the decade of military training I had before I encountered war. I would hear explosions in training and would dismiss them, with the stoicism that I thought indicative of a brave warrior. The first explosion that I heard in combat awoke the true instincts for survival. The noise and sheer power of the explosion made you realize that the training ground was long gone and that you had followed the Siren's song to its source. The noise reminded you that you were within death's grasp and you were in the storm.

EAR PLUGS AND BEES WAX

"Therefore pass these Sirens by, and stop your men's ears with wax that none of them may hear"

(Odyssey. Book 12, 188-191).

I have conducted dozens of live fire ranges during my years of military training and have shot hundreds of rounds of 5.56 and 7.62 ammo. I have fired my share of .50 cal. and thrown grenades during training. However, in training you always wear hearing protection. When you fire a gun wearing earplugs, you still feel the power of the bullet through the "kick" delivered from your butt stock, but the sound is muffled and you do not truly hear the weapon unleashing its fury while you wear ear plugs.

I likened wearing earplugs to the bees wax utilized by the rowers in Odysseus's ship. Odysseus instructed his men to stuff bees wax in their ears so that they could row close to the Sirens without going crazy. The rowers of this legendary ship knew they were in the range of these horrid tunes, but the Siren's song was muffled to them. Odysseus was the only one without bee's wax in his ears and the Siren's song drove him to the verge of insanity.

In combat you do not have the bees wax or earplugs in your ears. You fire your weapon and the men around you fire theirs. The sound makes your ears ring, a ring that all hunters and soldiers know intimately. If you want to hear it for yourself, just fire a firearm without hearing protection and the ringing sound of war will sing in your ears. Perhaps this truly is the Siren's song and for a fact it does drive some of us to the very edge of sanity.

PRAYERS AT WAR

I memorized the Our Father in Latin. I said it to myself during every action.

Paster Noster, qui es in Caelis. Sanctificetur nomen tuam. Adveniat Regnum Tuam. Fiat voluntuas tua, sicut in caelo et in terra. Panem nostrum cotidiam, da nobis hodie et demittte nobis debita nostra, sicut et nos dimittimus debitoribus nostris et ne nos inducas tentioatem sed libera nos a malo.....

QUIET

Winter in the Pesh seemed to enhance the natural beauty of the land. The air was cool and the skies maintained a deep blue appearance. I knew I would deeply miss Honaker Miracle and my men, but I was leaving at a good time. The incoming platoon leader would have ample time to learn this area of operation while the fighting was at somewhat of a lull. For myself, I found exactly what I was looking for in the infantry.

FROM CONDUCTING TRAINING TO COMBAT...

I bid my goodbyes to the ANP for the day and walked over to the rifle range on our COP. I was speaking with LT Evan Johnson. His ANA were conducting squad live fire exercises. I was at peace and my euphoria was still lingering from recently teaching. Evan and I were simply bullshitting, when I heard her sweet familiar whisper to the west. I heard the echo of battle. I heard her; the sirens of war once again sounded their tune of warfare and begged me to return.

The contact started with a few thuds and the unmistakable crackle of machine gun fire. In the span of two seconds my psyche transformed for battle. I knew it either had to be 1st Platoon or a convoy in contact around Mulkhana. The great cloud of the unknown instantly came overhead. I sprinted to the TOC while picturing the potential scenarios I would soon be wading into.

I walked into the TOC and ascertained as to the situation of the ensuing battle. I was informed that 1st Platoon was in contact to the northeast of Able Main. I quickly recorded the grids of both the enemy and friendly positions and ran to my barracks to prepare my men. I gave a warning order to SFC Staley and donned my armor, like countless times before.

It had been some time since my men and I were called to arms for a QRF mission. I felt the excitement of the coming battle flow through my body. I was honestly happy and excited to again lead my men into battle for at least one more time.

We mounted up and headed west at the gallop. We soon arrived, and set up over watch on the high ground to the east of Able Main. We began hunting for our prey. We learned that 1st Platoon initiated contact on an enemy patrol in the highlands; the enemy attempted to flee and sought shelter in a nearby cave. The opening of the cave faced directly east.

CAVE...

I repositioned my first section (two lead vehicles) so that they were facing the entrance of the cave. We moved just to the east of the Dag vehicle bridge. This new position provided our TOW with a clear shot directly into the cave's entrance. We stared directly into the blackness and held our position until 1st Platoon was clear from the surface danger zone of our TOW missile. If the situation permitted, it was always wise to clear friendly forces well out of the line of fire.

I stared into the black entrance of the cave. I knew that there were fighters in there, a few of which were horribly wounded. Able Main intermittingly fired mortars to suppress the enemy and destroy any thoughts of escape. We shook the earth around our enemy and kept them suppressed with .50 cal., until we could end them with a missile. Today we had the advantage; we waited to dispatch the lives of these men who wanted to destroy all that we stood for. They came to the Pesh valley for jihad; we granted them the paradise which they sought.

The final moments for the enemy inside the cave must have been horrible. Silence rolled over the land; that cruel silence that greets battlefields before it erupts into utter chaos. The valley lay quiet for a few moments. Perhaps they thought the battle was over as our mortars and machine gun fire ceased. Maybe they thought they would slip out after sunset and return to their refuge; maybe they were rejoicing.

Soon 1st Platoon was clear of our line of fire. I gave PFC Cortez the order to fire and, like so many times before, I signed the death warrants of our enemy. The missile was fired and I watched as the glowing afterburner sped toward the cave, spiraling as it went. It was a perfect shot, the missile exploded directly into the cave's entrance and its shockwave shook the valley. We delivered death to our enemy and continued scanning for any sign of life. There was nothing and the valley returned to the quiet of winter.

SKULLS

One afternoon I visited my favorite village of Sematan. The well we had recently commissioned for them was damaged. I assured them it would soon be fixed. They invited me for tea, and I happily obliged. We talked about the Russian occupation and I asked if any of them were fighters during that time. Many of them proudly answered with a "yes." One village elder stood up and began telling stories of battle. He told us that the mountains have caves filled with the skulls of the Russians. This former mujahedeen boasted that he had placed dozens of Russian skulls in caves just to the north of the village.

The children gathered round and listened to this elder as he continued to speak of battle with the Russian invaders. I smiled at this as I watched the children listening intently to his tale. As entertaining as I found these anecdotes to be, I realized that such tales of past battle and valor were one way how the Pashtuns preserved their martial culture. Story telling offered another glimpse into the Pashtun-Wali code. I witnessed a small lesson into the importance of bravery and fearlessness in battle. I looked at the faces of the young kids and teenagers who stared at our weapons and listened to the tales of war. I wondered how many of them would one day take up arms.

NEW MEN

As quiet as winter seemed to be, the enemy was kind enough to provide reality checks in the form of artillery attacks. I was walking about the COP one afternoon when I heard that horrible, horrible thud that mortars make upon impact. A round had landed just to our west. I sprinted to the TOC to see if I could gather any information. After receiving the situation report, I ran to my barracks and briefed my TOW crew. On the way, I passed one of the new mortar-men, fresh from the States. He was breathing heavily and was wearing the shroud of fear upon his face. This obviously was his first experience with incoming enemy mortar fire. I told him to report to his sergeant and not to worry, that everything would be okay. As I was comforting this young warrior, I realized that I felt almost numb to incoming fire. I had grown so accustomed to battle that incoming fire had become normal to me.

GOVERNOR VISIT

The provincial governor of Kunar province, Wahidi, came to our base. My platoon provided security for his arrival. As we moved into the district center, we were greeted by a Soviet style parade presented by the ANP. I had never before witnessed these tribesmen perform drill in the Western tradition. The new ANP district commander was a disciplinarian and had apparently made a positive impact on the ANP in our district. I was very impressed by their fervor, enthusiasm, and aggression in the ceremony. The ANP commander boomed commands, which rang across the makeshift parade ground.

My men assumed defensive positions on top of the district center's various towers. It was an inspiring sight to behold – ANA, ANP, and Americans holding the walls, shoulder to shoulder. Hope, like peace, came sparingly in these valleys. I fully absorbed the moment and felt as if our joint efforts were actually progressing in our area of operations.

The remainder of the day I trooped the line and talked to the various ANP and ANA. It was an amazing display of ANSF strength. The meeting continued all day and finally concluded before sunset. We returned to within our familiar walls as the day grew dark. I was happy to have been a part of such a historic visit.

ANA/ANP RELATIONS

These tribesmen that made up the Afghan Security Forces brought the attributes of the Pashtun-Wali code with them into these new security forces. Disrespect between themselves would not be tolerated and, at times, made situations interesting to deal with. I learned that the ANP at the District Center did not permit the ANA to carry their arms into their compound any more. This action was a direct result of the ANA doing the same thing to the ANP as they escorted the Provincial governor back to our fort the day prior. This was very embarrassing to the ANP.

LT Johnson and I coordinated a meeting between the ANA/ANP commanders so that they could come to terms. Evan and I waited until about noon one day for the ANP commander to return from a meeting in Asadabad. We spent a few hours discussing our thoughts and strategies in how to best find a solution to this matter at hand.

The ANP commander soon returned. Evan, the ANA commander, and I walked to the district center without escort, only ourselves. It was one of the few times I left the wire without my men – a rather interesting feeling and one I supposed that I would have to get used to.

We arrived at the district center and the two ANSF commanders sat face to face and spoke. The conversation was initially very heated. I watched as these two mature tribesmen conducted an interesting ballet of blame and justification. US forces commonly refer to this as the "blame game." It was my first time seeing Afghans utilizing Afghan logic on one another. You could sense the tension in the air, but each Afghan refused to break his composure. It was almost as if they were trying to see which of them had superior patience and it was intriguing to listen to. Eventually, through a bit of Evan's and my mentoring, the two soon came to a mutual resolution. They agreed they would allow each other's troops onto their respective outposts, providing key leaders escorted them. I was happy to have witnessed this ANSF partnership. The ANA commander soon took his leave.

Evan and I remained and ate a hardy lunch with the ANP officers. I looked at these foreign warriors and felt a feeling of intense sadness. I would soon be leaving them for FOB Blessing. I knew that I would forever miss breaking bread and drinking tea with such men. I would never forget these moments of simplicity. I remained after lunch and spoke with the ANP, named Sed Rackman, for a while. He told me of the many "benefits" of being Muslim; he had two wives and 15 children.

"WE HAVE TROOPS IN CONTACT"

My remaining time with 4th platoon grew shorter by the day. I began to savor the slightest nuances of each patrol we embarked on. Admittedly, I began to have a heavy heart each time I saw them. It was like spending your final days with a loved one, knowing that you had to leave them. I missed them even though I had not left yet.

We continued our patrols, keeping our stretch of road free from the enemy with our sheer firepower. Our first stop this day took us to Jubai. We halted and scanned those seemingly evil mountain draws but found no signs of the enemy. Nothing moved in those mountains.

We continued on our patrol all the way to the Kunar river road, without even a hint of battle. I was thinking that today would be an easy patrol and contact would not show her face. We were on our way to Shege West ANP station when the silence was broken by some unforgettable words over the radio, "We have troops in contact!"

SGT Richardson called me on the radio, "Did you hear that 46?" (6 is a call sign for leadership, my call sign was Dagger 46).

I answered, "Roger."

"Roger 46...they don't sound like they are doing too good."

I heard the distinctive crackle of machine gun fire over the radio and detected the elevated stress in the man's voice. He was trying to sound calm over the radio like we all did during firefights. We heard more radio transmissions, more stress, and more machine gun fire as we proceeded west. Once again, we waded toward the deep fog of the unknown that accompanies contact.

SGT Krueger said over the net, "I guess we just missed them huh, 6?" I concurred. We were just there. She decided not to bare herself to us then. I wondered why. Perhaps she was not ready for us. It could have been for any number of reasons. Perhaps the enemy was not ready; perhaps we intimated them by stopping and posturing in an aggressive manner. Who knows? This was just another variable in this constant arena of chance.

We moved west toward the sound of the guns. In my mind I was uncertain as to how I could best assist initially. It was not a wise idea to simply pack the road with more trucks. In an instant I decided to move our patrol onto the south Pesh River road. From that position we could effectively support the element in contact, as well as place more guns oriented toward the threat area.

We soon arrived at the battlefield, with smoke still rising from the recent mortar impacts in the two Jubai draws. We began scanning for our prey. The patrol in contact turned the battle over to me and their convoy continued moving west. SGT Krueger began suppressing suspected enemy targets with the CROW's .50 cal. We soon ceased our fire and allowed that eerie peace to roll in on the battlefield. We scanned the folds of ground and nothing moved. We all thought the battle was over, and soon headed east again.

"CONTACT RIGHT! RPG!"

Again it began with hellacious noise; I heard the distinctive boom of an RPG. A few seconds passed and the fog of the storm moved in. We all knew what had just happened, but were uncertain as to the total details. SGT Richardson came over the net and exclaimed, "Contact Right! RPG!" It was the clearest that I had ever heard his voice on the radio.

His vehicle was in the lead and was barely out of sight around a curve. As we waded forward into battle, I heard the roar of our lead M2 .50 cal. as it sent its payment of death unto the mountainside. PFC Mediola, of Saipan, was the lead gunner and today was his birthday. On his day of birth, death crept disgustingly close.

The remainder of my platoon and I soon rounded the curve. I looked into the draw where the RPG had originated. The smoke trail of this round still lingered, waving back and forth in the air as it told of the death that was intended for my men. However, the smoke trail also told us where the enemy position was. The enemy was hunkered down waiting for an opportunity to catch an American platoon off guard. Today would be the last time the enemy there would taste the air or see the sky.

Within seconds, my entire platoon arrived at the battlefield and began pouring .50 cal. and 7.62 fire into the draw. It's exhilarating to see the impacts of our machine gun fire at such close range. Tracer rounds traveled this way and that, tearing into the enemy's fighting position. We roared like a thousand lions in that instant. The enemy was close to us and I was somewhat concerned to call a fire mission this close to my men. I called for fire, adding range to my intended target, in case it fell short. The rounds impacted to the rear of the enemy, cutting off his retreat. The enemy had ceased firing as we continued delivering a punishing payload of death into the draw, denying the enemy of any chance of retreat. I would miss these moments a great deal.

I was in the process of refining a grid for an additional fire mission when Apache helicopters arrived on the scene, appearing in the sky over us. Apaches are truly powerful aircraft; their mere presence adds confidence to your psyche. I talked these archangels on to the target area and requested an immediate gun run. The Apaches did not want to risk firing over our head. My platoon moved north of the Pesh River via the Dag vehicle bridge. I then cleared the Apaches to fire. These angels painted the mountain a bright fiery orange with their unholy fire. I thanked the Apaches for their assistance as our predators of the sky continued on their hunt elsewhere.

I wanted to finish this fight with the assistance of mortars. I called 120mm mortars from Able Main. We watched the destructive fire of WP and HE mortar shells explode the mountainside to our south. The mortars landed perfectly and the draw was lit aflame in the failing light of the early evening.

SGT Krueger remarked, "Looks like they will not be collecting fire wood up there for a while." We all laughed. We had slammed death in the face of the enemy that day. Although this fight was a victory, it was a very close call as well. The difference of life or death for us was perhaps a matter of a few feet. Perhaps the RPG gunner missed because he moved slightly when he fired his rocket. Perhaps it was improper trigger control on his part. Whatever the case, be it God, or luck; I was thankful that fortune seemed to smile on us.

FINAL CLASSES

One afternoon I was spending some of my downtime writing in our platoon break area. I heard our 120mm mortars opening up. At times this was how I found out about an action beginning in our AO. I went to the courtyard and saw my friend, LT Eric Bruns, as he was registering his gun line. Eric was a very talented and battle tested fire support officer. I asked if I could have seven 120mm rounds for a new soldier that was recently attached to my platoon. Eric smiled and granted my request.

PVT Johnson, who the men called by his first name, Gary, had recently arrived in theatre. I ensured that each man under my command could effectively call for fire and did so with live rounds. By the time I taught Gary, I could teach a man to effectively call for fire in around 15 minutes. He called for fire for the first time. I smiled and felt sad; I knew this was the last time that I would teach a soldier on Honaker Miracle how to call for fire. I loved teaching the men how to make war.

In war you age, mature, and learn things quickly; you have to. If you don't learn these new skills, the valley will kill you. Untested soldiers and officers arrive in the theater of combat, much like newborn herbivores on the African savannah. The newborns on the savannah have to learn to walk and even run shortly after coming out of the womb. The same is for us that are new to war. We have to learn to walk and run in battle. We have to learn how to kill as well. If you are too slow to learn, you will be torn to shreds by the predators in the hills.

CALM ... TO FIREFIGHTS...

I was going on my last patrols in these villages on the Pesh River. I smiled as I saw children drinking from the wells we had helped build. It was hard at times to gauge victory in this land of chaos, but to give life is a victory in itself. After stopping at a few villages, we made our way to Sematan. I dismounted and moved to the rear of my convoy to pick up our medic, Doc Rojas. The day was quiet; the sea is always calm before a storm begins.

As I approached SFC Staley's vehicle, I saw him give the unmistakable hand signal, indicating that all dismounts needed to "mount up." I was confused for a split second, but did not question this experienced warrior. I sprinted back to my vehicle, yelling at the top of my voice for everyone else to do the same. As I ran to my vehicle, I heard the crackle of machine gun fire a few kilometers to my west. I ran faster.

Mounting up and gaining what little situational awareness that I could, I found that Able Main had received RPG as well as small arms fire. We carefully turned around and moved toward the sound of the guns. As we traveled west, I felt the shudder of the mortars impacting the earth and the storm of violence that began to envelop us. Once again, we waded into the darkness and into contact.

We arrived at the field that was the common battleground just to the north of Able Main. We began hammering the high ground with .50 cal. and began scanning for our prey, yet the soldiers from Able Main had beaten us to the punch. They had sighted the enemy and engaged with a javelin missile. It's always enthralling and takes your breath away to watch your .50 cal. rounds rip into the highlands as other ordinance slammed into the enemy. I would never forget these moments of tremendous intensity and emotion.

The action was over as soon as it began. We maintained a mounted over watch on these highlands, watching for any movement from our foes. Nothing stirred. The engagement was over and the valley returned to its deceiving calm and peace.

OVER-WATCH...

We woke for battle early one morning; my platoon quietly prepared their war chariots in the calm pre-dawn darkness. We moved via blackout (utilizing our night vision capabilities) through the darkness and headed on the South Pesh River road to set up an overwatch near Jubai. We began a slow crawl on the road. My IR beams, as well as SFC Staley's, were malfunctioning, making it very dangerous to drive. This danger was amplified on the South Pesh River road, whose shoulder is essentially a steep and dangerous 70-foot drop. We soon made the call to go white light, sacrificing some of the element of surprise for safety and made it to our over watch position without incident.

1st Platoon successfully air assaulted into the vicinity of the village of Dand, not far from the notorious Jubai draws. At first light, my interpreter heard a slew of enemy chatter regarding both 1st Platoon and my own position on his "walkie talkie." We heard one fighter say that he was preparing to launch his attack.

Following dawn, we displaced to the north of the Pesh River and set up near the Jubai ANP checkpoint, knowing that an attack was imminent. You could feel it in the air as we searched for our prey. 1st Platoon began to move on terrain where we were unable to support them. Contact erupted and we displaced in an effort to find our enemies. We heard that the enemy was ordering its elements to attack my vehicles and we prepared to meet them. No contact came our way as 1st Platoon continued moving down the high ground to safety.

A UAV (unmanned aerial vehicle) spotted the enemy and dispatched them; such is the nature of combat here. At times, your infantry is not the tool that kills the enemy. Rather, your infantry leaves the enemy no choice but to engage. Once they remove their shroud of civilian clothes and take up arms, they then become susceptible to sophisticated assets such as airpower, UAVs, TOWs, or artillery.

The fire soon ceased. My platoon held over watch on the high ground, covering 1st Platoon as they made it down to Able Main. We pulled within the walls of Able Main and picked up our commander. That day of battle ended without contact visiting us. I was thankful as all of the men from our company returned safely.

NEW PL

LT Florent Groberg arrived at COP Honaker Miracle. He and I became very good friends in only a short amount of time. Flo was a very fit and talented officer. I was happy that I would pass on 4th Platoon to such a capable warrior. I did my best to pass on all that I had learned in my eight months of combat. I began by introducing Flo (LT Groberg) to the various ANP positions in our area of operation.

Our first visit was to Shege East ANP. During our visit there, the ANPs showed me a small foot bridge about 200 meters west of their position. They expressed grave concern the enemy would have easy access across the river at night. The villagers had received permission from the local district government to build the bridge. I finally convinced the ANP that the bridge was easily defendable. I told them I would requisition some C-wire (concertina wire) and soda cans with rocks could act as an early warning device during the hours of darkness. They smiled and were pleased with my simple solution to their problem.

SHEGE...

We continued our patrols and demonstrated joint TCP (Traffic Control Point) operations with the ANP to Flo. Once the TCP was set and under way, I took Flo, CPL Dement and SPC Jones on a short patrol around this village. Our small fire team made its way through a field to the backside of Shege. We moved along this picturesque scene near the river and hopped over a few walls along the way. As I was scaling one wall near the river, it began to topple and fall while I was still on it. I landed and felt a bit embarrassed. Flo, the guys, and I had a good laugh.

We completed our short foot patrol and returned to the TCP. This enabled Flo to experience firsthand some of the frustrations in dealing with the locals. Several people approached the checkpoint and begged to be let through without waiting. I was always amazed at how many excuses Afghans could come up with to bypass a checkpoint.

I continued to show Flo all the areas for battle in our AO. I pointed out the danger area in the Qamchi draws as I thought about the fateful battles that we fought there. The well that we had commissioned in Qamchi a few weeks ago was complete. We stopped at the high school and briefly spoke to the high school teachers. Our patrol continued as we moved into the Qamchi bazaar and briefly talked to a few shopkeepers. We then crossed the river and did a quick walk to the girl's school.

ROCKS...

Flo would soon be able to experience the importance of restraint in this environment first hand. While we continued our patrol, a child threw a rock and struck PVT Johnson in the face. I was outraged at this but quickly reigned in my temper. The elders of the village were nearby and I demanded an audience with them. I told the elders I was embarrassed by this act, in particular since I had supported this village a great deal with reconstruction projects. I was very angry and wanted resolution immediately. What pissed me off the most was the amount of restraint my men utilized each and every day in these villages. We built a well only a few hundred meters away from one of our worst ambushes in our time in that valley. I was upset for my men, as this was a slap in the face to their efforts there.

For what it was worth, the elders seemed embarrassed by this act as well. They assured me this would never happen again. I was happy that my men had displayed restraint. Rock throwing can escalate into a very difficult situation if men are not trained to harness their force.

I had the utmost respect for the enlisted soldiers in this war. They had to balance their finely honed abilities to take life with an even stronger ability of restraint. In seconds they had to decide whether to employ their firepower or not. American soldiers in Afghanistan had to make life and death decisions every day. I will never forget them and the challenges that they faced.

LAST WALK UP OP ROCKY

As my legs burned on the climb, I knew this would be my final ascent to my beloved citadel of the Watapor valley. The ancient Mujahedeen Khan, was on top of the mountain to greet me and the rest of my panting soldiers as we reached the summit. We hugged one another and smiled, then set in our security positions. LT Groberg and I discussed the final preparations for a training fire mission using 120 mm mortars. As we waited for Honaker Miracle to approve the fire mission, Khan brought two plates of rice. We ate heartily and shared it down the line.

LT Groberg called for fire with great confidence. I was overjoyed to have passed on a critical skill that one day would not only destroy our enemies, but would also preserve the lives of my men. The thuds of the 120mm still seemed to spread chills of euphoria down my spine. I would miss these experiences with all my heart. I still do.

We joined Khan for chai. I introduced Flo to him and we made small talk. We talked on the roof of the only intact building on OP Rocky, a rustically made semblance of a small cottage. From here one has a commanding view of both the Watapor and Pesh valleys. Even though I knew of the horrible perils that existed in each of those valleys, I found this view to be amongst the most beautiful sites I'd ever witnessed.

KHAN

As Flo began to troop the line, I took the opportunity to speak with Khan about his history as a Mujahedeen. He recounted several battles that he had participated in against the Russians in the Pesh Valley. Khan had incurred one serious wound in his Mujahedeen career. He received RPG shrapnel wounds on his head. He showed me his scar with pride and a large smile.

Khan said he was 45 years old, but Afghans rarely knew their exact age. I placed him closer to the age of 55.

His first battle against the Russians was near the village of Corba, in the highlands near Able Main. He was about 14 years old at the time of his first engagement. His small group of fighters engaged a Russian column early one morning. The battle ended as the Russian Hind helicopters approached.

The mountains were safe havens to the fighters then, as they are now. He said that the Russians were afraid to pursue them. Even though the Russians wore no body armor, moving in this terrain was still hellacious. I thought these mountains must have rained hell upon the heavy motorized columns utilized by the Russians.

He said that men would learn how to fight from local Mullahs (priests) who did the majority of the recruiting. It seemed that religious zeal attracted the fighters to battle then, as they did during our war. In many ways the very nature of combat in Afghanistan has changed very little since the Cold War.

Khan was from a village not far from OP Rocky. During the Soviet occupation, he left home and lived in the mountains. I asked why the Russians were hated so. He told me of the immense cruelty the Russians demonstrated against the people. The Russians would come to villages and kill livestock for food. Many of the local villagers left the Pesh Valley and sought refuge in Pakistan.

I was sad to say good-bye to him. I hugged him and said, "*Salam Malekium*" to him one last time. I felt such a lump in my throat at that moment as I remembered the Afghan Election Day and how he employed the Dishka against our enemies. To this day I wonder how he is doing. As we ended our talk discussing warfare, he stated a perpetual truth, "Only the young enjoy war." It seemed that as I said my good byes to him, I was saying good-bye to that part of the Pesh River Valley.

REFLECTIONS

I would forever miss these talks and drinking tea with ancient warriors as I looked into the eternal valley of battle blanketed in a beautiful carpet of green winter wheat. The scene was enthralling and I will never forget my home there, my battles, and the people. Afghanistan will always hold a place in my heart and in my soul.

I knew I would always miss my platoon, these men who afforded me this warrior's education. I watched them – Jones, James, Krueger, Mendiola, Brenton, and Rojas – as they played hacky sack on a lazy afternoon. They were all smiling and looked like a bunch of high school kids hanging out during their lunch hour. A few months ago, Krueger and Jones almost fell in battle. By God's will and perhaps a bit of luck, they were spared from crossing the river Styx.

In war, the difference between life and death can be a matter of inches, or the improper trigger control of a PKM /RPG gunner. Here on the fringes of earth, life is so fragile. At times I wrote only meters away from where enemy mortars and rockets smashed into the ground.
As my final days came to an end on the COP, I spent a good amount of time in reflection. The only battles of my life were fought less than three miles from where I sat and wrote. Some were fought on foot, while others were mounted. Some at dawn, some at noon, and others under the shroud of darkness. However, each one was special to me.

RIFLE EXCHANGE

Following breakfast one fine morning, Flo and I exchanged rifles. Dement, Flo and I walked to the rifle range on our outpost. I was able to zero this new rifle with only six rounds and Flo was able to do the same with mine. I was well into my final days spent on the line, the very tip of our efforts on the frontier of freedom. I cherished these final moments with my men – their smiles, their jokes, and their non-stop bullshitting.

Flo and me in Sematan.

NEW ANP COMMANDER

Flo and I visited the new District ANP commander. He spoke to us and shared a couple of Afghan proverbs. The first was, "Untie a knot with your hands, not your teeth." This seemed to be in line with the patience which the Afghans utilized to solve problems. The second was a short story regarding an Afghan woman in Russia. Each morning she poured water on the ground before sweeping, to keep the dust down. She repeated the same process day in and day out, even when it was raining. While it was raining, someone said, "Why are you still pouring water?" She replied, "The rain is God's work, the sweeping is mine. I must do it because the rain will not always be there." This story seemed to illustrate the stubborn and persevering nature of the Afghans.

LT Groberg did a wonderful job in fulfilling his role as the Afghan Police liaison. I would miss these small meetings a great deal. My experience in the Pesh valley was almost like being governor for this small part of Afghanistan. As Flo was taking time to get acquainted with some of the ANP, I locked eyes with the new ANP chief and his officers. I stared into their dark eyes and studied the dark wells that looked stained by decades and centuries of warfare. Their lives had been formed from years of battle. They looked at us as we spoke in a positive tone; they heard these charismatic speeches before, time and time again. They knew this land and the many challenges that lie ahead.

The ANP chief had recently returned from the Muslim pilgrimage (Hajji) to Mecca. He said he was approached by a couple of Arabs while he was in Medina who inquired as to where he was from. He replied, "Afghanistan." They asked if he was fighting the Americans. He said no, and that he was actually helping the Americans. It was interesting to hear of our enemy speak of Jihad, amidst the Hajj. Some of them seemed to speak of war in the presence of God.

BATTLEFIELDS

Battles here, like in ancient Greece, are typically conducted on the same pieces of ground over and over again. I took Flo to all of them so he could know the ground that would soon offer battle. In ancient Greece, the battles were conducted on the flattest terrain possible, so Herodotus tells us, "*they search out the smoothest and fairest plain that is to be found in all the land, and there they assemble and fight*" (Herodotus, The Histories, Book 7, chapter 2). These ancient fields served as combat dance floors for generations.

In the Pesh valley, the enemy favored mountain draws as their continual arenas for battle. The folds in these ancient rock formations provided our enemies with several important fundamentals of terrain necessary to conduct attacks upon us. The draws offered expedient entry and exits, as well as both cover and concealment. You learned to look at a draw as a place of danger. Everyone that hiked or drove past these draws sensed the dangers that could at any time emit from these places. In some respects, patrolling near these mountain draws was like moving past a petrified dragon. You moved past these draws and gazed at them in a way a child might walk past a horrific gargoyle statue and feel a bit of fear in them. You just never knew when this stone dragon would come to life and attempt to breathe fire upon you and your men.

ANA DINNER, STORIES

The ANA battalion (*Kandak*) was soon redeploying to Jalalabad and hosted a large dinner on the ANA side of our outpost. The ANA presented a meal that seemed to come out of a feast that I imagine a Pashtun chieftain would have attended in the days of old. The ANA had even slaughtered a cow in preparation for this meal. District Governor Zalmay was in attendance. I broke bread with Governor Zalmay and these BDU (camouflage) clad ANA Warriors. As I sat eating in this circle, I smiled. I loved these meals, as I felt the centuries of culture embedded in this tradition.

Following the meal, we engaged in small talk. Knowing that my final hours were fast approaching, I took some time to ask Zalmay about his combat experience, in particular against the Russians. All men, regardless of their ethnicity, love to tell war stories.

SAYING GOOD BYE

I traveled to all my ancient villages to introduce Flo as well as say goodbye to them. As I spoke with the elder of Anderrsille, I told him I was sad to be leaving him. I was sad to leave all of the ancient villages and elders. I told him that I would forever cherish my time there. For months I had walked in a foreign and ancient world. I considered this part of the valley my home. As my final days approached on Honaker Miracle, I felt like a grade-school boy that was being forced to leave the neighborhood where he grew up. I grew up in this part of the Pesh Valley. Not to sound too cliché, but I think it was there that I finally became a man.

MEETING WITH ABIB OF SHENIGAM VILLAGE

During my last days on Honaker, Abib came to the base to talk about the Shennigam footbridge (Indiana Jones bridge). He knew that I was leaving and came close to almost begging for this bridge. I assured him that it was in the final stages of planning and development. I took some time to talk to him about his history and the history of his village.

He told me his family's roots came from Nuristan (the land of light). Nuristan was just to the north of the Watapor valley. His father moved from there into this village. His hazel eyes and scraggily beard indicated his Nuristani descent. His father could speak both Nuristani and Pashtun and had blue eyes. His father, like many Nuristani's, was taller than many Pashtuns. I inquired as to why this might be. He replied that the Nuristani diet concentrating on the staples of meat and milk, combined with the cold weather, produced these physical attributes. It reminded me of how Caesar described the Germans, in his *Gallic Wars*.

He was around 15 years old when he first saw Russians in the Pesh valley. He told me that they would fire artillery and kill without regard. He stated, "They brought nothing with them, but war." Like many of the former refugees here, he moved to Peshawar, Pakistan for a large part of the Russian occupation. His brother was an ANP chief a few years ago and was killed by the Taliban. He now cared for his brother's children.

We ate lunch together and soon it was time for me to bid goodbye to him. I hugged in the Pashtun way and looked into the depths of his beautifully painted hazel eyes. His village would get their bridge before too long.

PASSING 4TH PLATOON

The time for me to relinquish command of 4th Platoon finally arrived. It was very hard to do, but a natural thing in an officer's career. I sent 4th Platoon up OP Rocky under the full command of 2LT Flo Groberg. I remained behind and packed for my upcoming move to FOB Blessing. SGT Krueger and SPC Stacey remained behind in the event we needed to conduct base defense or to provide TOW capability in the valley should QRF be needed. This day there would be no battle.

That afternoon, two ANPs, Abdul and Dost came to the base to talk and wish me luck. We grabbed food from the chow hall and ate in the shura room. I asked them about their first engagements in battle. They enthusiastically told their stories. As always, I enjoyed sharing tales of combat with my fellow warriors; I listened intently. They enjoyed speaking of their valor. It appeared that telling war stories in a manner where we seem braver than we actually are was a universal trait amongst warriors. I felt like I was in a small tribal camp, eagerly listening to the tales from the older warriors. I would forever miss moments and opportunities such as those. Following the stories about firefights, Dost said something that was indicative of a man who has seen too much war in his life, "There is nothing exciting about war."

GOOD-BYE TO 4TH PLATOON

I awoke my last morning at Honaker Miracle and enjoyed a hardy breakfast. I would miss Combat Outpost Honaker Miracle, which had been my home and dominion for the past eight months of combat. This outpost was my dormitory during my university of war.

I bid my farewells to CPT Conlin and the 1SG. I walked to our war room for one last time and gave a small farewell speech to my platoon. I used the "linemen" story that I heard during my first year of football, when I was thirteen years old. "You are all linemen. You will do 99% of the work and get less than 1% of the glory. And you will get hit every single play." I used that analogy in describing the role of the infantry. I was sad bidding them my farewells. I owed them everything.

REFLECTION

I knew that I would miss the line and my platoon with all of my heart. I truly found everything that I had been searching for. Combat was no longer this imaginary object. I knew then that I would forever miss these days of commanding 4th Platoon. I considered my time with 4th as a gift from God. My experiences in leading 4th Platoon numbered like the stars in the night's sky. Memories of war, different patrols, and different villages formed different constellations into the orbits of my mind, each with its own truth.

Coming in from a patrol.

My time in the infantry company was unforgettable. It encompassed several explosions in the main emotions in life. I forever missed the line and the challenges that it presented me. The greatest victory for me in the Pesh Valley was not losing a man from 4th platoon. I prayed that God would spare them for the remainder of the war. I bid my farewells and left with a heavy heart.

LEAVING HONAKER

4th Platoon mounted up and staged their vehicles online so that they could transport me to FOB Blessing. Looking upon 4th platoon prepared for a combat patrol filled me with deep chills. I would forever miss my time in combat with them; to me, they were my family. I could recognize all of them, even by their coughs or when they cleared their throats. They were some of the bravest and finest warriors I have ever known.

They and this land have served as my true school of warfare. Rather, I should say that the Pesh Valley has been my university. My lectures have been the countless patrols that I have gone on; my tests were the many actions I have shared with them. My bad grades have been our damaged vehicles and seeing them after an RPG ripped through our MRAP. My all nighters have been atop OP Rocky or our burning truck sunrise. Our final exams together have been on Election Day, or the close ambush in Qamchi. Our pop quizzes were the numerous occurrences of incoming that we have reacted to, manning the TOW in search of prey.

I owed these men my life and my "quintessential" degree in warfare. I shall forever look upon these days with nothing but smiles. I hoped they would always be as proud of their service in the Pesh River Valley as I was of them. Regardless of whatever fate becomes of this valley, their acts of valor will forever live within the pages of my heart and soul, as well as this book.

I mounted up for the last time in 4th Platoon's vehicles. I was no longer a platoon leader; today I would be their passenger. We continued toward FOB Blessing. We moved west and after passing Able Main, a nearby patrol reported some enemy chatter. We prepared for contact. You could feel the entire crew in the MRAP tense and prepare for a fight. Flo was commanding and I was riding in the back of the MRAP, staring anxiously at my map so that I could best advise if I needed to. I had joked with Flo that he had yet to have his final exam of the relief in place process, a firefight. As we moved, we thought that contact was imminent. Flo stated, "All right! Final exam time!"

We passed through untouched. I arrived at Blessing and linked in with the Battalion S-2 (intelligence) shop. SPC Burr used a truck and helped me with my baggage from the motor pool to my barracks. I bid my farewells to SFC Staley and SGT Rich. It was a new chapter for 4th Platoon and for my military career. However, first I would go home for R&R.

As I was settling in, I was notified that I was on a manifest for a helicopter bound for Jalalabad that night. I confirmed this with my good friend, LT Tom Halverson, who was serving as the S-3 Air. Instantly, I was overjoyed.

The remainder of the day I completed packing for leave and prepared myself for my new career field. I visited with my friend, Gator Company XO, LT Mike Luth, formerly of Dagger Company. I felt at peace.

R&R

It was the middle of the night as I sat in the HLZ passenger terminal awaiting my flight to Jalalabad. This terminal, as we called it, was nothing more than a wooden shack that we call a B-hut. It began the first of my many hurry ups and waits on my way to the U.S. There was an interesting assortment of soldiers and contractors waiting for a ride to JAF.

The hour grew late as I waited for a bird made of steel to take me clear of the 2-12 IN line. Our helicopters arrived at FOB Blessing. We boarded and flew through the darkness. The first stop was in the Korengal. The second was in my old fort, COP Honaker Miracle, whose signature was quite noticeable from the illumination of newly installed solar lights in Jumma Gundai and Shamir Kowtz. We touched down briefly, dropping off contractors, and soon left.

We flew away, and left my battlefields behind in the dark night. My Qatar kala, my Jubiai, my Mulkhana, my Qamchi, and my Shege were behind me, as they were soon engulfed by the blanket of darkness. I was soon clear of the 2-12 IN line. We got to Jalalabad, landed, and remained there for the night.

JAF

I was at JAF awaiting my flight to Bagram, a step closer to home. Even with the promise of peace and happiness so close, my mind still drifted to my men, the infantry, and the battles that I left behind in the Pesh valley. Those moments were forever inscribed into the tablet of my memory and will forever be a part of me. I took a small plane bound for Bagram Air base. I scanned the landscape from above as we traveled, and saw larger versions of the villages that I was so familiar with. I already missed my little villages that could transform from innocence to dread within the eternity of a second.

OFF THE LINE

I was off the line and my days of closing with the enemy were over for the time being. Although, I was at peace, having survived my infantry trials and longing to see my beautiful homeland, I still heard war's sirens singing their song. She continued to call and entice me with her seductive images and sounds of battle. I could not believe that I heard her song when I was so far off the line and heading home. I have heard of other warriors speaking of missing war. I now found myself longing to be in battle once again; I could not believe it.

Her songs leave out integral elements of battle. She does not sing about fear or worries of your men being injured or killed in battle. Her song does well to leave out these key components. Perhaps, if she sang so, men would not fantasize about her so much.

BAGRAM

I landed at Bagram. The scene captured a mixture of military personnel, as well as a myriad of civilians conducting their travels to various NATO installations. These large American air bases such as JAF or BAF presented the feeling of overwhelming firepower and complete superiority in the Afghanistan war. It made one very proud to behold such a majestic display of power. However I had also seen the limits of such power in the valleys near my old outpost. Now more than ever I understood Hadrian's Wall. I understood the challenges of holding highlands with heavy forces against an unconventional opponent. It seems that we built a version of this Roman wall in our FOBs and COPs. We attempted to hold a line and spread light.

At Bagram, we signed over our rifles. With that act, we gave up our ability to take life at close range. I had my weapon next to me at all times for the past eight months. I felt naked without this piece but would not need it where I was going.

KUWAIT

I arrived at Ali Al Salem Airbase in the country of Kuwait. It was my first time in this land that was once the objective of the first Gulf War of 1991. On the short bus ride from the airfield to the LSA (life support area), the first thing that I noticed was the road. I thought to myself, this ground was very flat. An MRAP would have no problem maneuvering here.

The warriors around me were bound for home. Like me, the perils of combat and the many graphic sights of the land had changed many of them. We envisioned our homelands and loved ones.

Night in the Kuwaiti desert was cool, with a slight breeze. It was very quiet, as there were no Kiowas, Apaches, artillery, or sporadic bursts of machine gun fire that greeted the air. We moved far beyond the jaws of combat. In Kuwait I signed over my body armor, the armor that I wore on countless combat missions. Parting with that armor told me that I was safe.

I rested there with other warriors from my battalion. It was so peaceful as we exchanged war stories and made small talk. I soon understood why infantrymen loved bullshitting to such an extent. It was very therapeutic.

SUNRISE

I looked to the east on our flight from Germany to the USA and saw my first American sunrise in over eight months. I had never seen a sunrise at 20,000 feet. It was a deep reddish orange color. This light promised deliverance from the Sirens, at least for a couple weeks. I would be free from the unmistakable crackle of machine gun fire, the mind-sickening booms of RPGs, the powerful thuds of artillery, and the sound of Apaches or Kiowas. I was at peace, safe and happy.

Flying at altitude, I studied the American landscape intently. I felt a deep pride as I looked upon the roads and the cities of all sizes. My pride came from the fact that these cities were free. With the exception of occasional crime, these cities did not have ambushes, RPG attacks, IEDs, and suicide bombers. With as much potential for violence that the world has; our walls still held. Our expeditionary forces have brought our steel across the Atlantic and to the enemy's havens. We met them on the field in the deserts and the mountains instead of our main streets at home. We had brought steel and fire upon our enemies. We had brought fear and terror to those who attempt to destroy our ideals and us. I was honored to have met the enemy in battle. I felt fortunate to have led young Americans in combat. We held the enemy at bay in my sector; this was one of my greatest honors in life.

My warrior heart shall forever be in the Pesh and Watapor valleys of Afghanistan. It is there where I found this so called "contact." It was there where I furthered my education of officer-ship. Afghanistan was my true school of war and combat. I was thankful that I was blessed with such a compliment of brave, strong, and intelligent warriors. They afforded life to one another and to me. They permitted me the opportunity to bring steel upon our enemies. I owe the warriors of 4th Platoon a lifetime's worth of gratitude. I will never forget their voices, nor their acts in battle. Together we harvested our enemies upon our fields of battle.

As I approached the end of my flight, I could clearly see my beautiful snow covered Rocky Mountains. These mountains were not the bastions of the enemy, as they are in the Pesh valley. Rather, they were bastions of beauty and freedom.

HOME

A break from the lines is one of the more enjoyable parts of warfare. I was free from the Siren's songs and her seductive grips and was at peace there; at least initially I was. I spent hours at a comfortable and quiet coffee house in Colorado Springs and thought of the Pesh. As I was reading the New York Times, men of my battalion were fighting for their lives. It was amazing to think that only a week ago I was on Combat Outpost Honaker Miracle in the Pesh River Valley. I was in the small villages of Andersille speaking to the elders. I was finishing showing the AO to my new friend, LT Florent

Groberg, who is now in charge of 4th Platoon. I did not engage in battle while we were conducting our Relief in Place (RIP). I wondered if he had engaged in battle while I was home. As brutal as the war was in Afghanistan, most Americans would never know of the horrors and perils of hell that their young patriots from around the country faced there on a daily basis.

MEXICO

I traveled to the Baja peninsula in Mexico in an effort to find peace and beauty. I spent a few evenings on the beach at Cabo San Lucas and simply listened to the waves gently roll onto the shore. It was almost as if I could sense and hear the earth breathing as I watched the sunlight dance upon the surface of the ocean. My opponents in the land of the mountains certainly have never beheld such a sight in person. Unlike us, they lived their lives in hardship. If they were to see this, I am sure they would see it as Western decadence. One evening a storm approached from the west, reminding me of the storm just beyond the Pacific and the mountains. A plane moved overhead, one of the first planes that I heard fly over in peace. There was no need for a show of force from this bird. This bird would not drop bombs to melt the earth. I attempted to make peace in one of the most beautiful places on Earth, yet chaos haunted me and followed me even there to that Latin paradise.

FEBRUARY 2010

A PEACE HARD FOUND

I spent some time during my R&R in Michigan visiting family. Finding peace in my homeland was not as easy as I had envisioned. It is strange to think that at times I had more peace within the storm than I did at home. Perhaps I thought that once one makes peace within the winds of the tempest; it was difficult to find it on the calm lake.

I sought the ideal of peace as I did the ideal of combat. Perhaps some warriors, such as me, must travel through an Odyssey before they are granted this long awaited rest. While on R&R I thought that perhaps Homer wrote the Odyssey to explain how hard it is to go home after adventuring at war. Like Odysseus, I faced many monsters on my travels home. I faced my own Cyclops; perhaps we all do.

SCHOOL VISIT

While waiting to head back to the front, I was snowed in for a few days in Dallas, Texas. I stayed with my sister, Rachel, and her husband, Dave, who lived nearby. It was nice to spend my last hours of peace with my family.

One day I accompanied Dave to his school. He taught English at a high school in the city of Plano, Texas. I spent my day speaking with both 9th and 10th graders about my various experiences in Afghanistan. I missed the peaceful confines that a school seems to give off. I looked upon these youths and their innocence and was happy to know they have never heard the sickening thud of a mortar, or the crackle of machine gun fire. They knew only of peace and safety. It was a nice short extension to my leave, but I was once again bound for the front.

GERMANY

On my way back to the front I stayed in Liepzig, Germany for about a day as we waited for our aircraft to undergo maintenance. We stayed in a small part of the terminal that had a sleeping area and a cafeteria. The environmental transformation a soldier experiences upon entering the jaws of the beast is almost humorous. We spent time in this terminal with modern luxuries such as coffee, Wi-Fi, and plenty of German sausage. However, soon we would leave this place and head toward the lines again.

I had not heard the echoes of combat in almost four weeks. In the airport, some of the thuds of moving cargo seem to have stirred my beast within. Soon I would no longer be able to ignore such sounds; they would be a call to battle.

As I sat and waited at the Leipzig terminal, I saw a myriad of different faces, patches, and uniforms. Many were going back to the front, as I was. I could identify who was heading to the lines for the first time. They had a different look upon them as they prepared to move toward the beast and into the storm. As I sat there in the pseudo cafeteria writing, a Marine rifle company conducted their final formation before continuing on toward their destination. I watched them as they broke into separate platoons for final instructions. I was able to relate to the young untested lieutenants who attempted to appear confident in front of their men, as I did not too long ago. Many of the Marines were smooth faced LCPLs who had not yet been touched by the rigors of combat. They had now been lured in by the Siren's song to the lines.

My time in limbo was soon over and I continued east.

ARMOR

Shortly after arriving back in Kuwait, I had redrawn my body armor from the storage facility. My body armor and helmet were easy to find, as it was the dirtiest set. As I picked up my armor I could instantly sense the months of war upon it. When I touched my armor, I could hear the Siren's song, even at that distance from the front.

My armor had both weighed me down and protected me. It took liters of water of sweat from me. Touching my armor after R&R was like reconnecting with a lover after a large expanse of time. I knew it's every curve, every line, its weight, and its touch. Likewise, the armor knew all of me. It carried the fear I had shed in battle. We held each other in the direst moments of my life.

Armor is such an ancient thing. Although it has evolved, in many ways it is still the same. From the Greeks, to Rome, to knights, to now, men have depended on it to preserve themselves. It has taken many forms, hardened leather, bronze, segmented metal, plates, chainmail, flak jackets, and now the 21st century inventions of plate carriers and the IOTV (improved outer tactical vest). It seems that armor has evolved very little over the centuries. My armor consisted of plates flanked by Kevlar; nothing too futuristic about it. I am sure that a Roman or Greek would be amazed that a cuirass has evolved so little in the centuries of organized warfare.

BACK TO THE FRONT

We soon were on our way back into Afghanistan. We flew in a C-17. As we approached Bagram, the crew chief began preparing his body armor, signaling that we were preparing to descend, once again, into the storm. I felt it deep within. It's an amazing thing to watch a soldier put his armor on; the age-old ceremony of preparing to brave the storm. I stopped briefly at Bagram, where I was reunited with my rifle. It felt reassuring to have my machine of metal at my side again. I would need it before long. We continued toward our valley by stopping at Jalalabad.

A MISSED FLIGHT AND A RIDE NORTH

I was set to take a Chinook back into the Pesh Valley but the aircraft had mechanical problems and did not fly that night. I decided to jump on the Fox Company Combat Logistics Patrol that was moving out the next morning.

I linked up at the F Co. TOC in the early morning hours, before the sun had kissed the sky. I found it comforting to listen to the soldiers prepare for this long convoy by bull shitting. It felt good again to be amongst brothers in arms as I prepared to again enter the jaws of the beast.

We began moving north around dawn. It was my first time to move at length in the Kunar river valley.

Like the Pesh valley, this valley was adorned with the savage beauty that I came to expect of Afghanistan. The sunlight danced beautifully upon the green fields of winter wheat, but these glimpses of beauty were as temporary as the brief periods of peace there.

Contact soon erupted in the area known as Chow-Kay. The Combat Logistics Patrol did an excellent job in repelling the attack by utilizing M2 and MK19. I smiled during the firefight, happy to be back again within the embrace of battle. The platoon spotted their enemy and ended them with a TOW missile. It was a fine battle and a fitting welcome back to the battlefield. Our massive convoy continued north.

BOOM!

It began with a noise, ungodly loud. My ears were ringing such that I thought I was deaf. At the same time, it was almost as if there was no sound at all, like sound itself was sucked in by this explosion. This "silence" seemingly took dominance over the scene. This surreal silence is difficult to explain, but for a moment the blast was as a black hole is to light. It became a vortex pulling in all peace, life, and sound. It was the essence of fear, seeking to end us. IEDs do not pick the cowards from the brave; it does not matter to them. These horrible inventions are continually used against our allies and us. They sought to tear our limbs from our bodies and end us. Then there was a red and black curtain of sorts emitted from the explosion. We were covered by black smoke and asphalt, which swallowed our vehicle. The shroud of death engulfed us for an instant. Death himself came very close and covered everything. I whispered, "*God.*"

Our MRAP was lifted off the ground about four feet. My head slammed into the roof of the vehicle's armor; luckily my helmet took most of the blow. I saw stars and in a millisecond I remembered my own rollover in an MRAP months ago. I prepared myself, as I was on the verge of unconsciousness. I was reeling from the pain as we landed, and was unsure if we were upright or not. Luckily, the armored beast landed on all four wheels. No one spoke for a few seconds. Each man, like me, was waiting for the pain to register in our brains.

In that tenth of a second, I could feel the warm red blood begin to run down my knee. I was uncertain as to how bad it was. I imagined that I had a piece of shrapnel in my leg as the pain began to surface. I felt like yelling in pain, but did not want to cause panic in my truck. I moved my hand over my wound and noticed that it was cut. I felt more blood running down my leg. It was not too bad. I placed pressure on it and sighed with relief. I wiggled my toes on both feet, just to be sure. My head pounded. I was thankful to be alive.

As I became self-aware once again, I looked to the men in the rear of the truck. They all appeared only slightly wounded. I could see particles of earth still falling from the explosion. As the smoke cleared, I could the see the crater that almost brought death to my comrades. I physically touched the gunner. It was a CROW truck, so the gunner sat inside the truck with us. He was still entranced from the blast. I asked if he was okay. He answered, "yes." I then checked LT Chad Kunzler, the officer who had 4th Platoon before me. He was bleeding a bit from his arm. Again I feared the worse but he assured me it wasn't bad. The interpreter also had only a minor wound. I informed the vehicle commander that no one was hurt too badly.

Our MRAP limped slowly from the crater as the F Co. platoon attained situational awareness and called up the report to the nearby FOB Fortress. I was still trying to make sense of what had just happened. Once more I had escaped the shadow of death.

Chad and I dismounted to assess the damage to the MRAP. The adrenaline in my body helped to silence my pain and permitted me to climb out of the truck. As I dismounted, I racked a round into my rifle for the first time since I came off leave. As I climbed off the truck, my eyes scanned diligently for any secondary IEDs or ambush positions. We found that the front axle was bent and the MRAP had extensive damage to the undercarriage. We would have to limp the vehicle to nearby FOB Fortress.

I stayed at FOB Fortress, manned by elements of the 173rd Airborne. The medics patched me up good enough so that I could walk. It turned out that one of the platoons on FOB Fortress was the same platoon that Honaker and Miracle (of who my COP Honaker Miracle was named after a few years prior) had served with. I thought that to be so ironic. Many of the NCOs in the platoon told me that they remembered when COP Honaker Miracle was composed of only a few gun trucks and C-Wire. We exchanged stories of the battlefields that we both shared. It was certainly an interesting crossroads of battle.

The following day, the warriors from the original COP Honaker Miracle gave me a lift to JAF. Medics at JAF changed my dressings and ensured me that my injuries were not too extensive. I soon moved to FOB Blessing. This time, I took a Chinook.

GRIM REAPER

Shortly after arriving at FOB Blessing, I was assigned with the grave responsibility of being a SCMO (Summary Court Martial officer), to inventory the personal effects of one of our fallen comrades in arms. The assignment came shortly after my own close encounter with death. I accepted my orders and tried to do the best job that I could.

I began to inventory and pack the fallen warrior's effects, which included his body armor. His armor was kept in a black garbage bag because of its grotesque state, as it was soaked in his blood. You could smell the unmistakable scent of blood when you came near it. I was carrying this bag to a building when we received incoming fire. I sought cover in a nearby building. Two soldiers happened to run into the building as well to take cover from the incoming. As we were all waiting for the artillery duel to be finished, one of the soldiers said, "I smell blood." I said nothing.

Inventorying his personal items was very difficult for me. I saw pictures of his children and drawings that his kids made for him at school. The artisan responsible for these drawings was probably around five years old. I packed them neatly and carefully as his family would soon receive them. At one point I had to stop because I had to vomit. His room reeked from the blood soaked armor inside the garbage bag. I saw more pictures and child artwork and was simply overcome with emotion. I ran outside and puked up my lunch. A medic who happened to be walking by asked if I was sick. I told him why I felt sick. He said he was sorry and moved on. After an hour or so I returned to complete my task. This was one of my hardest duties in my entire tour.

ALLIES

FOB Blessing had a district center just outside its gates. There I met more Afghans who worked in the security forces. It was always wonderful spending a night filled with the nuances and customs of the Pashtun-Wali code. We discussed many things, ranging from fighting the Taliban to poetry and history. The simplicity of good talk, food, and tea was wonderful. I found peace that reminded me of my days as a platoon leader.

Drinking tea with the Afghans was simply wonderful. As a former platoon leader, I realized the importance of this custom. For just a few moments, serving and drinking the tea was all that mattered. Even there, where life can be snatched from a man in seconds, the roads explode, and every mountain may hold an ambush, all of that was silenced for just a few minutes. All that mattered in those short moments of time was tea, smiles, and conversation. I truly enjoyed such time with these Eastern warriors. They told me a popular Afghan proverb that helped explain the importance of teatime and the Pashtun-Wali code, "the greatest wealth in life is manners."

MORTUARY DUTIES

I prepared the deceased's personal effects and waited for a Chinook helicopter to Jalalabad. Sitting there under the full moon near the Blessing HLZ was a bit unnerving. I chatted with the men of A Co. mortars who offered me a cigar, which I graciously accepted

We made our flight to JAF without incident. While the other passengers walked to the passenger terminal, I waited by myself between two Chinooks with the soldier's personal effects. It was a beautiful night with the sky illuminated under a full moon under Orion's watch. It was calming to be there, not a soul was around me for at least 300 meters. That was the furthest that I have been from another American while in Afghanistan – it was calming and solemn.

I soon took a C130 to Bagram airfield. I passed off the deceased's personal effects to the mortuary affairs office. It was the saddest thing I have done in combat. As we entered the hanger, there was a Humvee with a casket with an Afghan flag draped upon it. It was a solemn moment, displaying the ultimate sacrifice for liberty not only amongst Americans, but Afghan's as well. The warrior's belongings that I prepared would soon be bound for the United States. The cost of liberty is terribly high at times.

BAGRAM REFLECTION

I stared off into the distance at the Hindu Kush Mountains. These ancient fortresses have seen many a foreign banner come and go. They have seen empires march out and soldiers from all corners of the world encamp at their feet. These mountains served as a constant reminder of the enemy's power. We had our missiles, our radars, our maps, and our aircraft; but still the enemy held the ground. They operated just under our noses or, perhaps more accurately, we operated just under theirs. These mountains still warned me of the perils held in her valleys. Visitors to Afghanistan would be wise to listen to her warnings.

MARCH 2010

SPRING

Spring fast approached and with it came a new promise of life, but the approaching warm weather melted the snow in the highlands and reignited the promise of warfare as well. The enemy's supply routes would soon reopen. They spent the majority of the winter in wait; their springtime offensive would soon begin.

I was still at Bagram waiting for my passage north. During a meal, a group of people from Kosovo sat next to me. I made talk with this seemingly friendly group of contractors. A company, called Flour, employed them and they worked in the maintenance field. A few of them had been in Afghanistan for just under five years. We relied on these civilians for some of our life support and various maintenance tasks. It was strange to see people trade one war torn land in exchange for another. It was almost humorous the amount of opportunity that war provided. If not all roads led to Bagram, quite a few did. I found passage north back to my valley and again rejoined my brothers in arms upon the line.

ANA AT BLESSING

Most American bases in Afghanistan have some sort of compliment of ANSF quartered there. Although they shared the same perimeter with us, stepping onto their side of camp felt like you were walking into an entirely different world. Time simply went by slower for them, as it seemed to for all Afghans. I took the opportunity to introduce myself to them as soon as I could. I initially spent some time meeting the various officers from the ANA battalion at FOB Blessing. The majority of their conversation centered on issues regarding supply and logistics. Apparently one common factor for all the Afghan security forces was their insatiable need for supplies. Each meeting with our allies illustrated their lack of logistical strength. The meeting concluded with a fine meal consisting of bread, meat, and rice.

I also noticed that many Afghans, the security forces included, took out their prayer beads from time to time while speaking to us. They chanted their silent prayers while speaking to the western infidels.

SUNSETS

I utterly enjoyed these moments when the sky was painted with such beauty and gentle winds blew from the east. One evening I was sitting near the flagpoles at FOB Blessing and heard the American flag rustle in the wind. The sight of our colors in the wind inspired me and warmed my heart. They represented the very liberty that we attempted so hard to protect. We attempted to bring our torch of liberty there in that valley of fire.

As I wrote in my journal, I wondered who would read this work, "I wonder where you will be when you read my words. Will you be in your home? Will you be in a library, at a university, or a coffee house? Let me tell you of this land in this moment. It is one of those light-blue sunsets right now. No orange light because of the clouds on the horizon, rather, a calm quiet blue evening. I'm sure you know the type."

This savage beauty composed of rugged peaks and ridges surrounded me. In the distance I could still see snow atop a few mountains. The snow would soon melt and empty its waters into the Pesh River. The fields were painted in beautiful green on the valley floor. They formed such a lovely carpet. The winter wheat was dotted with several clumps of wild flowers that resembled dandelions.

I looked at the city of Nangalam and recalled moving through it with my men. During sunset I rarely heard the clashing of steel and learned to embrace the peace while I could, even if it was just for a few moments. I learned to embrace such moments of peace while we had them. The call to prayer echoed off the sides of the mountains in the distance. I looked to the mountains that surrounded me, knowing there were undoubtedly fighters kneeling and submitting to God. At this time of day I especially took time to gaze upon the magnificently rugged mountains. They were the perpetual and silent observers of what has been endless chaos in Afghanistan.

Few things gave me more peace than sunsets in the Pesh River Valley. Their beauty was almost indescribable. Each evening I watched as the sun shed its last peaceful dim rays of light unto this perpetual canvas of war. The heat left the valley and offered only calm. Sunsets brought peace to this land of war. Although I came within inches of death there on so many occasions, this timeless beauty continued to enthrall me. I sighed as I gazed upon the rugged ridgelines with trees and outposts upon them.

I found my warrior self here, and the chapters of my first war shall always live in the rocks of Afghanistan. The Pesh valley will forever be *zma Mectab di Jang*, my school of war.

ANP AT BLESSING

Some evenings my comrades and I would venture out to the nearby district center without a large escort. It would only be two or three of us and although the district center was only a 20-meter walk from our gate, it felt very exciting to walk there on our own. I approached the Afghan guards at our main gate and said to them, "*Swalay-day Mungz larsha*." We are going to the district center. The ANA soldier on guard smiled at us as we opened the gate. I racked a round into my rifle for our short walk to the district center.

Our ANP brethren always welcomed us as they bid us to sit and join them for a meal. "*Cane na, cane na*" (sit down, sit down), they would say to us as we entered their dining room. I truly enjoyed the simplicity of dining with the Afghans. It was these moments of smiles and pleasantries shared over tea that I loved almost as much as combat. This was my Afghanistan, with its savage beauty, its moments of ferocious battles flanked by rugged simplicity. Everything, for me, seemed as it should have been – two American officers outside our walls shrouded in darkness. We sat in our simple cement building in a dimly lit room and became a part of this ancient tapestry.

I spent many evenings at the District Center, speaking and listening to the Afghans. I studied them, as they undoubtedly studied me. I loved listening to their stories of early combat. Surin, one of the ANP, told me about his early career in the ANA. He kept a very western style moustache and was educated. He knew that he risked his life by working with the coalition. He gave some good advice when we parted ways for the night, "Fighting sounds so sweet when you hear about it. But it's horrible when it happens."

I thought it was good and very realistic advice.

COMBAT FROM BATTALION STAFF – "FOG OF WAR"

Viewing combat from my new position at the battalion level was a vastly different experience than as a platoon leader. Contact was not met with a violent reaction. Instead, we had to be calm and collected, so as to better support those in the fray. Upon receiving a report of contact, we sought to support our comrades who were locked in battle. Watching combat from the battalion level was another valuable lesson into the concept known as the "fog of war."

This "fog" makes up the great expanse of the unknown when an element makes contact with the enemy. In any engagement there are always several key attributes that are unknown in the first few seconds, and even after hours. Acting as the higher headquarters, you want to know as much as you can about the ongoing action. You want to know if there are any wounded, if so, how badly? How will they be evacuated? Is there any damage to the vehicles involved? If there is damage, how bad is the damage? Does the element in contact have sufficient supplies to continue the fight? How are the friendly forces responding? Does the element have enough ammunition to continue the fight? Are there any drones or aircraft to support the fight? If so, how long will it take to move those assets to them? Once the aircraft arrive on station, how much time will they have on station? If supported with helicopters, how far is the nearest place for them to refuel and rearm? Does the element in contact need QRF? If so, how long will it take QRF to get to them? What is the size of the enemy force? Is the enemy going to reinforce their position or break contact? What kind of weapons is the enemy employing? Is there a threat to aircraft that will respond? Will the enemy attempt to ambush our own QRF? Where are the potential locations for IEDs or ambushes on the way to the fight? Do we have the exact location of our friendly forces? Are the friendly forces separated or together? If separated, do we have the exact location of every element? Do you have grids to the enemy? Can we drive MRAPs on the road to the element in contact?

The above stated questions only begin to denote the massive details that make up the phenomenon known as the "fog of war". At times, even the element in contact can only answer a few of these. Sometimes, the best way to support battle is to simply not bother the infantry company in contact and allow them to fight the battle at hand. Learning to wait in this manner is known as battlefield patience. It is not an easy lesson to learn, nor is there a clear-cut way to employ it. Every firefight is different. Certain elements may be repeated, but no story of an action will ever be the same. This is an important lesson whose teachings and frustrations are repeated through every relationship between higher and lower echelons in combat. There can even be chaos involved with three platoons attempting to support one another, let alone a battalion to a platoon.

OP APACHE

Whenever my duties permitted me to, I still managed to go out on patrols. I awoke early one morning and was stopped by the HHC XO. He invited me to accompany a patrol to OP Apache, not far from Blessing. I went with some men from our S2 section and from Headquarters Company. We moved to the west on foot outside the walls of Blessing. I was happy to leave the wire again and fall back into an infantry tactical column. It brought back such vivid memories of leading an infantry platoon. I smiled as I racked a round into my rifle and headed out on the march.

We moved to OP Apache, passing small shops, old men, and children on the road. I smiled as I corrected some of the soldier's spacing on the road. Some of them were clearly not accustomed to patrolling and, at times, bunched up. I instructed them to keep their spacing and not give a PKM gunner a present by allowing him to kill two Americans with one burst of his machine gun. After a kilometer or so, we began our ascent up to OP Apache. The walk up this rugged trail reminded me of my beloved OP Rocky.

The patrol up the small mountain was invigorating. I felt alive again as my breath quickened, my heart rate increased, and my leg muscles burned under the weight of my armor. I felt like an officer on the line again. As we walked, I scanned the highlands and secretly wished for the crackle of gunfire. I constantly scanned the terrain, looking for places to set up a support by fire in case we came into contact. During our rest on the climb up, I again reminded some of the less experienced soldiers to keep security while halted. They grumbled, but one stern look from my battle-experienced face silenced their complaints.

We reached the top and were greeted by the ASG (Afghan Security Group), a pseudo paramilitary force for hire who wore uniforms and helped guard coalition bases and outposts. OP Apache was a formidable position and was both well guarded and armed. Following a quick orientation of the surrounding valleys, the ASG served us tea.

The tea was wonderful, as always, and was a release from all the ravages of war. It was pure and very real. I conversed, using my limited vocabulary of Pashtun, with some of these Eastern warriors. They were impressed with my knowledge of their language as I asked them where they were from and about their families. I typically made small talk by asking the following questions (the spelling of the words are phonetic), "*Salam Malekium. De kum zei* (where are you from)? *Wa da la dei* (are you married)? *Koronany de sang ga day* (how is your family)? *Su manchuan la dei* (how many kids do you have)?" In the conversation they told me an Afghan proverb, "*Awal Zan, Ya Jahan* (First yourself, then the world)."

NEW DUTIES

I began to embrace the importance and gravity of my new position, which focused on studying the enemy. It was very strange at times to read about the enemies that I fought against for nearly nine months of my life. The explosions, the mortar impacts, the recoilless rifle rounds; they all had names and faces. I began to know our battlefields in more ways than simply places that seemed to spawn muzzle flashes. It was certainly interesting to add a different layer to my knowledge of warfare in these lands.

Although I was no longer prowling the valley in search of a kill, I realized I was still at the fringes of earth, living out my boyhood fantasy. Fire missions were commonplace out of Blessing, as the mighty 155s screamed punishing rounds toward the enemy. I heard their impacts as they crashed upon the earth and sent their echoes off the surrounding mountains. It silenced any thoughts of peace and drove home the fact we were still very much at war. I was fortunate enough to view it from both the eyes of a platoon leader as well as a staff officer.

The Pesh Valley continued to mesmerize me. In the moments following a fire mission, this valley would change from a stormy sea to a peaceful mountain lake. It was certainly deceiving at times. The Pesh valley had such a deep deception. Its ability to fool a warrior was certainly uncanny. In some respects, the beauty of the Pesh valley resembled that of a rose bush. You fell in love with its beauty but forgot about the sharp thorns that can draw blood. This place had such deep parallels of violence and beauty.

ARTILLERY

Throughout my days at Blessing I heard outgoing 155s almost daily. Their shock flowed through me like nothing else. I remembered the first time that I heard such thunder claps. The mighty guns were only 400 meters away from where I wrote each day, but I felt the shock of the cannon blast through me each time. It was like feeling a mighty wave while standing in the ocean; it slams you like nothing else. It is a wave of sound, power, and utter terror. Each mighty boom was an addition to the song of war that continually played in my ears.

UAVS

We brought death to our enemies utilizing a great slew of weaponry. The staff aided to bring UAVs (Unmanned Aerial Vehicles or commonly referred to as drones) into battles. I was amazed by this new era of warfare, where these vessels of steel without human pilots inside of them swam in the dark ocean of the sky searching for their prey. We saw our enemy through the UAV's lifeless camera eyes. Taking human life with a UAV is certainly a new concept to warfare. Life can be taken without a single muzzle flash, or bullet tearing the sky. It provided insight into this new chapter of modern warfare in the 21st century.

A UAV glides across the sky like a great white shark swimming in the sea. Its eyes transport images across mountains, oceans, and continents. Seeing a UAV is somewhat of an eerie sight, an aircraft without a cockpit or pilot. It is almost like seeing death himself inhabiting this body of flying steel. UAVs do not know fear and do not hold back. They do not worry about their own flesh becoming victims and they only seek to destroy. I felt fortunate that I was able to watch them engage in battle. UAVs will continue to be an important element of future wars, as they were in this one.

SPRING

The signs of spring continually appeared in the valley as the trees began to bud leaves, adding more green to the scenery. The perpetual power of nature continued its cycle amidst our war. The earth did not pick sides in this war. Nature continued with its cycle of life as we continued in our struggle. This war was deeply interwoven into the shadows of the planet. We held our frontier outposts as beacon fires in this black night. Our patrols were lines of torches attempting to light the darkness.

There were several signs that announced that spring was approaching. The returning warmth in the air reminded me of my first impressions of this land, and its intensity. I could feel the heat in this ancient land and I could see convection waves as I looked toward the mountains. It would not be long until the heat of the day began to take its toll upon the infantry who roamed these mountains in search of their prey.

PASHTUN-WALI CODE

My understanding of the Pashtun-Wali code came slowly. Learning this ancient culture was not as simple as reading a guidebook. You had to learn it with patience and experience. I continued my visits with the ANP. At times they told stories that helped to unravel some elements of the Pasthun-Wali code that reigned over the land. They told me how some tribes in the Pesh valley have settled feuds in the past. At times families give an offering of sheep or a woman. Exile is also another method of resolving disputes. Regardless, the key to solving many disputes in the Pasthun-Wali code was to offer generous compensation for losses or disrespect. This could be done either in blood, or as previously explained, a payment of sorts.

Each visit with the Afghans provided yet another piece to the puzzle of deciphering this warrior culture. I think that by the end of my tour, I had just begun to understand the Afghans. To understand them is to understand a world ruled by chaos, with intermittent glimpses of peace. Understanding them was like nothing I had ever attempted before in my life. You could not use western logic to understand them. However, the longer you were at war and experienced the violence of epic scale in the valley, the easier they became to interact with.

NANGALAM

I continued to learn of the surrounding area around FOB Blessing by joining patrols whenever I was afforded the opportunity. One afternoon I accompanied a patrol to Nangalam and Menagai. I was unaccustomed to walking in such a big village. Nangalam was a far cry from my quaint Sematan in the Watapor district, but it was a good feeling to move under armor and rifle again. Nangalam was the largest village that I had ever conducted a dismounted patrol in. There were several blocks filled with different shops. Hordes of children followed us on our patrol, egged on by my limited knowledge of Pashtun. Nangalam was the hub of commerce for all in this rustic valley.

We soon turned north and entered the mouth of the Waygul valley. It was beautiful, and the valley's green carpet was spotted with yellow flowers. The flowers provided me with visions of hope and peace that resided just beyond the mountains and the sea. It looked like a meadow from some fairy tale. The beauty of this place never ceased to amaze me.

As we patrolled north toward Menagi, I could not help but to be almost hypnotized by the valley's beauty. Although I had fought here for almost a year, I still found this place to be amongst the most beautiful sights I had ever seen in my life.

Spring time. Flowers in bloom heralded the gates of hell.

I looked to the north as we walked. To the north laid Nuristan province, "the land of light" that fostered some very fierce fighters. This Waygul valley was a gateway of sorts to that land. A place called Wanat was close by. It witnessed, in 2008, one of the worst losses that American forces have ever sustained in Afghanistan. I found it ironic that the gates of hell were marked with such beauty, heralded by flowers in bloom.

ELDERS OF THE KORENGAL

We hosted a shura at the district center with the elders from the notorious Korengal valley. I always enjoyed looking upon these collages composed of different elders. Each man had a uniquely different look to him. Some had very dark eyes and dark hair, while others had almost a western look. One man in particular had striking green eyes deeply embedded into his harshly tanned and weathered face. He did not utter a single word, but was my favorite character in the room. He had a hint of eyeliner tracing his eyes. I was told that they painted their eyes in this manner in remembrance of their prophet.

Although I never worked with these particular elders or visited them on patrol, the scene was very familiar to me. These men knew only survival in this war-torn land. I felt as if I had listened to their grievances and promises dozens of times before. Their homes encompassed this battlefield that seemed to engulf all of these valleys. They lived amongst war all of their lives. Their culture, in many respects, was a culture of war.

ATTACKS AT BLESSING

Springtime brought increased attacks upon FOB Blessing. We continued to receive RPG and small arms fire a couple of times a week, bringing back those familiar primordial feelings that I felt during firefights. It had been a while since I had heard the clashing of shields. Within seconds of hearing the fire, that ancient serum, adrenaline, once again coursed through my veins. Admittedly, I craved the feeling of combat as one might have craved a cigarette or a hard drink. I smiled whenever I was afforded a glimpse of contact.

NIGHT HUNT

One evening I joined a night mission with PSD (Personal Security Detachment) platoon. I was grateful for the invitation and to have another opportunity to enter the storm. As I prepared my armor and my night vision goggles, I felt the overwhelming feeling of excitement that precedes a mission when you think that contact is imminent. I have felt anticipation or had butterflies in my stomach before, but the anticipation prior to a dangerous mission cannot be replicated. I vaguely knew of the plan, but it didn't matter to me as I was anxious to rejoin the hunt for the enemy and prepared my armor carefully.

I linked up with them on Blessing in the dark of the night. Before we departed for battle, we conducted the American pre-battle ritual of bullshitting. We relaxed our minds and spoke of anything but the patrol. I passed the time talking to SSG Carver and a few other soldiers, watching them smoke and smile as their faces were illuminated by starlight. The red bulbs of their cigarettes glowed in the darkness.

The sky was filled with all the stars. I looked to Orion and breathed deeply. I remembered when I first noticed Orion on that starry night in August of 1998 when I was that young 18-year-old Marine recruit. Those fields in South Carolina seemed so distant.

The time to mount up arrived and we moved east toward COP Michigan. Driving in the darkness was such an exhilarating part of war. We moved silently in our armored beasts, moving slowly on the road like panthers stalking their prey. We soon arrived and stopped at my old COP Michigan. It was nice to see my old home and men from my company. My former company commander, CPT Eastman, briefed the mission. I clasped arms with LT Gabriel Dearman and wished him luck for the mission ahead. It was good to see my comrades prior to wading into the unknown. We soon moved east, in the darkness, toward Tantil.

DARK WATER... A RIVER

We set in mounted over watch on the Pesh river road as Dagger Company moved into the valley south of Tantil. We wanted to move our MATV's (trucks) across the river, in order to support the dismounted forces in the valley. I dismounted with a few of the men for a leader's recon, so we could attempt to find a river ford on foot. We moved in the still of the night, utilizing the cover of darkness and the noise of the moving river. It was always thrilling to walk under the guidance of the green light from our night vision goggles. As we walked on the shore of the river searching for a place to ford, the scent that reminded me of a fresh water lake reminiscent of my youth entered my nostrils. It is always strange during war when visions of innocence and lands far away come to mind.

We stopped along the shore and made our first attempt at crossing the river. I could not believe that I was actually trying this. It was exhilarating, yet I was keen to exercise caution. I stepped into the Pesh River and allowed the war to engulf my body in a different way. It was my first time stepping into this river that I have lived and fought by for the past year. The waters were cold and sucked the warmth from my body. The current was stronger than I had anticipated. Our squad continued into the river. The recent snowmelt of spring had raised the level a few feet in the past weeks. As I waded deeper into the river, the cold water cut through me like a knife. We pressed our luck a few meters more as the water level continued to raise. It was at that moment when my confidence in moving our trucks across the Pesh diminished. We pulled back, in hopes of finding a more suitable ford.

We moved on the shore again and the cold wind sucked the heat from our wet bodies. We again pushed into the water and made it a bit farther this time, but again, the river proved too deep. We pulled back to the shore. The mighty Pesh River proved impassable for vehicles that night. We would have to keep our heavy guns north of the river. As I kneeled on the shoreline, I felt like a character straight out of some adventure about war. I was in paradise there under the stars; my body soaked with ancient waters from the snow melts of the Hindu Kush. Even as I write, I can still hear the Pesh River quietly flowing upon the land.

We returned to our MATVs and held mounted over watch. Dagger Company finished their sweep and did not receive contact. Instead, the enemy attempted to flee the area. Our air power found the enemy as they attempted to flee in the dead of the night and made quick work of them. They shook the valley with overwhelming firepower. Seeing explosions in the night's sky was beautiful to my eyes, as always. Your heart simply smiles when you know that the enemy met his end. I will never forget moments such as these. I smile now as I write.

We all mounted up and returned to our fort, returning just as the sun was touching the sky. It was a beautiful morning on the lines.

INVITATION FOR BATTLE

One evening SFC O'Connor invited me to accompany a patrol to Asadabad. I did not have to go on this patrol. I could have easily said no and gone along with my night. However, the Siren's still drew me to their song. I thought perhaps I could experience another battle and graciously accepted the invitation.

I awoke that morning and prepared for the patrol, again conducting the ceremony of dressing in my armor and ensuring I had enough ammunition. I linked up with the PSD convoy and mounted up in SFC O'Connor's vehicle, along with SSG Carver. We departed our FOB and headed east. It was interesting to look upon my old battlefields from the back seat of a vehicle. Seeing these lands from this new angle was a different perspective for me. The valley was green and alive, bringing hope and new life into the world. It also breathed new life into the war here. As the heat intensified, so did the fighting. The heat melted the snow in the mountain passes of the Hindu Kush, opening the supply lines for the enemy, awakening the war season.

Moving east we came across a platoon from A Co. near the Sheriak valley. They informed us that they heard icom chatter which stated, "Here they come…

get ready." I felt the primordial self begin to surface and prepared myself for the upcoming engagement. My muscles tightened as they always did before a fight. I took a deep breath. I nearly forgot how icom chatter affects one's mindset, even before hearing the first bullet tear the sky. Hearing a report of the enemy talking is almost like hearing gunfire. You knew they were watching you, waiting to launch an attack. It was such a strange thing to hear the enemy who were deeply hidden in the rocks. You prepared for combat, even without the firing of a single round.

But combat did not greet us in that instant. We continued on our mission and made it to ABAD. We picked up a few soldiers who were returning from leave and soon were on our way into the Pesh valley again.

"WE HAVE SHOTS"

We were moving west, had just passed the mouth of the Sheriak valley, and halted. I heard SFC O'Connor, repeat the call over the radio, "We have shots!" Battle began.

PSD returned fire with .50 cal. and MK19. Within seconds the mountains to our south erupted with impacts from a hail of American gunfire. I loved watching the impacts from our munitions slam death back into the mountainside. The sight sent chills down my spine, and instantly I felt invigorated.

SFC O'Connor and I dismounted. I handed some MK 19 ammo to the gunner, SPC Lavery, as I stepped out. He continued hammering the highlands with his 40mm grenades. I could hear enemy bullets tearing the sky around me. It had been a few weeks since I last heard incoming bullets whistle about my ears. I smiled, but at the same time I clenched my stomach and prepared for the fight. SFC O'Connor began engaging with his M4. I did the same.

In battle I would smile, but it would be inaccurate to say that it was a joyous occasion. It wasn't; it was horribly dangerous and the lives of our comrades were at stake. I often wondered why I smiled in firefights. I felt dread in these moments, but I think I smiled to make myself brave. I smiled because it made me focus away from the fear of death. I tried to take pleasure in this horrible deed that we were partaking in. Perhaps it can be likened to being motivated to take a horrible shot of whiskey. You know that it will taste horrible and probably harm you, but you do it, while attempting to seem fearless. It worked… sometimes.

I was not acting as a platoon leader in that battle; I was a rifleman and a warrior. I, for once, became the violence and vengeance. I did not have to exercise restraint and fully embraced the moment. I allowed myself to remove the restraints of an officer in battle. I permitted myself to drink of that strong wine called combat without regard. I allowed the drink to flow throughout my blood as I smelled the truth of combat, allowing myself to be lost in that sweet tune of the Siren's song. It almost felt as if I was seeing battle for the first time. I did not have to worry about calling for fire or maneuvering the element; I simply enjoyed the moment and experienced what my men must have felt like during our own battles.

The enemy intermittingly displayed their positions through their muzzle flashes in the highlands. More bullets tore the air around my head and I saw their impacts slam around our vehicle. I began squeezing off rounds, pounding the mountain with lead from my rifle. I kept squeezing off rounds and, without realizing it, had gone through an entire magazine. I was in complete euphoria and felt invincible. I smiled as I changed magazines and continued to pour lead onto the highlands.

After my third magazine, I slowed my rate of fire. The enemy continued to trade rounds with us. I began firing controlled bursts onto the highlands. I can still see the smoke rising slowly from my barrel. The rounds seemed to almost eject from my rifle in slow motion. I heard my brass fall upon my feet as I sang my paean (war song) with my rifle. I moved close to SFC O'Connor as he readied his AT-4 (rocket launcher). I fired from his left side, providing covering fire. His AT-4 malfunctioned. He rotated to his rifle and continued shooting. It was such joy creating a line of battle with another warrior. He shot at our enemy, a few rounds at a time. This was a beautiful sight, one that will forever be with me.

I moved to the left of the MATV. Again, I smiled as I continued shooting. The enemy's rate of fire began to slow. I watched the impacts of my rounds land near the muzzle flashes. Staring at the highlands through my rifle sights was simply beautiful. I saw a few of our enemy attempt to move out from under our murderous fire. They appeared as flashes of cloth slithering like snakes under the boulders. My ears rang of the Siren's song, with the piercing ringing tone that those of us that have fired weapons know so dearly.

To you, my reader, I am not sure what you are feeling as you read this, but I felt pure energy at that moment.

There is nothing else like it, returning the very death that the enemy wishes upon you.

In between magazines I checked on our medic, SSG Carver. She was busy keeping the children away from our vehicle. They collected brass from our expended bullets in the midst of these battles, risking their lives in the middle of firefights. It was a horribly sad thing to witness. What was more; it was experiences such as these, which made combat even more normal to these children. They grew up in these battles and would run amongst our gunfire. To most children, they would only know this scene by watching a movie. Most kids would never even dream of running into a firefight where machine guns and mortars explode, but here in the Pesh River Valley, these battlefields became their playgrounds.

SSG Carver continued pulling security and continued to scan her sector. It was the first time that I was near a woman in the grips of combat. She seemed almost to bring some calmness into this storm, smoking while scanning her sector. I asked for a puff from her cigarette; there was something magical about having a puff of tobacco amidst the firefight. I returned to the battle.

We kept the enemy suppressed with our bullets. Soon, 120mm mortars out of COP Michigan began landing on the field of battle, which further ignited my lust for combat. The plumes of the white phosphorus smoke slowly rising made me feel like I was a lion seeing a wounded animal. I kept up my fire, changing magazines, and placing the empty ones into my cargo pockets.

Kiowa helicopters arrived at the scene. I was down to two magazines and SSG Carver gave me a few of hers.

I wanted to have a few extra in case we decided on a ground assault. I moved to the contact side of the vehicle and provided a bit of cover fire for SFC O'Connor as he talked the Kiowa helicopters on to the target. They made several gun runs and delivered death unto the enemy.

Soon silence dominated the valley; neither a shot nor a sound crept over its floor. Smoke simply hung in the air and rolled off the highlands from our munitions. We continued to scan; not a living thing stirred upon the mountains. The engagement was over and this valley of death once again fell into its disguise of a peaceful slumber.

DARI HAR

I continued volunteering for patrols, as I wanted to savor a few more sips of war before we returned to peace. On this occasion I joined a patrol to the village called Dari Har. I linked up with the patrol and was overjoyed to be amongst riflemen again. I smiled as I listened to the patrol leader give his brief. We were soon on our way.

We moved and crossed a small tributary of the Pesh River. The entire time we were flanked by dozens of kids, ranging from the ages 7-18. Two 18 year-olds in particular had amazingly fluent English and were both aspiring to be interpreters. On the approach to Dari Har, we crossed a wooden bridge, built a bit more solidly than my Indiana Jones Bridge in the village of Shennigam. The bridge even had a handrail, a rarity in this chaotic land. Like most bridges in Afghanistan, the walkway was extremely bouncy as we crossed in our full armor. We continued our journey along the Pesh River and walked along a very large retaining wall next to the village mosque. We stopped at the mosque and the ANA that accompanied us conducted a meeting with the mullah.

We maintained security on the outside of the mosque, forbidden to enter such holy sites. I climbed a small part of the draw near the mosque. Draws, if you remember, were the favorite engagement areas of the enemy. The men from the patrol assured me they had never been attacked in this area, but my senses were heightened as we climbed. I watched the high ground for any indications of movement. We completed the short climb and moved to assess a tree-planting project sponsored by our forces. I made small talk with the Afghan farmers who were always amazed when they saw an American speak Pashtun. They offered me water from a natural spring; I had a sip. We soon picked up and traversed the ground toward Blessing, it was a wonderful day to be alive.

NANGALAM

With time, Nangalam became more familiar to me. On one afternoon patrol, Dagger 4th Platoon passed me as they were on their way to Blessing. I saw my old MRAPs and soldiers and smiled as they rumbled by me. We walked into the village of Nangalam. I stood guard over our leaders as they spoke with elders. I was taking the role as a rifleman on security, like my men had done for me on several occasions. I practiced my Pashtun with the children that were nearby. I bought sugar bread for the soldiers I was with. I felt as if we were knights in a medieval village as we stood in our armor, leaning against the mud-brick alleyways. I smiled at the simplicity of the moment and its pure ruggedness.

DISTRICT CENTER VISIT

I took each opportunity that I had with the Afghan security forces to learn more about this culture that was deeply embedded in war. Many of the Afghans that worked as ANP or ANA were *mujahedeen* against the Soviets. They had an intricate knowledge of the nature of war in Afghanistan as well as insight to the native warriors that fought there. The ANP chief had told us we play an intricate game of cat and mouse with the enemy. The cat waits to ambush. We traded roles from time to time. The Afghans told me, "We wait. It is our culture." Honestly, the Afghans were, at times, some of the most patient people that I have ever met in my life. They seemed to be able to wait out wars. The enemy we fought combined incredible elements of patience and violence.

PERSPECTIVE

I felt fortunate that I was able to experience warfare from different vantage points. I missed my days of patrolling the valley with 4th Platoon, but was happy that I could see this tale from the eyes of a staff officer and occasionally as a rifleman. As a rifleman, I was able to see war as it unfolds before one man's eyes. Admittedly, there was something appealing about taking a spot on the line and not worrying about the fire and maneuver aspects of battle.

As a staff officer I was able to observe the brain that ran this powerful beast known as an infantry battalion.

I supposed that learning the true art of war required viewing the chaos from several vantage points; not only on the line of battle, but also on the staffs of battalions and brigades. I took my position on staff to further my education into the art of war and to serve the battalion with the best of my ability.

FIGHTING SEASON

The fighting season returned to our valley with a boom, literally. As the heat appeared to awaken the enemy from their hibernation, Blessing began to receive a slew of artillery and rocket attacks. It seemed to awaken the storm, as battles sparked up all across our line. With the return of the fighting season, I wondered how many more battles I would see before leaving the valley. As I soon found out, I would continue to witness several attacks.

The mountains looked different in the increasing heat of the spring. They appeared more menacing. Perhaps it was because I recalled the physical cost that it took to move up these monsters under the weight of full armor, ammo, and weapons. The heat brought war and would inevitably bring more death.

Even amongst the growing chaos of war, I was honored to have been a part of such a journey. I felt lucky to have been a character in that epic journey of life and death. My experiences in combat answered a myriad of personal questions for my life's passion into the military arts. I could hardly believe at times that I was an officer and had helped to destroy our country's enemy. To this day, the gravity of what my men and I did there is somewhat staggering.

APRIL 2010

"SOLDIERS WIN BATTLES. STAFFS WIN WARS."

Spring arrived and the valley was adorned with the scent of both battle and the perfume of flowers in the air. My education into warfare as a junior officer continued as I learned the ropes of a staff officer. My experiences were not as chaotic as my days on the small outpost, however they were an equally important part of this experience called combat. Lessons had to be learned quickly there, as they were on the line.

An experienced field grade officer helped me find meaning in my newfound position. During a conversation, he said something to me that I think all junior officers should hear during their transition from leading in firefights and they become a part of a staff. He told me, "Soldiers win battles. Staffs win wars."

This quote certainly denotes the grave responsibility that those tasked with planning operations must deal with on a daily basis. While on the line, it was easy to see the glory of destroying the enemy from a hail of gunfire or a TOW missile. On the line, your grit is tested in combat and the dozens of ambushes you lead your men through.

Life is much different for a staff officer. He fights every day as well; but in a different manner. He slaves for hours and days in front of various maps, trackers, and computers. He attempts to make a balance of available men, air power, artillery, MEDEVAC, assets, and reinforcements. The staff officer aims to present a calmly templated plan for an operation. The plan will look neat and will be adorned with blue arrows, enemy locations, and may even include imagery of the terrain. He knows the chaos awaiting the men on the ground; these men form the points of the large blue arrows that adorn the maps displaying the upcoming operation. The staff officer attempts to do his best to make an outline to guide the chaos that will undoubtedly envelop the forces involved in the fray of battle.

Mistakes or oversights at the battalion level did not seem grave at first. However, I soon came to find out that a missed step at staff level could have devastating effects for a platoon or company in contact. Staff is definitely not a glorious portion of warfare. You rarely had a chance to see the effects of planned firepower as it devastated the enemy, but you did relish in victory. You felt satisfaction in knowing that you aided those that were about to face the perils of hell with all the firepower and medical support at your disposal. You planned for victory.

UAVS

Throughout my time in staff I was able to peer through the eyes of a UAV on numerous occasions.

These futuristic aircraft never ceased to amaze me. UAVs are certainly a revolution in military affairs. When I think of them; hunting with hounds comes to mind. In this relationship, I was uncertain as to which one of us was the hound and which was the hunter? Like hunting for boar or fox, we relied on these flying hounds of steel. Perhaps a more suitable analogy would be to liken UAVs to falcons utilized by medieval hunters on the plains. They rested upon our airfields and flew out on the hunt when we beckoned them. We saw through their eyes that had no blood, soul, or fear. We peered through the eyes of our silent aerial hunters whose pupils pierced the darkness and detected the heat of the enemy's bodies glowing in the night. These unmanned flying predators hunted by tracking the heat generated from the warm blood that flowed through our enemies.

They circled our prey when they found them. These soulless flying aircraft waited for orders from their human masters to rain hell upon the Earth. Once we gave the order, they shredded our enemy into a blood-filled mist of fiery destruction. I wondered to what extent they would further impact warfare. Time will tell.

ATTACKS AT BLESSING

The fighting season provided me with several reminders of the deep sensations of battle. I was awakened several mornings by the hail of gunfire. I would slip on my boots, grab my rifle, and make for the TOC.

At times while sprinting to the TOC, I could hear the rounds whistle over my head; it was strange that such a noise became normal. You could tell when rounds were meant to kill you or not. From the battalion TOC, I watched the massive counter-attacks with 120 mm mortars and 155 mm artillery. Although I missed leading the counter-attacks, I smiled to myself when I heard platoon leaders over the radio call for fire and make adjustments. The battalion had just received a few new platoon leaders. I instantly recognized the new ones and their uncertain voices over the radio, as I remembered my first times calling for fire as a green platoon leader.

CHANGE OF COMMAND

I watched the A Company change of command. The occasion drew forth our comrades from COPs all along the line. I loved days such as these when my comrades from different COPs came to visit. I saw my comrades, LT Mark Zambarda, 1SG Varrs, CPT Eastman, as well as 4th Platoon. It always filled my heart with happiness to see my comrades and their smiling faces. I hoped to see them smile in our homeland. Dement was now a SGT. I recommended him for his battlefield promotion to SGT shortly before leaving the platoon. It was good to see my men move up through the ranks.

As with all such ceremonies, they play the Star Spangled Banner. Every man under arms saluted and paid respect to our colors. I sang the song silently to myself as chills slowly rolled down my spine and stared at the flag as it waved in the wind.

Such simple moments put our efforts in the Pesh in a stunning perspective for me. I believed we were in the valley to protect our families and our homeland against an evil that wanted to destroy us. It was beautiful to see our flag fly high with the blue skies and the savage beauty of the mountains serving as the backdrop. We fought there for each other and our country.

REFLECTION

Sunsets continued to serve as my time of reflection. Following dinner, I would sit and stare into this magnificent valley as I wrote in my journal. I peered east into what looked like a tapestry of beauty and divinity. The view down the line displayed some of the most dangerous places in the world; and they were simply breathtaking. At each sunset I felt the gentle foreshadowing breeze of the coming evening. I peered east and saw the descending ridgelines flanked by beautiful white clouds. This was one of the most beautiful sites that I may ever set my eyes on. I gazed upon the mountainsides around me and saw the small brown villages dotting the terrain. I was at peace amidst all this chaos.

TANTIL, FIELDS OF GOLD

I was tasked to go to Jalalabad to see to a few administrative duties. I hopped on the Combat Logistics Patrol and traveled east through the Pesh valley. The wheat fields traded their deep emerald green for their golden yields and were ready for harvest. The wheat was knee high and painted the valley with gardens of golden majesty. Women and girls wearing brightly colored dresses were harvesting the fields.

We received sporadic gunfire from the north as we passed Tantil. We halted, presented ourselves for battle, and sent a few volleys of .50 cal. into the highlands. I prepared myself for action. We continued to scan the highlands, but the fire was merely harassing, as the enemy did not commit to battle. I sighed, as I had hoped for action.

We continued east, passing the Sheriak valley when one of the jingle trucks lost a front tire. He could not have picked a worse area to stop. I dismounted with some of the men and cautiously scanned the highlands where contact seemed to erupt out of nowhere. I peered anxiously at the ridgelines over us and waited; no enemy was there today. We assessed the situation and decided to limp the jingle truck to Able Main, rather than present such a target to the enemy. We continued east and soon left my familiar Pesh valley and turned south on the Kunar river valley road, bound for Jalalabad. We passed through a few urban areas and reached the outskirts of Jalalabad.

Driving into Jalalabad was an entirely new experience for me; it actually had lights and buildings. Jalalabad was the most civilized place that I witnessed during my tour in Afghanistan. It was night while we were driving through it. Seeing a city illuminated set my mind and heart at ease; as it felt safer. Seeing Jalalabad definitely told you that you were far from that valley of chaos and death.

KORENGAL PULL OUT

Our forces conducted a planned realignment in the Korengal valley. As my battalion prepared to pull out our senior officers gave some excellent guidance. They said, " Every unit in this battalion needs to be ready in a moment's notice to move to the sound of the guns, wherever those guns may be."

They spoke of the delicate manner at hand with this move. I never fought a battle in that valley, but the stories I traded with other officers and soldiers spoke of hard fought victories. A great deal of American blood, money, and time was spilled into that God forsaken place. We would return that valley to the darkness it came from. Our forces tried to tame that frontier for about five years. I hoped that no more of our blood would be spilled there. The booms of 155's, 120's, 81's, TOW missiles, .50 cal., 7.62, and 5.56 had erupted from our small fortresses in the mountains. Countless bombs and missiles were utilized in defense of our outposts. Thousands of Soviet style rounds have been slung against our walls. The pullout from the Korengal valley went as smoothly as one could have hoped for. The valley had been the dance floor for countless battles. I prayed for all of the men that gave their lives there in that fold of darkness.

BACK TO THE PESH

When my business at Jalalabad was complete, I linked up again with Fox Company as they prepared for another long patrol into the Pesh valley. The troops around me looked tanned, dusty, tired, and battle hardened. We moved north, back into the belly of the beast.

We soon arrived in the Pesh valley and moved through my old and beautifully familiar battle space. I loved to look upon my old battlefields and my villages. They were my home for so long, and during one of the most influential times of my life. I smiled to myself as we passed through my old Andersille, Shege, Qamchi, Semetan, Shennigam, Mulkhana, and Jubai villages.

We halted at Able Main for about thirty minutes. Our convoy was escorting a few Afghan jingle trucks (semi-trucks) laden with supplies. Some of the drivers were new and had apparently lost their nerve before we reached the Sheriak valley. They changed a tire for what appeared to be no reason other than regaining courage. They were scared. I spoke to them and told them not to worry, that we would protect them. With fear still in their eyes they reluctantly agreed.

We continued west. I started rhythmically tapping my magazines on my body armor as we entered the vicinity of the Sheriak. I understood why the ancients would at times beat upon their shields prior to battle. Tapping on something helps to cool the nerves, but this tapping on my magazines seemed to awaken my ancient self. I smiled as I looked to the highlands, secretly longing for another engagement, but today we passed through unmolested. Not a single shot tore the sky.

MY 30TH BIRTHDAY... AFGHAN LOGIC

I turned thirty years old in the Pesh River Valley and spent my birthday at the district center, attempting to gain support from elders against the enemy. I participated in that intricate dance known as "attempting to influence an Afghan," which is essentially a circular conversation. The Afghans are masters in this art form. They almost appeared to have a natural resistance to any Western logic. The Afghans have the ability to frustrate the wisest and most patient of warriors. Anyone that has ever dealt with these tribesmen will tell you, they can be some of the most frustrating people on earth to speak with.

Patience with the Pashtuns is amongst the most important factors that one must remember when engaging in talks with them. Succeeding with these tribesmen called for a different way of thinking. Although I was aware of this necessity, it was still challenging each time. The key during these interactions was not to become frustrated. It seemed that victory in Afghanistan, even at the personal levels, demanded the most steadfast of patience.

KORENGAL SHURA

Soon after our force realignment out of the Korengal valley, a large number of elders, to include the Korengalis, attended a shura at the district center next to FOB Blessing. This was the largest collection of Afghan elders I ever saw at one time. This shura provided me with some of the most valuable insights that I learned about this war torn Afghanistan. The Afghans themselves taught these lessons.

Some of the district leadership stressed the important of unity with the elders. Sher Badir, the district governor, stated that without the support of the local people, a government is nothing. He spoke of the tough times that had continuously fallen upon Afghanistan, starting first by discussing the Russian times. He stated, "We defeated the Russians, but we have not made any progress in thirty years. All elders have a part in maintaining security. Without security, life is nothing." Another local Afghan leader stated, "Every Afghan has a mental disease, because we have had war for thirty years."

We listened with great interest as many of the Afghan leaders spoke about the ongoing war in their valley. Our officers gave a speech of their own, "Make tomorrow better than today. Let your children and your grandchildren say that you, their fathers and their grandfathers, took a stand and stopped thirty years of war. War is not a normal thing. You have made it normal." It was a fine speech.

The scent of onions filled my nostrils as I listened to our translator speak the words of the elders. In this room of concrete and no electricity, the scent of onions was sweet and seemed to set this scene of an ancient meeting just right. The room was full of roughly forty elders. All of the attendees had different colored beards, red, black, gray, and white. It was such an interesting collage of Afghan and American warriors. I continued to listen and studied these elders who have known so much chaos and strife for most of their lives. They did not look like the soul-less remnants of men that one might imagine after decades of war. Instead, these men looked hardened, strong, and prideful. These Pashtuns were definitely a living, breathing culture of warriors. War was their reality and all they have ever known.

Perhaps, I thought, this is why warfare remained so prevalent in Afghanistan. To the Pashtuns that lived in the Pesh valley; tribal war and war against outsiders was simply a way of life. Maybe it was to all Afghans, as they experienced war all of their lives. The children of the Pesh utilized our areas of firefights as their playgrounds, picking up our expelled brass. Gunfire, explosions, and death were as common as the planting of fields in the spring and the harvest in the fall. Perhaps, I thought, the Afghans did not see a need for a decisive season or a few years of war. There was no need for the war to stop for them. To them, war was a part of a never ending cycle and simply a part of life. Maybe this is why war continued there, seemingly without end.

I had only lived in the Pesh Valley for about a year, but I understood war there. War was no longer this obscure figment of my imagination or dreams. War was now a routine part of my life. It was as normal as eating lunch or taking a shower.

BARBER

At times I saw our enemy only as an unconventional opponent attempting to fight for their own beliefs. However, every now and then I was reminded of the evil that we faced there. The enemy was composed of men who took innocent lives. Whether it is on Manhattan Island or in a dusty room in the Waygul valley, purposely killing innocent people is wrong. Such was the nature of the evil that we faced; this place was a land truly drenched in both evil and darkness.

Early one morning I was walking to get a haircut, following my morning run at the gym. As I walked toward the barber's shed I learned that our FOB barber, Abrahime, was killed in his village last night. Abrahime was asleep in his house and, in the dead of the night, the enemy snuck into the house and put three bullets into his chest. Sadly, the first thought I had was, "It looks like I can't get my haircut today." It was a very practical thought. It was then when I realized that I might have been at war for too long.

Regardless of the fate of our efforts there, I hoped that people would understand that we attempted to bring some light and order into this war torn land. The barber's name was Abrahime. It is strange to think that, had he never been killed, I would have never written his name down in this, my chronicle of war. I was rather fond of this man. During my haircuts, we would talk in the little Pashtun that I had learned. I was somewhat saddened by his unanticipated loss and prayed that God would give him peace.

This was Afghanistan, and life continued almost without a ripple. The Afghan civilians that chose to work with the coalition played a risky role in life. I felt more hatred toward the enemy. It was one thing to clash steel with us, the ANA, or the ANP. To murder a civilian is different.

We spoke about the barber's death with the ANP. They did not appear to be concerned about this matter. Like most disasters or tragedies in that country, it was taken lightly and without much worry. That valley was a place where death seemed like only a minor inconvenience.

GRIM REAPER...

Although our tour was almost over, our men continued to fall in battle. I was again assigned to inventory the effects of another fallen soldier. SGT Nathan Kennedy of A Company fell in battle. I prayed for him and for his family as I inventoried the fallen warrior's personal effects. As normal as war and death was in the valley, inventorying a fallen warrior's effects was horrible to do. The price of liberty is painfully high and I prayed that

Americans would never forget their sacrifice. My fallen brother's items were soon ready for shipment.

I awoke early one morning and prepared for my long voyage to Bagram. I was staged on the HLZ waiting for my helicopter. My Chinook landed and elements of the 101st Airborne Division arrived. As I approached my bird, a LT that I recognized walked off the helicopter. He was a classmate from the Infantry Officer Basic Course. In the few seconds we shared, we smiled and clasped arms. It was always nice to see a face from the past.

We left Blessing in the daylight. It was strange moving the fallen's effects through the very valley that took his life. It was my first time seeing the Pesh valley from the air in the daylight. I was naming all of the engagement areas as I flew over them. There, hundreds of feet above the Pesh river road, I was safe from the many ravages that plagued troops traveling on the road. The Sheriak was down there, as always tempting a fight. We pressed on, briefly stopping at my old fort, Honaker Miracle. I was able to exchange a quick greeting with LT Bill Fiorito. As we flew away I was also able to catch a glimpse of the newly built Shennigam footbridge. It looked a great deal more solidly built than the Indiana Jones Bridge.

I arrived at JAF without incident. In the evening, JAF received indirect fire. It interrupted me on mile seven of a thirteen-mile run. I sought cover with some civilian contractors in a bunker near the gym. We waited out the attack and made small talk until the all clear sounded.

The war followed me everywhere; it was simply a part of that country. It was in its rocks, its air, it was everywhere.

MAY 2010

RELIEF IN SIGHT

Our final month of battle had arrived. It seemed that with the hurricane of emotions that one experiences in combat, time tends to fly by. Elements of the 101st Airborne Division began to trickle into our large gateway of FOBs. I was making my trip to Bagram with SGT Kennedy's effects and watched as the 101st Airborne began to arrive. Fresh faces from Fort Campbell, Kentucky were walking about with their distinctive patch. Some of them were young privates and officers without combat patches. However, many were the mature NCOs and officers who had been baptized by war long ago. It was interesting to see so many chapters of war that were about to start, when my own was about to end. It seemed that this Afghanistan continued to draw more and more warriors into this seemingly perpetual arena of war.

It was another beautiful sunset, but that ancient beauty came with a high tax. I heard news of yet another man from my battalion who had fallen in battle. As I stared into the sunset, I offered prayers for him.

Following my prayers, I overheard an incoming group of soldiers from the 101st receiving a brief from their 1SG. They asked their 1SG questions about their perspective FOBs. The soldiers asked about things that mattered to them in combat. They wanted to know if they would get mail, if they had Internet and if they had showers there. The 1SG answered his men to the best of his ability. His face had the look of too many deployments, but a great deal of experience. You could see the true responsibility in his position; he knew he was taking his boys into a hell. Perhaps he wondered how many of them would fall in battle.

I continued to watch the 1SG as he dismissed his soldiers. He remained by himself and lit a cigarette. This rugged infantryman placed a foot on a box and stared off into the sunset. He exhaled smoke from his tobacco, but I think it was something else. The grave pressure of leadership looked to be hanging in his smoke. I wish I had a camera at that moment and had taken a picture of his face. I would submit a picture of this man's face to Webster's so that it could be next to the word "concern" in the dictionary. This man had seen his share of war before. There was no mistaking what awaited his men, and he knew it.

BAGRAM

My travels soon took me to Bagram. Although I did not hear the sounds of battle around my ears, the imposing Hindu Kush continued to whisper of the dangers that lay within its peaks. I delivered SGT Kennedy's effects with care and said a final prayer for my fallen comrade.

I did not linger in Bagram and caught a C-130 bound for Jalalabad. I was surrounded by several troops from the 101st Airborne. I looked at the young ones who did not have a combat patch as of yet and smiled, as I knew that they would soon receive their baptism in battle.

We boarded the C-130 bound for Jalalabad and I was looking forward to completing my travel early in the evening. Exhausted from my travel, I fell into a very deep sleep. I was awakened unexpectedly by a loud noise, a flash of light, and I could have sworn that the aircraft shook. It felt as if we were in contact for a split second, as if an IED or some sort of a missile had exploded near us. I thought I was dreaming, as no one in the aircraft reacted. Thinking that I was merely seeing things, I closed my eyes and went back to sleep.

We landed, but we were back in Bagram. We were informed that our plane had been struck by lightning. I returned to the passenger terminal and spent my time speaking with a platoon leader from the 101st Airborne. He, like me, arrived in theater without combat experience. He asked me a few questions and I told him what I could, remembering when I was in his shoes nearly a year ago. It was certainly strange to watch as a new chapter of war began to unfold before my eyes. In just a few days, they would be at their COPs, relieving ours and other units. Soon they would be in the midst of their own battles that were not yet known.

ARTILLERY

I longed to return to the line as I waited at Bagram. Thinking about it was quite ironic, that I wanted to hurry back to a place of absolute danger as our battalion continued to be hammered by the enemy. FOB Blessing continued to receive increased rocket and mortar attacks. The enemy was targeting our 155s with seemingly accurate and precise fire, but my brothers-in-arms were there. I wanted to return to them and finish my tour with honor. The enemy continued to bleed and hammer us. We continued to lock shields and bleed them as well. We held the line.

SOME OF 4TH PLATOON LEAVING

After not too long, I made it to JAF. This time lightning or any other obstacle did not hinder my voyage. I spent a day or so there, waiting for the next logistics convoy to head north. As I was walking to the F. Co. TOC, I saw some familiar faces that made my heart glow – SGT Richardson, PFC Cortez, and Mendiola. They were amongst the first of our soldiers to begin their long journey back to the United States. I was overwhelmed with happiness as I saw my men smiling and free from the grips of death. I spoke with them and saw they were simply so happy as they knew that their battles were over. I shook hands with each of them and wished them a safe journey back to the States.

Seeing the men from my platoon drove home the honor of leading Americans. Our soldiers sacrificed so much of their freedom and happiness to come serve at war. They were volunteers who joined the Army not merely for college money or medical benefits; they joined to be a part of the infantry. They joined to fight and to meet the enemy in gut wrenching firefights. I have never shared better company in my life than I did with my brave soldiers. After I wished them all safe travels, I headed back into the belly of the beast.

A BEAUTIFUL SIREN – DEATH IN DISGUISE

For the last time in my Afghanistan tour, I linked up with the Fox Co. Combat Logistics Patrol. The voyage through the Kunar and Pesh valleys continued to present me with a tapestry of savage beauty. The winter wheat, which had carpeted the valley floor in an emerald green, had traded its color for a beautiful carpet of gold. The fields were alive with the harvest and were dotted with dozens of women and children reaping the wheat. The scene looked like something out of a medieval farm. Bundles and bundles of wheat were scattered about on the valley floor, waiting to be collected.

A large part of me was amazed that I could still appreciate such beauty in all of this chaos. One would think that after the carnage and death imposed by this valley, that the sight of it would sicken me. Nothing could be further from the truth. The beauty continued to take my breath away. In some ways the beauty of Afghanistan was a Siren herself. This Siren enticed me with her bosom of mountain peaks, ancient valleys, and farms. On each patrol she seduced me with her beautiful curves that made up the ridgelines of the highlands, her beauty simply enticed me. She attempted to disguise the true horror of death that waited for us in valleys and mountain draws.

I took a deep breath as we moved past my old battlefields near Honaker Miracle. I missed them. It felt like I was driving past my old elementary school in my hometown. I saw myself in these battlefields as we passed them and felt a waterfall of emotions as we continued west. A part of my warrior self would always be in these valleys, I felt in many respects that I had become a part of that land.

PREPARATION AND TRANSFORMATION

FOB Blessing had both the feel and the sounds of transition. On a daily basis, men from the 101st prepared themselves for the battles they would soon fight. I heard the unmistakable firing of M-4s at the rifle range as men zeroed their weapons. I also heard the echoes of 40mm grenades as soldiers practiced with their M203s. The explosions upon the rocks and gunfire brought forth a multitude of memories from my own firefights. Very soon the 101st would attempt to tame these lands. Very soon it would be their war.

A strange feeling of combat *déjà vu* occurred one afternoon as I was outside my quarters writing and enjoying a cigar. The 155s opened up with their murderous fire, supporting an action some miles away. At the same time, about six newly arrived soldiers from the 101st were walking by. At the sound of the guns, a few dropped to the ground and a few ran for cover. The few of them on the ground looked at me; sitting crossed legged smoking a cigar, paying as much regard to the outgoing fire as one gives to the chirping of birds. I said, "Well, boys, that was outgoing."

They asked, "Really? How the hell can you tell the difference between outgoing and incoming?"

I told them, "You'll know." I smiled and continued to enjoy my cigar. I remembered when I first learned that lesson of what outgoing sounded like. It was a fitting moment in my experience at war.

HEARTBEAT OF WAR

The Pesh valley seemed to live with the perpetual heartbeat of war. I heard it thud, thud, and thud incessantly. These thuds were carried by the 155s that tore the air and sped their payloads of death onto the enemy. What did those large cannons tell us? What did those cacophonic yells say to us? What did they say to the enemy?

The incessant yells of battle told me that this war was far from over. Yet, my time on the line was almost complete. They told me that at that very moment, young fighters fueled with religious zeal were preparing for battle. Some of them were from Afghanistan and others were from those far corners of the earth where the Quran is the law. As I fantasized about going to combat, these men did the same. Many of them imagined fighting us here in these valleys. These fighters prayed to their god and I heard their reminders five times a day.

I looked at the Afghans – the ASG, our interpreters, the locals, and the workers on our FOB. They were an entire generation at war and had never known peace. They have probably never known a month in their lives without hearing a bullet tear the sky or a blast echoing through the valley.

I saw such epic sights each and every day. Scattered small groves of trees broke up the terraced farmlands. Ancient mud-brick houses clung to terraces. Kiowas, angels of death, flew overhead, their black shadows silhouetted in front of these jagged rocks. They landed to refuel and rearm. I saw the dust rising from their rotor wash. I saw a Mosque painted white, with its small minarets pointing toward God. I saw the Nangalam traffic circle in the distance. I saw those powerful descending finger-like ridges pouring down onto the valley floor. These cascading ridges looked like waterfalls perpetually set in stone.

As I looked over the mountains and the blue skies, I heard a plane, one of our angels, patrolling the skies. I looked, but did not see him. A gentle breeze blew and birds chirped in the trees. I heard the cheering and the clapping of hands from a cricket match that some Afghans were playing near the HLZ. All was at peace; all was quiet for a few moments. One learned to appreciate the small moments of peace there, like a cold drink of water on a hot summer's day.

At times I watched the battles near COP Michigan and listened to the 155s punish the highlands incessantly with their payload of death. The ridgeline was on fire and our entire world seemed to be aflame. The mountains were on fire and smoke rose slowly into the heavens. Smoke hung there and lingered like death, a constant reminder of war and the perils that hunted us as we hunted them.

The highlands southwest of COP Michigan were alive with smoke and dust rising from 120mm mortar explosions. At times it was hard to fathom that we dropped such firepower only a few kilometers down the road. Chaos became normal; it gave us death, and at the same time delivered chaos to make the land quiet again. Our drums of war continued. Such was the nature of this Afghan war. Death surrounded us and utilized epic natural beauty as its camouflage. That was a rather strange thing, I think. It explained how these scenes of intense beauty inhabited the same space as death. The Pesh embodied a true paradox; as beauty and death occupied the same space.

Still contact tempted me. Like a temptress, an evil woman that you know will hurt you, but you still wanted her. Secretly I wished for one more engagement, so I could feel the beast flow throughout my body once again. At the same time, I realized I was fortunate to be alive and, for the most part, unscathed during my experience in that grand adventure known as war. This land and its collage of a vast amount of sights, sounds, and feelings would forever hold a special place in my heart and my education as a warrior. As strange as it sounded, I knew I would miss that God forsaken valley. It was my finishing school into the perils of combat.

INCOMING

During my final days on FOB Blessing, we continued to take artillery fire. The sound of the impacts made you shudder. They reminded you of the true danger that existed just beyond our walls of stone, men, and C-wire. The sickening thuds of indirect fire were echoes that I will always hear; regardless of how far from this vortex I may travel.

I awoke some mornings to the sickening sound of incoming rounds. The sound of steel munitions smacking the earth was unmistakable. They exploded and sent their shrapnel swimming through the air in search of prey. They swam to find limbs to rip apart and to rob the earth's warriors of their lives. More men were wounded and another MEDEVAC bird landed, taking the wounded away.

One round landed on the FOB and shrapnel peppered the door to the latrines. I walked in and noticed the damage, chipped concrete in the washroom. The shrapnel had cut deep into it. I couldn't help but think about the effects the shrapnel would have on living flesh, causing much pain and perhaps death. We continued to prepare the 101st for their time in the Pesh, while at the same time attempting to protect our forces during this transition. In many ways it was like shoveling a driveway full of snow during a snowstorm. You attempt to clear as much as you can, but it is difficult as the snow continues to fall. It was the same for us there; we attempted to pass on our lessons to the 101st while at the same time fighting it out with the enemy.

IED NEAR THE GATES

I awoke one morning to what I thought was outgoing 155mm fire. At the time I thought it sounded a bit strange, but did not think twice about it, dismissing it as nothing more than a fire mission. As the dust settled, literally, I walked outside and found that it was an IED explosion within sight of the gates of Blessing. It wounded a few ANP and Afghan civilians. The valley still screamed for blood and continued to harvest lives.

As a warrior and a scholar, I learned volumes upon volumes in that valley. I would always miss my daily lectures in the auditorium created by the mountains. The lessons here were certainly hard driven, lessons that soldiers would never forget. These lessons talked about the truth of life, the truth of death, and the truth of war.

AFGHANS

I spent my final days in the Pesh River Valley studying all the subtleties of life in the world that surrounded me. I watched a group of ten or so young Afghan men working on our FOB, laying a brick walkway of sorts outside the chow hall. They were being watched by an ASG who sat on a shaded perch with his AK lying by his side. He sat in what we called the "Hajji squat style." That style of sitting involves having your feet flat and bringing your rear-end down to your feet, as if you were doing a deep squat. The workers took turns working in the heat. The exploding booms of the outgoing 120mm did not startle them, as they no longer startled me. They were born with such noises and treated our firepower with about as much regard as we give to honking horns in a busy city.

During our final days we were continually serenaded in battle as our FOB continued to receive indirect fire. I heard the unmistakable crash of incoming rounds and the unmistakable sound of danger. They utilized their AGS-17 against our ranks, their version of the MK-19. CPT Migliaro and LT Chris Capaso were wounded, but thankfully only with minor shrapnel wounds. We were so close to leaving and men were still being hit in battle. We replied with our own steel and cooked the mountainsides with our fire.

A PLATOON ON THE MARCH

On one of my last evenings I watched my friend who I attended Infantry officer course with, and his platoon, prepare for a mission. It was a beautiful sight and reminded me of my time with my own platoon.

SIREN'S SONG

Watching infantrymen prepare for battle in the cool evening under a full moon was calming to me. That image reminded me of the feelings that enthralled me about warfare; a perfect and beautiful sight to my eyes.

They moved out and began their climb up one of the hellacious mountains. As always, men move differently when moving toward contact. They prepared for battle; you could see it in each of their steps. The near full moon illuminated the way as they moved like Greek Hoplites climbing on a night raid toward a mountain fortress. I closed my eyes and listened to them walk. I could faintly hear their footsteps and the soft creaking of equipment. I sighed as I missed my time with 4th Platoon, but smiled knowing my men were safe. I stayed and watched the patrol until it crested over a ridgeline and the men were out of view. I looked to the stars in the sky and smiled. It was another one of those hundreds of moments forever burned into the canvas of my memory. The Pesh valley was the true picture of a warrior, of the infantry, and of war.

LEAVING THE DARKNESS

It was very surreal when I received my orders to leave the valley. As evening approached and the full moon peaked out of the east in the failing daylight, I gazed upon the rugged and sparsely vegetated mountains. It was the final time that I would see the Pesh Mountains under the dim light of a sunset. I felt sad to leave my school of war and knew that I would forever miss this place. I will never forget the lectures, the lessons, and the trials that we endured here. I will never forget the sacrifices paid by my men and those of my brothers-in-arms. I found a part of myself there and I left a part of myself as well.

I wrote my final journal entry only meters away from the chapel whose roof had a hole in it from a rocket attack only hours before. It was a ferocious looking hole through the tin sheet roof. With its jagged edges, the hole looked like it would slice your hand open. I breathed deeply as I was sad to leave my first war.

The final evening was quiet, not a sound from our guns or theirs ran across the land. The land seemed to almost stand still, with the exception of a slight breeze. Perhaps the valley was sad as well. I stared at her with tears welling up in my eyes. I stared at her as a man staring at his lover, knowing that he had to leave her forever.

I took my time as I gazed upon the valley for the last time. I experienced a waterfall of emotions. I saw a world isolated by centuries of warfare. I saw the mountains stand as giant memorials to fallen warriors. These natural monuments of stone stood there, seemingly immune to the tons of explosive ordinance that we have continually cast upon them. In that valley I saw war. In that valley I learned of war and learned what truly was in my heart. With a deep sigh I placed my journal into my pocket and moved to gather my armor and bags.

As nightfall set in, illuminated by a full moon, we moved to the Blessing HLZ, waiting in the late spring night. I gazed upon the dark outlines of the mountains that surrounded us. Finally, two Chinooks landed and their rotor blades came alive with light from static electricity. Laden with baggage, we piled into the Chinooks. By the time we loaded, it was nearly dawn and the landscape was already lit in an eerie pre-dawn darkness. We lifted into the air and left FOB Blessing. I was beginning my journey east and away from my first war.

As we moved, I gazed upon the mountains from the windows of the chopper. The mountains watched me silently as I left them. These mountains held many secrets of war and violence within them. They knew they were not alone. They would soon pay witness to the vicious battles the 101st were sure to fight against the enemy.

We made a hasty stop at my beloved Honaker Miracle. We were only there for a few moments, yet a multitude of memories and emotions fell upon me. As supplies were unloaded from the aircraft, I reminisced over the familiar surroundings: the walls of the COP and the mountains. I said my goodbyes to war. I felt sad to leave the ground that we fought so passionately to defend. We lifted into the air and I took in my battlefields for the last time, viewing these places that I knew by heart. I breathed deeply as we flew farther away from these lands. I had a lump in my throat and felt tears well up from deep within me as we continued east. I thanked God for sparing the lives of my men, and my own. My adventure in the Pesh River Valley was over. I would miss my time there. Our bird of steel left the Pesh valley behind.

We flew toward the light of the new dawn and turned south into the Kunar River Valley.

I was free of the Pesh valley, but the valley will always hold a grip on me. A part of me will forever be in the Pesh River Valley. A part of the Pesh River Valley will always be in me.

JAF – BAGRAM

We spent but a few days at JAF. The echoes of the savage 155s and 120s were far off in that dark valley to the north. The echoes of war were kept far from my ears and echoed to me no longer. I assisted with a few administrative tasks and prepared for our final moves to Bagram and home.

Soon we were set to leave JAF. We waited for our C-130 on the airfield. A full moon displayed our shadows on the ground. It was beautiful to look at the shadows formed by the outlines of warriors with armor and rifles in hand. Our dark forms appeared to me like ghosts of a time long forgotten. Our battles were over and we boarded the C-130 that transported us to Bagram.

Redeployment was a strange purgatory of sorts that encompassed waiting, cramped quarters, and more waiting, but it provided me time to reflect on some of the deeds that we had conducted at war. I had drunk heavily of the wine of war. I indulged in war and enjoyed every moment of it. I looked upon the snow-capped mountains of the Hindu Kush far off into the distance. After one year of constant firefights, ambushes, IEDs, and artillery attacks, the warnings that these mountains gave to outside invaders still proved true. They told us to stay away; the mountains do well to warn the foreigners.

These snow-capped fortresses told the ultimate truth of war here. They seemed to say that war in Afghanistan is as timeless and eternal as the mountains themselves. Even with all of our technology, these ageless barriers mocked us. They limited our all-powerful might. They watched us, as we watched them. The war would continue.

GOOD BYE...

I watched my final sunset in Afghanistan with a heavy heart and sighed deeply as we waited for our plane to Kyrgyzstan. The sun slowly dropped and shrouded the land in darkness.

As LT John Cumbie, LT Greg Sullivan, and I waited to board our C-17, we caught a beautiful moment; we watched the full moon as it rose over the horizon. The glowing celestial body slowly moved atop the mountains and was a memorable site. It was almost as if this land of war was saying its goodbyes to us. For me, that moment was the perfect way to bid my farewell to this place called Afghanistan. I silently kissed this place goodbye. We boarded a C-17 bound for Manas, Kyrgyzstan. The war was now behind me.

MANAS, KYRGYZSTAN

We rested in Manas and walked without our rifles; we would not need them for some time. It was hard to fathom that I was free from the war. The graceful and delicate beauty of the Kyrgyzstani women was a welcoming sight. Their beauty had such a calming effect on me. I dined and soon changed into a clean uniform, which had not seen or heard the ravages of war. It was innocent, untouched, and clean.

My adventure was fast coming to an end as we waited for our passage back to civilization and to the light of the world. We would soon return to the very democracy that we defended. I wondered what would be the fate of Afghanistan. Although my unit left that dark valley behind, those battles undoubtedly continued. I could almost still hear the guns bellowing. Time is the ultimate judge of warfare, and time would only tell.

GERMANY-USA

We arrived in Frankfurt, Germany. I felt at peace amidst the green fields of Frankfurt, once a focal point of WWII. Those green fields were adorned with dandelions. We waited for our plane to refuel and resupply. Our soldiers rested outside the terminal in the smoking area. I shared a smoke with one of the men. The day was beautiful and was adorned with pure blue skies. This day was one of the most beautiful and peaceful days of my life. It was quiet there, we were safe, and I did not hear the terror sounds of the artillery, machine guns, or 40mm. The war was behind us.

PVT Martinez of my old platoon was there, on his way home. I shook his hand, overjoyed to see him. All of the men of my platoon survived. Flo successfully finished leading them to peace. I was honored to have fought with them. My time with 4th Platoon was amongst the happiest times of my life. I was honored.

Our plane was soon ready. I sat next to Flo and my friend, Tom Goodman, on the flight back to the United States. I felt comfortable and at peace with these two officers from Combat Outpost Honaker Miracle. We spent the flight exchanging stories and laughing. We had survived our first war as officers. I was happy and at peace. We soon landed in Colorado Springs, Colorado, USA.

The 4th Infantry Division band was there and greeted us, playing the theme to the original "Rocky" movie. It was somehow fitting. We left our airplane and walked in a long line to the building where we would turn in our weapons and be driven to Ft. Carson. I smiled as I peered to the west and saw the beautiful Rocky Mountains. These Mountains were the symbols of peace, rather than warnings of war. I sighed with a breath that embodied relief, but the sigh also embodied sadness for leaving Afghanistan. The great adventure and my dream of leading men in combat had been fulfilled. I had followed the song of the Sirens to its source in the Pesh River Valley. I had seen the Sirens.

I left the war, but I think the war never left me.

DEAR SIRENS...

So this is what it is like to go to war. More so, this is what it is like to come home from war. After our yearlong menu of battles, I leave you to sail across the world to my homeland.

So, my beautiful Sirens, our paths finally crossed. You were everything that I had imagined you would be. You were beautiful, you were exciting, you made me feel alive, you made my heart pound, and you made me sweat. You made my stomach tighten, you made me feel dread. You tore the bodies of men apart before me. You hurt my men. You tore at my body. However, you taught me the importance and value of life.

I will miss our chance encounters. I will miss you as you cry for me. I will miss your scent. I will miss how you made me feel. I will miss the fear, the exhaustion and the pleasure that you covered me with. I became drunk with you. I wonder when I shall see you again. I look forward to our next date. Even now, with peace so close, I yearn to see you again. I want to trade steel in our embrace, perhaps we will soon.

Until then I will think of your song.

THE ALLURE OF THE SIRENS

As fate would have it, I found myself at war again only four months after returning from Afghanistan. 4th Infantry Division asked for volunteers to work in their headquarters in Iraq. I had not yet seen the lands of Mesopotamia, so I volunteered. This time I would not be in charge of men on the line. Instead, I worked in the great eye of the storm that is a division headquarters.

I lived at a place called COB (Contingency Operating Base) Speicher. It was essentially a fortified base camp around an airfield in Tikrit, Salah Ad Din province, Iraq; the hometown of Saddam Hussein. The sheer size of the place was monstrous as compared to the small outposts in the Pesh River Valley. The life support area where I lived was almost as big as COP Michigan. I would not meet the enemy in combat there, but the Sirens continued to sing to me from time to time. They teased my ears and my passions.

There I could usually only catch the faint tune of the Siren's Song. Some nights I was serenaded by a familiar sound as I walked across the desert floor. M2 .50 cal. echoed across the dark desert's sky. Orion was there watching me as the echoes of the .50 cal. reminded me of the truth of war and her chaos. It reminded me of the sheer violence involved in combat and of those savagely beautiful places far removed from the never-ending coffee pots of a division headquarters.

SIREN'S SONG

One night, I was eating dinner with my mates, CPT Adam Smoot, CPT Dave Danford, and SGT Phil Bates. We were enjoying our meal, bullshitting care freely as soldiers do. It was then I heard her voice. I heard the unmistakable impact of indirect fire. I recognized the faint "whang" in the distance. I knew without a doubt that it was a 107mm.

It had been several months since I heard her tune. My primitive nerves that had lay dormant for months came instantly to life. My warrior soul and memories were resurrected. The men around me stopped mid meal. You could see it in their faces and I felt it. It was dread, a feeling that nothing else compares to. It is one of the near unexplainable truths of war.

Dread is one of the attributes of warfare that I failed to properly describe in my writing in Afghanistan. As exciting as combat was, it was dreadful. This was an emotion that you tried desperately not to think about too much. If you did, you would not dare take part in combat. This feeling was one of doom. It was death knocking on your door, but it became easier to brush off with time. After a few firefights you learned to ignore it. You had to.

I also felt something else when I heard the explosion of the rocket. I felt joy and happiness. It felt good to have fear re-injected into my blood and psyche, as the beast within began to rise. My altar to war buried deep within my heart was again made ready. My candle of war was once again lit aflame. I loved it.

Although I would not be leading a counter attack, I enjoyed being in the midst of danger again. Hearing the Siren's song after so long confirmed a few things about my heart. I still lusted for her. I wanted another night to approach her under the horrible sound of gunfire and the explosions of artillery. I wanted to sweat and breathe deeply as I embraced, in my armor, these princesses of evil.

I lusted for combat. I thirsted and fantasized for these Sirens still. Although I knew the perils that would await my flesh and the flesh of my comrades in battle, I still wanted it. I lusted for it more than anything else. Perhaps I listened to the song of the Siren's for too long. It seems that combat has indeed touched me. It has touched me like nothing else in my life.

Oh how I miss thee.

Sweet Sirens

You pull at my heart and soul

Stronger than any desire I have felt

Sweet horrible Sirens

I followed your songs

To the Mountains

the valleys

And into the dark desert

I have seen you

touched you

heard you

As you have touched me

I wonder if I will always miss her. It's very strange. For me, I met one of my most dangerous and passionate loves in the Pesh River Valley of Kunar Province, Afghanistan. She teased me in Mesopotamia from time to time.

However, this experience of war is not free. There comes a toll you must pay to visit these Sirens. It is more costly to some than others. But, we all lose something in war. Some of us lose our lives and others lose a limb. Some lose a girlfriend or a wife. Some of us lose our soul and some lose their minds. Some of us lose a part of or all of the above.

Even with this heavy cost, I think that men will continue to fantasize about these Sirens. Do you?

I suppose if there is one truth about war and her Sirens; it is that once the Sirens touch you, you are changed forever.

If you choose to take this path to the rocks, take heed in the warning the Odyssey tells us:

> "First you will come to the Sirens who enchant all who come near them. If anyone unwarily draws in too close and hears the singing of the Sirens, his wife and children will never welcome him home again, for they sit in a green field and warble him to death with the sweetness of their song.
>
> There is a great heap of dead men's bones lying all around, with the flesh still rotting off them. Therefore pass these Sirens by, and stop your men's ears with wax that none of them may hear"
>
> (Odyssey. Book 12, 188-191).

USEFUL PASHTUN

1. How are you?	*Sang gay?*
2. How is your family?	*Coranay, de sang ga day?*
3. I'm doing good.	*Jorday.*
4. Good	*Hooday*
5. Yes.	*Woah / Ha.*
6. Thank you very much.	*Deera Mananna.*
7. Where are you from?	*De Kum Zei?*
8. I am from...	*Ze De…*
9. How old are you?	*Su Kaland Ye?*
10. What is your name?	*Num de cheri?*
11. My name is...	*Zma num...*
12. Where do you live?	*Cherta osa gay?*
13. Where are you going?	*Cherta Zei?*
14. How many kids do you have?	*Su Manchman la day?*
15. Good evening.	*Spag po her sha.*
16. Sit, here.	*Dalta, Cane na.*
17. Bridge	*Pul*
18. Gun	*To- pac*
19. Knife	*Chalku*
20. Give me	*Raka*
21. Bread/food	*Dough di*
22. Water	*Ow Bah*
23. Girl	*Jeni*
24. School	*Mectab*
25. Book	*Kitab*

26. Counting	
1: *Yo*	
2: *Duo*	
3: *Dree*	
4: *Salur*	
5: *Penza*	
6: *Spag*	
7: *Wu*	
8: *Ota*	
9: *Nun*	
10: *Las*	
27. Fight	*Jang*
28. Infidel	*Kafer*
29. Explosion	*Chow denna*
30. Father	*Plar*
31. What does your father do?	*Sta Plar, saw a zei fa la rey?*
32. I lived in Kunar for 1 year.	*Ze osage in kunar for la pa yo kaland.*
33. Month:	*Mes.*
34. Friend / My friend	*Dost / Zma dost*
35. Come here.	*Dalta rasha.*
36. Go over there.	*Shalta rasha.*
37. Run.	*Manda.*
38. Go / go home.	*Za / Core Za.*
39. Make a line.	*Landa jorkay.*
40. Slowly	*Kala la*
41. Hot	*Germeda*
42. I'm scared.	*Wali eregay.*
43. Dead	*Morsu*
44. Army	*Urdu Milu*
45. Little	*Lig lig*
46. We… / lets go.	*Mungz…. / Mungz Zu.*

47. What is the name of this village?	*De kum kalay?*
48. Elder	*Malek*
49. Mosque	*Jumed*
50. Happy Eid.	*Eid Mubarak.*
51. Stop.	*Wodrega.*
52. Today	*Nun*
53. Tomorrow	*Sa Ba*
54. Yesterday	*Pa run*
55. Good bye.	*Hoday paman.*
56. Peace be upon you.	*Salam al malekium.*
57. I understand a little pashtun.	*Ze poigie lig lig de pashtun.*
58. Ready?	*Tiara?*
59. Wait.	*Sab brey woka.*
60. Wait 5 minutes.	*Sabrey woka penza minute.*
61. How is qamichi village?	*Qamchi kay de sang ga day?*
62. Enemy	*Doosh men.*
63. You know?	*Ka na?*
64. Step by step	*Kedam- y- Kedam*
65. Beatiful	*Hi-sta*
66. Monday	*Do shamba*
67. Tuesday	*Say Shamba*
68. Wednesday	*Char Shamba*
69. Thursday	*Panj Shamba*
70. Friday	*Jumma*
71. Saturday	*Shamba*
72. Sunday	*Yak shamba*
73. Brother	*Woor*

ACKNOWLEDGEMENTS

Thank you to my parents: Claudio and Tereza Salinas. Thank you mom for all of those constant rides to Karate and your love. Dad, thanks for all our "patrols" in the woodlands of Michigan. Even with all the training I have received in the military, you'll always be a better shot with a rifle than me. To my siblings: Rachel, Claudio Jr., and Melisa – thank you for always being loving and supportive as I continue to travel to the corners of the Earth. Special thanks to my beloved Claire – you provided me with the love and support that I desperately needed in one the most challenging chapters in my life.

My good friends: Drew DaRonco, Brent Insco, Cary Ossiff, James Trumbly, Alex Edwards, Brently Moats, Derick Carver, Leon Landa, Eric Guy, Thatcher Merrill,

Kyle Whipple, Isaac and Seth Williamson. Your bonds of friendship and support have lasted through years of not seeing one another. Thanks for always being there for me.

Throughout my career I have had many mentors that nurtured me in my education of the world and war. Thank you to my professors Dr. James Holoka, Dr. Steven Ramold, Dr. Robert Citino, Dr. Matt Schumann, and Dr. Walter Moss. Special thanks to all the officers and noncommissioned officers in the ROTC program at Eastern Michigan University – I will never forget those vital lessons of tactics and leadership.

A special thank you to Mr. Bob Babcock and the entire team at Deeds Publishing. To put it simply, you made my dreams come true.

Thank you to those who allowed me to utilize their photographs in this book. A few of the photos were taken by men who served in this sea of chaos with me, to include Louis Martinez, Julius Ventura, Juan Herrera, Joseph Dement, Tyrel Richardson, and Neil Shea. I extend special thanks to the photographer, Eros Hoagland, whose expert work is displayed on the cover of this book.

Most of all, thank you to my fellow warriors under arms – past, present, and future. All of you have sacrificed so much for our country. No words ever written will be able to pay true testament to what you have done and continue to do.

ANTONIO M. SALINAS

Antonio Salinas was born and raised in Allen Park, Michigan, a suburb of Detroit. He was the third of four children born to Claudio and Teresa Salinas. His youth was spent dabbling in combative sports and hunting in the woodlands of Michigan. Upon graduating from Allen Park High School in 1998, Antonio enlisted in the United States Marine Corps where he served as a geospatial intelligence analyst, then a martial arts instructor trainer, and later an intelligence chief. Following his time in the Marines, Antonio attended Eastern Michigan University and gained his Bachelors in History and Political Science. Antonio then pursued graduate school where he enrolled in Army ROTC and attained his Masters in History. Antonio was commissioned as a 2nd Lieutenant in 2007 and has served in both Afghanistan and Iraq. Antonio currently lives in Colorado Springs, Colorado where he continues to serve in uniform as a Captain.